JESSICA LIPSKY

IT AIN'T RETRO

DAPTONE RECORDS & THE 21ST-CENTURY SOUL REVOLUTION

IT AIN'T RETRO
DAPTONE RECORDS & THE 21ST-CENTURY SOUL REVOLUTION

JESSICA LIPSKY

A JAWBONE BOOK

PUBLISHED IN THE UK AND THE USA BY
JAWBONE PRESS
OFFICE G1
141–157 ACRE LANE
LONDON SW2 5UA
ENGLAND
WWW.JAWBONEPRESS.COM

ISBN 978-1-911036-73-9

PRINTED IN THE CZECH REPUBLIC BY PBTISK

1 2 3 4 5 25 24 23 22 21

CONTENTS

AUTHOR'S NOTE: IT'S NOT WHAT YOU KNOW...

In 1998, I was a tomboyish, cow-licked kid whose taste for bell bottoms and paisley had yet to come back into fashion. Peering over the cliff of puberty in the era of boy bands and Britney Spears, I was quickly realizing that I had an exceedingly unpopular taste in music—which I played loudly, constantly, on a boom box my folks had purchased for my ninth birthday.

Popularity was a concern, sure, but I could not listen to "... Baby One More Time" even *one more time*. When Spears's debut was unleashed to worldwide obsession, I wasn't caught up in the hype. The manufactured perfection of The Backstreet Boys, N'Sync, and the like are embedded in my brain, and yet I don't remember actively listening to any of these groups. Nothing about their sound felt engaging, and even though I could handle being marketed to, my burgeoning angst wasn't down with the pop I was being digitally dosed with every afternoon on MTV's *TRL*.

But I had to pretend like I dug it. After all, enduring pop music is a rite of passage among every alt kid, and a resumé-worthy skill. I was somewhat successful because I had a secret love, and we got down every morning before I went to school.

KFRC 99.7 FM in the San Francisco Bay Area—an oldies station that played sounds from approximately 1956–74—saved me. It was a sonic elixir of classic rock, Summer of Love hits, and, most importantly, soul. The station opened my ears to the sounds of Motown, Stax, and Chess; made me dance; and drove me to buy books, CDs, and movies that evoked

★ ★ ★ ★ ★ ★

sounds of the era. I called the station almost every morning from age nine to make requests and answer trivia. I wished so badly that I lived in a time where this music permeated like Britney Spears did, where the sounds of The Shirelles, Otis Redding, The Temptations, Martha Reeves & The Vandellas, and Booker T. were known by my peers. Where vocal harmonies weren't autotuned, and actual musicians were highlighted.

But those dreams made me sound like an old man, and they would make me deeply unpopular among my peers. So I told no one and shared no music.

By October 2007, I no longer thought about Britney or boy bands, and I felt confident that my distaste for such tunes made me cool. Smoking a joint as I perused the stacks at KUSF 90.3 FM, a San Francisco community radio station where I had a late-night show, I landed on a CD with an orange cover featuring a proud but serious Black woman. The album looked vintage, but I didn't recognize the Daptone Records label, so I pressed play on track 2, "Nobody's Baby."

A simple walking bass line was interrupted by a woman's voice crying "Whooooweeee," a powerful alto commanding you to pay attention to her tale of independence, told over a late-60s-style horn arrangement. *Holy shit*, I thought, after skimming through the liner notes. *This is new*. The sound of Sharon Jones & The Dap-Kings catalyzed something deep in me, and one of the band's songs would make an appearance on nearly every show of mine for the next two years.

It also, in an instant, gave me a swell of hope for more modern sounds in soul and funk. Although I was a few years behind the curve (Sharon Jones & The Dap-Kings already had three records out), I felt as if that moment was the start of everything—the start of the soul revolution.

It turns out that my lifelong musical quest was rooted in something much more common: I was too young and in the wrong city. Had I been ten years older and living outside of the Bay Area suburbs, I could have heard DJs bridge the gap between funk and hip-hop at LA's legendary Root Down party, or at Frankie Jackson's long-running Soul Kitchen in New

★ ★ ★ ★ ★ ★

York. These deep diggers—along with dozens of other DJs and collectors across the country and in Europe—had fueled a soul fire, keeping alive a culture that valued older, raw-edged music.

What I couldn't have known, or perhaps even dreamt of as the pop of the late 90s turned into the indie rock of the mid-2000s, is that musicians were also itching for something soulful. In New York, Gabe Roth and Neal Sugarman built off their shared interest in rare funk records and recorded a slew of LPs and seven-inch singles with their friends for the hell of it. Closer to home, musicians at the cross-section of LA's turntablism, funk, and breakbeat DJ scenes played together at parties and formed a cohort of funk diggers called The Breakestra. These burgeoning modern funk and soul sounds first percolated locally, then cross-pollinated in hipper places. The rest of us were left to wonder how the hell Avril Lavigne's "Sk8er Boi" was nominated for five Grammys.

The soul revolution has given rise to dozens of artists, each with their own unique influences and style. Indie groups from New York, California, Indiana, and Washington have grown from the family tree of Daptone and Sharon Jones, sprouting new soulful communities. In the mainstream, artists such as Amy Winehouse, Bruno Mars, Aloe Blacc, Alabama Shakes, and Leon Bridges created funky pop that similarly iterated on the sounds of the 60s, 70s, and early 80s. Heavy bass, breakbeats, and raw vocals made appearances in hip-hop, reggaeton, and rock, developing into today's most popular sound that you didn't know you were listening to: the sound of Daptone Records.

INTRODUCTION: SOUL EXPLOSION

Forty or fifty musicians are swarming behind the scenes at Harlem's famous Apollo Theater—they're jamming in small groups backstage, performing personal pre-show rituals, shit-talking around an overfull beverage table and clustered in groups, watching from the wings as their friends work three nights worth of sold-out crowds into a palpable frenzy. The Apollo residency was a reunion of sorts, an occasion for a family of musicians who had played together in various funk, soul, jazz, and Afrobeat projects for nearly twenty years to celebrate what made them unique: a dedication to showmanship, a highly attuned ear for and devotion to music made in the 60s and 70s, and an appreciation for the collective spiritual bond which informed the intensity of their shows.

Each night of the Daptone Super Soul Revue, held during the mild early winter of December 2014, was a chance to revel in the unifying, groovy power of soul music in all its forms. Every musician who had worked with Brooklyn-based Daptone Records took the stage in a series of continuous sets, adding and removing players (most of whom performed with multiple groups) and equipment between bands without intermissions or curtain calls. Mississippi-based a cappella group The Como Mamas and locals Naomi Shelton & The Gospel Queens brought devotional music from the church to center stage; instrumental groups The Sugarman 3 and session musicians Menahan Street Band performed meditative cinematic soul and hybrids of jazz and boogaloo; Antibalas and The Budos Band delivered their respective versions of Afro-funk euphony; during an interlude, Dapettes Saun & Starr reminisced about performing

★ ★ ★ ★ ★ ★

at the Apollo's amateur night as young women in the 1980s. Nearly the whole of the 1,500-capacity theater stood from their chairs, compelled to dance and pay witness to the heartfelt, heavy, and energetic performances from Daptone's headlining acts: Sharon Jones & The Dap-Kings, and Charles Bradley, also known as the "Screaming Eagle of Soul." As an independent, musician-owned label that made most of its money on the road, orchestrating a hometown soul revue was a dream come true.

A soul revue like Daptone's hadn't been attempted in decades, its success a tribute to the label's pioneering and often defiant ethos. Daptone took a page out of the book of James Brown, whose residencies at the historic venue in the 60s and 70s were so legendary that they were commemorated in multiple records. Sharon Jones had first performed at the Apollo in 2007, her mark ("Love ya! Sharon," written in silver ink) gracing the venue's famous wall of signatures alongside those of Paul McCartney, Al Green, Prince, Tony Bennett, rapper 50 Cent, and President Barack Obama—though the Super Soul Revue was a markedly different occasion. Beaming from ear to ear, Jones readied herself in a series of sparkly dresses and strappy two-inch heels in dressing rooms once used by beloved divas Billie Holiday, Diana Ross, and Patti LaBelle—each a force of personality with a fervent fanbase, though their energy was surely eclipsed by Sharon's. "She belongs here!" Apollo historian Billy "Mr. Apollo" Mitchell asserted to the revue's documentarian.[1]

But the road to sold-out Apollo residency wasn't linear, or even paved, for most of Daptone's musicians. Some first overcame illiteracy and homelessness, others a lifetime of rejection by record companies or decades working multiple jobs to support their musical passions when the only gigs were at underpaying clubs. The majority were simply nerds, obsessed with rough cuts of funk and soul from the likes of Motown, Stax, Brunswick, or Dynamo records. And, while record-collecting and crate-digging culture was having a moment at the time of the Daptone Super Soul Revue—largely due to the label's unwavering commitment to its favorite genres—the popularity of 60s and 70s era soul had long been relegated to oldies radio, hip-hop samples, and overly nostalgic film soundtracks. By the mid-1990s, when Daptone precursor Desco Records came into the world, funk in the key of The J.B.'s was only relevant for its breaks, and Aretha Franklin—the Queen of Soul and an idol of Sharon Jones—was waiting to exhale.

In 1996, Franklin was in between albums and was considering delving into more acting. That year, she was also featured alongside popular R&B artists past and present on the soundtrack for the hit dramedy *Waiting To Exhale*. Franklin's "It Hurts Like Hell," a contribution the *New York Times* noted for its "letting-it-all-out pop-gospel anguish," was critically well received but didn't enter the Hot 100 charts.[2] As the sixth single to be released from the soundtrack, it seemed as if Franklin's pop relevance was buried in favor of the R&B and hip-hop fusion that was steadily climbing the charts.

By then, most of Motown's major acts had been inducted into the Rock and Roll Hall of Fame—becoming not so much has-beens as a reflection of what once was. Charting R&B artists such as Mary J. Blige and Destiny's Child were less living in the shadow of 60s and 70s soul and funk but instead standing on its shoulders, eschewing the grittier sounds of those earlier generations. While rock had responded to the slickness and excess of the 1980s by stripping down to a grungier, moodier core, soul had mostly taken the opposite path, embracing a slick, hyperproduced style that was as sexy as it was radio friendly. Live instruments were replaced by sequencers, drum machines, and samples; vocals became increasingly acrobatic. Although this era undoubtedly birthed classics like Janet Jackson's "That's The Way Love Goes," its perfection could be suffocating and even lifeless. With the exception of Lauryn Hill's 1998 smash "Doo Wop (That Thing)"—which employed 60s-era harmonies over hip-hop rhymes and juxtaposed New York in 1967 with the contemporary city—radio hits had long moved on from the sounds Aretha Franklin forged.

More experimental, less commercially driven musicians responded

★ ★ ★ ★ ★ ★

by fusing their modern sound with a crate-digging sensibility. Artists like Jamiroquai and Sade, along with the Solquarians collective (whose members included now-household names Questlove, Erykah Badu, Mos Def, and D'Angelo) iterated on the grooves from their 1970s childhoods to pioneer neo soul—an aesthetically slick mix of soul, R&B, and hip-hop that was sultry and cinematic, perfect for an "urban" audience who wanted an antidote to gangsta rap, misogyny, and the overindulgence pervasive in much of the Top 40.

Neo soul took inspiration not from new technology or techniques but from the raw, unpolished sounds found in the backroom and dollar bins of record stores. Rare groove—another roots- and digging-oriented music culture—came up alongside neo soul. This amorphous genre focused on the (often extremely rare) original songs sampled in hip-hop, and, together with house-influenced acid jazz, introduced audiences by the crateful to masterful 70s B-sides. But rather than be content combing the stacks for such tunes (though they were certainly diggers), the folks at Desco created those records from scratch. Or at least a shelf full of records that could be confused with obscure rare groove tracks.

Located a short subway ride downtown from where Hill filmed the video for "Doo Wop" in Manhattan's Washington Heights neighborhood, and a few dozen blocks from the Solquarian's base at Electric Lady Studios, Desco Records' studio at 440 West 41st Street was a come-up. The spacious but dingy set of rooms nestled in the basement of an apartment on the outskirts of Manhattan's theater district were just a few blocks from the heart of New York's seedier past—the infamous 42nd Street sex show and prostitution stroll. While the "Deuce" provided much inspiration for now-famous funk anthems from the 1970s, the 90s had brought much change. New York's once squalid and dangerous midtown was scrubbed to a gleaming, sanitized sheen beneath an onslaught of developer dollars. Yet despite this corporate-sponsored spit shine, the grime was still caked in the corners.

★ ★ ★ ★ ★ ★

This was where Desco Records was born: a musical innovation that sounded like a blast from the past but was created in the shadow of a new millennium. And it was from here, over the course of several years, that the sweat-soaked funky soul cooking in Desco's basement studio would spur a revolution.

Born of necessity (a label would give an air of professionalism to the randomized auditory whims of its founders), the independent, "retro"-sounding Desco was co-founded by bassist/songwriter/producer Bosco Mann (government name Gabriel Roth) and French funkophile Phillip Lehman, an eccentric producer from a monied family who had left a previous life as a Parisian street artist for the rarified world of raw funk singles. Hopped up on the hunter-gatherer adrenaline familiar to most vinyl junkies, Desco set out to recapture the wild spirit and unpolished sound of a criminally overlooked and underappreciated genre. With Lehman on drums and production, and Roth engineering while playing bass and also producing, Desco recorded funk in the style of early 70s James Brown, soul-jazz, and Afrobeat with a growing and diverse cast of horn players, singers, and percussionists who would later define the genre of modern soul.

Although Desco's funk didn't have much in the way of a roadmap, it had many sonic idols. Desco followed in the tradition of legendary labels and countless unrecognized, unheralded recording houses, but the music coming from this West 41st Street studio was different. Like their 60s and 70s forebears, Desco's outfit had swinging horns, bouncy bass lines, chugging percussion, and voices at once sandpaper rough and velvety smooth. But this modern era of funk, and the soulful sound that followed, differed in rawness and its disregard of modern recording processes. Desco favored rich, warm, and gritty analogue production—the kind found on beloved James Brown records and obscure funk 45s alike, with a heavy dose of East African heat from the likes of Matata (a Kenyan group whose 1974 album *Independence* was on repeat),, and the great Fela Kuti.

Roth and Lehman brought musicians into a single room and preferred

★ ★ ★ ★ ★ ★

to record them live to tape—a setup that could create an enviably tough sound with the right combination of talented players. Where Desco's influences had broken the mold to create some of the baddest bands, the fledgling label was determined not to fuck with greatness. Instead, they looked back and dug deep.

"[Phillip] is a crazy collector. I had some records, but he had *crazy* records," Roth told *Wax Poetics* in 2010. "Fela, James Brown, The Meters. They seem real obvious now, but at the time it wasn't like there was a lot of funk bands that were into that. All the funk bands were into P-Funk and that kind of sound, you know? So at the time, it was a little rebellious and raw, even though it may seem a little tired right now."[3]

The term funk, like all good words used to describe music, is uselessly vague. It was used as early as 1907 on New Orleans jazz musician Buddy Bolden's unrecorded tune "Buddy Bolden's Blues" (aka "Funky Butt"). It's been applied to everything from James Brown's smash hit "Papa's Got A Brand New Bag" (1965) to the up-tempo Watts 103rd Street Rhythm Band's "Spreadin' Honey" (1967) and the acid-damaged weirdness of Parliament Funkadelic's 1971 album *Maggot Brain*, all the way up to the 1990s socks-on-cocks thrash of the Red Hot Chili Peppers. But in its earliest, truest form, funk is raw and driven by its rhythm section, with a heavy dose of horns—a sound captured on nearly all Desco records. But as funk gave way to disco, and disco to house music and EDM, then to a million other genres, auditorily pungent funk music became hard to find and almost entirely the arena of collectors.

Desco first tapped into this fiendish need for rare, obscure and lost sounds by releasing fake kung fu soundtracks, then 70s-style funk records as The Soul Providers—an eight(ish)-piece proto-group to the hugely popular Dap-Kings, who served as Daptone Record's house band and provided instrumentation for Amy Winehouse's *Back To Black*, among other pop projects. They recorded a group of local teenagers called The Mighty Imperials, who played in the style of early Meters, as well as Afro-funk from The Daktaris and soul-jazz from The Sugarman 3. So seismic

★ ★ ★ ★ ★ ★

were those first few years that Naomi Shelton Davis & The Knights Of 41st Street would record "41st Street Breakdowne" in tribute to the studio that got the whole ball rolling.

But it was a studio on Long Island that would be the site of a fortuitous meeting of Roth and the woman who would lead their motley band of funkateers. In 1996, The Soul Providers were laying the instrumental backbone for singer Lee Fields when Roth envisioned three backup singers to provide harmonies on the lightly misogynist track "Let A Man Do What He Wanna Do." When his tenor sax player showed up the following day with only his girlfriend Sharon Jones, and not the three vocalists he'd promised, Roth was irked but curious. Jones—a somewhat stocky Black woman with box braids, a bold attitude, and at least a decade on most of The Soul Providers—sang the harmonies with precision but left a real impression by channeling her trademark sass on a quasi-novelty tune called "Switchblade." Compact in stature but fierce in performance and personality, Jones believably promised to "cut you so bad your mama won't recognize you." She had the whole studio in stitches. "Switchblade" was Sharon Jones's first record with Roth, and their unlikely musical chemistry would bubble over for the next two decades.

The laissez-faire reign of Desco Records in New York's burgeoning revival sounds community was short-lived, though, despite a sizeable output of hot wax. Lehman and Roth parted ways in 2000, leaving the latter "broke and brokenhearted" but on the precipice of something huge.[4] Precipitating a larger cultural shift, both Desco founders left Manhattan for the outer boroughs to focus on different sides of the same soulful coin. Lehman favored tougher sounds and founded Soul Fire Records; Roth moved his operation to Bushwick, Brooklyn, and started a label focused on expertly polished (but never overdone) mid-to-late-60s soul and funk—operating as Daptone Records. By combining their love of 60s and 70s sounds with a growing appreciation for Afrobeat and acid jazz, as well as the city's world-class musicians, the two jumpstarted the modern soul/funk renaissance.

The spark of this renaissance didn't occur exclusively in the dank, well-isolated confines of Desco's studios—they were part and parcel of a renewed interest in raw, danceable music that was swelling simultaneously in New York's underground and elsewhere in the country. Before Desco came on the scene, New York City was a veritable buffet of nightlife opportunities, and hungry clubgoers in the late 80s and mid-90s could sample from hip-hop, house music, disco, and funk. And, while Roth, Lehman, and their friends were among the first to put a modern NYC spin on funk, Frankie Inglese and Jack Luber (collectively known as Frankie Jackson) were ahead of the game with their Soul Kitchen DJ night. The roving Monday-night dance party began in 1989, attracting diverse fans of breakbeat, hip-hop, and funk to a slew of clubs in Manhattan—Vandam, S.O.B.'s, Brothers BBQ, and Wetlands, among other locales—for years before shutting down and rebirthing its sloppy funky mess in the aughts.

Elsewhere in the city, the producer and songwriter Mark Ronson was making a name for himself at the Sweet Thing party on the Lower East Side. His pan-genre tastes and expert blending of funk and associated flavors brought Ronson mainstream attention, and also helped cement the link between disparate genres through a party-ready soundtrack. Operating from the LES underground, the Empire State Soul Club's monthly night of high-speed soul records tapped the netherworld of garage fiends, mods, and northern soul fanatics, then cemented their common musical core. "We started doing it because there was nowhere to go and hear this stuff. Then I realized, well, we have to do it ourselves," ESSC DJ Warren Lee told the *New York Times* in 1992.[5]

This blossoming of New York's subcultural milieu was the result of a larger revival: New York City was flush and quickly shaking off the impressively gritty look of its 70s and 80s heyday. The reign of Mayor Rudy Giuliani had spurred a targeted and widely criticized schmutz-reduction policy known as "broken windows" policing that saw crime rates drop drastically. Neighborhoods previously considered dangerous, out of

★ ★ ★ ★ ★ ★

the way, and unwelcoming were now gentrifying—creating a slow death rattle whose contagion would spread to many previously "cool" New York neighborhoods for the next twenty years and draw droves to a city that felt simultaneously edgy and safe. Similarly, young people were making more money under the economic boom of the Clinton years and during the first Dot Com boom than they could spend on rent (which was devastatingly cheap compared to 2021 standards), coke, clothes, or concert tickets. Those who weren't raking it in or getting sent to Riker's Island in Giuliani's name could afford to live in Manhattan for relatively little money, creating an artistic paradise.

Yet the city's underground—which had not yet moved en masse to Brooklyn and Queens—had begun to mix and question the roots of its existence. In a city known for its plethora of arts and deep history of riotous subculture, why was it so hard to find an independent band? Fans and musicians in New York's indie-rock scene, which would birth The Strokes and Yeah Yeah Yeahs, took the raucous, impassioned sounds coming from local dive bars and made a chord-by-chord crawl to superstardom.[6] Whether the soul and funk scene was directly inspired by this move or simply caught the contact high is unclear, but as New York and the rest of the country fell face first into the uncertainty and shock of a post-9/11 world, creating music that was unpretentious and spoke to the soul felt ever more important.

Although New York may feel like the center of the universe, Ronson, Frankie Jackson, the Desco crew, and others were certainly not alone on an island. The funk producers' obsession with collecting and emulating the rare, raw funk 45s that would come to define those early revolutionary years is not dissimilar to England's northern soul scene of the 1970s, in which young, mostly white working-class kids voraciously collected rare American soul 45s and would journey from the far reaches of the region to amphetamine-fueled all-night DJ dances.

★ ★ ★ ★ ★ ★

Thousands of miles removed from the grit, grime, and supreme funkiness of Manhattan, the vast swathes of Los Angeles and Orange counties might not seem amenable to the raw soul and funk sounds culled from the hardest of East Coast nights. Yet Los Angeles, without a doubt, has deep roots in the soul revolution. The sprawling city was once home to much of the soul music industry—including Motown's headquarters, beginning in 1972; *Soul Train*'s famous stroll; and the site of the WattStax benefit—and was a profitable place for touring and homegrown bands such as War, Shalamar, and The Brothers Johnson. Yet such sounds had fallen out of popularity by the early to mid-80s, when hair metal and pop reigned supreme along the Sunset Strip. Meanwhile, punk rock had already become part of the DNA of the area's youth culture and pushed older soul sounds further to the margins.

Just as New York experienced targeted policing, Los Angeles in the 90s was reeling from gang and police violence that didn't look much different from events of the 60s and 70s. An explosion of West Coast hip-hop—which simultaneously explored bravado and brutality, achieving mainstream, multi-ethnic popularity while largely targeting a Black audience—relied on lesser-known funk and soul to create now iconic beats. Members of LA's thriving "alternative" communities of mods, soulies, and skinheads were also looking toward the past, obsessed with many of the same deep cuts. In a city so sprawling and mythologized that it seems on the outset to be devoid of any true identity, these subcultures thrived on and took notice of soul and funk sounds. The city's loosely defined limits, incredible diversity, and unofficial systems of identity politics created commonality when mainstream culture didn't offer much to hold onto—and soul music provided the connective tissue for many of these communities.

Meanwhile, generations of Latino and Chicano kids in East LA and an as-yet-ungentrified Echo Park spent their evenings cruising the city's boulevards, listening to the radio and making dedications to their friends and lovers. They favored sweet soul music from the early to mid-60s—love songs as well as catchy garage ballads—played by DJs like Godfrey Kerr,

★ ★ ★ ★ ★ ★

Dick "Huggy Boy" Hugg, Art Laboe, and Casey Kasem, and made popular by Thee Midniters and Brenton Wood. Even as tastes changed from generation to generation (and pop radio favored classic rock, hip-hop, and indie), lowriders, pachucos, cholos, those who don't define themselves by a subculture considered listening to oldies radio a birthright; the twelve-volume oldies bootleg set *East Side Story* a sought-after prize. The sounds of the 60s were passed from parent to child, all along the boulevard, without much expectation that those sounds would be recreated, live, in later years.

At the same time, DJs and musicians born during the WattStax period of LA funk and soul were experimenting with the nexus of acid jazz, breakbeats, and hip-hop. Influential party The Root Down, which spun off from hip-hop night The Breaks in 1997, mixed turntablism, MCs, and live music (including a set by an early days Black Eyed Peas) for what founder Carlos Guaico, aka DJ Loslito, would call a "discerning crowd that wanted to hear something not so commercialized, so Top 40."[7] The Breaks was a "weekly watering hole for a particular set of artist/musician/record collector" and the site of "a very, very intense emotional connection with the music." DJs would often stay after hours, enjoying long conversations about the new music they discovered. Those live players morphed into a funk group called The Breakestra, launching the West Coast wing of the revival, and inspiring dozens of bands in California and beyond in the 2000s. At Long Beach–based soul night Good Foot and later Funky Sole—a spinoff project from one of The Root Down's founders—DJs applied their fervent collecting of raw soul and funk to packed clubs. The result was a culture of vintage-sound appreciation that crowded dancefloors across the county's eighty-eight cities week after week, proving that soul was still relevant, even if there weren't many opportunities to hear live bands.

The funk and soul revolution was well underway in America's coastal cultural epicenters—to say nothing of the music that would come from Chicago, Texas, Indiana, and elsewhere—fueled by passionate bordering on obsessive collectors and musicians, and loved fastidiously by subcultures

★ ★ ★ ★ ★ ★

in a pre-internet age. These people found each other before the advent of social media, sharing records, sound, subversion, and musical talent to create a potently revolutionary sonic underground that would be quietly nurtured while indie rock and electronica had their time in the sun. By the time smartphones, Facebook, and Twitter became ubiquitous, the revolution—which had largely shifted its focus to mid-60s soul—was afoot, and a second generation of bands was lining up to drip heavy sounds into the ears of hungry fans.

Pop mega-hits such as Mark Ronson and Bruno Mars's "Uptown Funk"—as well as critical darlings like *Coming Home*, Leon Bridges's 2015 album of R&B meets early 60s soul, and upstarts Alabama Shakes—are but the outer layers of a seriously groovy musical onion (green onions, to be exact, if Booker T. & The MG's have any say in it). At its core is a soul generation who, unable to find the music they wanted to hear, felt compelled to create it themselves and share what they found. They struck a balance between paying homage and iterating on greatness, employing a fly-by-the-seat-of-your-pants approach to collaborating and punk ethos that disregarded popularity in favor of a feeling and a vibe. True to its name, the renaissance in funk and soul music is heartfelt.

"I really, personally, never tried to be somebody I'm not. Or tried to emulate some music, or tried to steal some history or tradition that I'm not a part of. What I try to do is make records that sound good to me, and make honest records," Roth concluded in that 2010 interview with *Wax Poetics*, adding that much of his success can be attributed to like minds. "I really try to write with my heart and play with my heart."

CHAPTER ONE
DAMN IT'S HOT: NYC AT THE CENTER OF THE UNIVERSE

Gabe Roth first arrived in New York as a teenager, departing the sunbaked, tree-lined avenues of California's Inland Empire for Manhattan in the early 1990s. He landed at his sister's apartment near Columbia University—a quick train ride away from where his future brewed inside a dark bar, next to a crate of vinyl records. Back home, Roth had been playing drums with his friends at local coffee shops and stroking a long-held obsession with the nasty, tonally fucked-up blues albums he found at Riverside record stores and flea markets.

"I had one record that was called *One String Jones*, and this is some dude with, like, a two-by-four with one string on it and, like, a pint bottle, just sliding up and down. And there's something about it to me—I just wanted to hear the rawest music I could. Everything else kind of felt like bullshit to me at the time," Roth says, any sense of teen angst absent from his recollection.

Roth's sister had a roommate who, by virtue of geography and age, had been blessed with a knowledge of funk. He turned Roth onto James Brown's *Funky People*—a now-rare compilation of artists who recorded on the Godfather of Soul's People imprint in the early to mid-70s—and the commanding, sexy voice of "female preacher" Lynn Collins, the punching horns of Fred Wesley, and Maceo & The Macks quickly invaded Roth's spirit. Together, they ventured downtown to the Soul Kitchen, a party where deep funk and breakbeats were served up along with chicken wings and forty-ounce Colt 45s, sometimes with a helping of a live band. DJs

★ ★ ★ ★ ★ ★

Frankie Inglese (who Roth would come to know well in later years) and Jack Luber were among the leaders in a city that was beginning to once again dabble in the sounds of funk; their Monday-night vinyl-only gig was packed with gyrating crate diggers, models, it rappers, veteran party people and hip-to-the-scene regular folks. How a curly haired, likely wide-eyed teenager from Riverside managed to sneak into one of the dopest parties in the city, however, has been lost to time.

Like any smart DJ, Inglese had a diversified sound, and had been spinning house and hip-hop at a trendy electronics store-turned-nightclub called Nell's on 14th Street and 8th Avenue prior to cooking with gas at Soul Kitchen. "I was also playing funk, soul and disco, but wanted to do something where I could just play those records out, exclusively and in their entirety," he later said.[1] At the time, club culture favored mixing funky breaks—essentially the heaviest parts of a song that were sampled in hip-hop—rather than a full recording. "One of our first spots was Brother's… we brought in a shitty sound system and set it up in the back, and it just took off from there. We went from Brother's, where we had like 50 people, to 1,500 people plus, with crowds lined down the street to get it." Much like funk itself, Soul Kitchen was indulgent, inclusive, and freeingly groovy. Speaking to the *New York Post* in 2009, Luber said, "It's about white girls dancing with Black guys with the look on their face like, *I can't believe I'm dancing with a Black guy and drinking a 40*, and Black guys thinking, *I can't believe I'm dancing with a white girl and she's drinking a 40*."[2]

If the night was eye-opening for Roth, it also sent a systemic shock to other attendees who pushed aside tables to dance to deep Marvin Gaye tracks, extended James Brown cuts, and anything particularly heavy from Bootsy Collins, The Meters, and Rufus (with and without Chaka Khan). "I used to go every week and loved the fact that it was similar to the rare groove scene I knew in the UK," said Maurice Bernstein, founder of the famed Giant Step rare groove/acid jazz parties, which took up residence in the city in 1990. "Seeing that party grow in popularity, it gave me the confidence that there actually could be a market to do shows with soul

★ ★ ★ ★ ★ ★

and funk artists in NYC."[3] With Soul Kitchen as their guide and England's acid jazz clubs as inspiration, Bernstein and partner Jonathan Rudnick put on shows with Maceo Parker, Isaac Hayes, The Ohio Players, and George Clinton as the Groove Academy. They also started Giant Step, a long-running party that debuted at S.O.B.'s—a club on what still feels like an oddly desolate strip of Varick Street—and was both a DJ gig and concert. Giant Step provided a stage for rappers and jazz musicians such as Jamiroquai, Digable Planets, The Roots, and The Fugees, along with a house band, to improvise over prerecorded hip-hop and funk.

By the time Roth returned east to attend New York University in 1992—where he obsessively listened to *Hot Pants*, James Brown's 1971 LP (and, stupefyingly, his 32nd studio album), as well as more obscure Brown cuts like "Gettin' Down To It" and "Dooley's Junkyard Dogs"—the city was in the throes of the golden age of hip-hop and was simultaneously experiencing a revival of interest in the breaks that formed the backbone of its original sounds.[4] Before gentrification crept through the city, live music flowed out of dozens of venues north of Houston and on both sides of the Bowery, catering to rock, country, punk, and hip-hop heads. Clubs thrived just south of Midtown in the Flatiron District, west to the Meatpacking (which had yet to be transformed by trendy retail and the Highline park), down to Tribeca, east into SoHo, and throughout the Village. But while you could occasionally see R&B heroes such as Ray Charles, Booker T. & The MG's, or a half-in-the-bag P-Funk at Tramps on 21st Street, new funk—delivered live and in the flesh, the kind you wish you could take intravenously—had long left the five boroughs and mostly lived on among record collectors.

Although club culture thrived in the 80s and 90s, DJ culture hadn't yet put needle to wax widely in the city's bar scene. Those spaces that did have two turntables, a mixer, and a halfway decent sound system developed devoted followings and attracted some of the city's leading DJs. Behind the wheels of steel, DJs such as Frankie Jackson, Stretch Armstrong—who, along with Bobbito, influenced a generation through their early morning hip-hop radio show on WKCR 89.9 FM—and, later, a young Mark Ronson (then DJ Sparks Ronson) mixed hip-hop, R&B, and classic funk together at downtown bars and clubs, soundtracking the grit and grandeur of NYC nightlife. Yet, years before Gabe Roth would make his own indelible mark on the New York scene; before Giant Step would create a nexus for neo-soul artists, tap dancers, and twenty-first-century hip-hop; and prior to Frankie Jackson catching the ears of models Christy Turlington and Naomi Campbell and du-jour artists like LL Cool J, a trio of DJs were pushing the needle further back to the sounds of the 60s.

Helmed by the tiara-topped Connie "The Empress" Francis, Warren Lee, and Jeff The Chef, The Empire State Soul Club convened once a month on Thursday nights to pay homage to obscure 60s soul tunes, semi-forgotten Stax Records wax, and other labels with verve. Just as their northern soul counterparts did across the pond in the 1970s, ESSC created a safe haven for soulies from the mid-80s onward—a place full of good grinding music, devastating love songs, and dancefloor crushers like Eddie Floyd's 1968 horn honking single "Big Bird." Empire State Soul Club was grounded in subculture, and its DJs went to great lengths to keep its members informed. They put out a ten-page biweekly newsletter with playlists, scene news, and even a gossip column written by Lee under the pen name Nikki Crush called "We Will Crush You," and created their own merch, including a much-coveted wristwatch. But although they offered membership cards early on, ESSC wasn't exclusionary. "On a normal Thursday night," the *New York Times* reported in 1992, "the club attracts some two hundred people, ranging from die-hard soul fans to students and Wall Street workers. Its mailing list has such ultra-hipster names as Fred Schneider from the B-52's; the cartoonist and playwright Lynda Barry . . . and the film maker Jim Jarmusch, who has been spied wearing the official Soul Club watch."[5]

"Everybody came," says Francis, who had been experimenting with soul records under a variety of banners since the early 80s. "There were no barriers, and that's what was great about it. It became the experience, and it was

★ ★ ★ ★ ★ ★

embraced by the community. I was always so overwhelmed at how embraced it was. The thing about soul music is that it truly speaks of an experience. It's the saddest songs about heartbreak, loss, discrimination, struggling for your place in society; being seen, heard or recognized, set to some of the most beautiful pounding, driving rhythms. Gorgeously orchestrated and all sung with an emotion that you can't deny. It just pierces the heart directly whether it moves your feet or your soul. It comes from a place that's so deep inside, that I think that's why everybody finds something in it."

The Empress—a sharp, fast-talking redhead with a slight drawl courtesy of her native Jacksonville, Florida—told the *Times* that soul music is "her real calling ... I absolutely have faith in anything that the needle touches; this is my art." ESSC's manifesto shared a similar passion and intensity: "What we do is for ourselves, our members, and any other interested parties ... in that order," its newsletter declared in 1989.

DJ Matt Weingarden "immediately fell in love" with Empire State Soul Club when he first walked through the door at North River Bar in Tribeca—the club's locale circa '95. A native of (but not too fresh from) Detroit, the soul cradle of America, he was so blown away by the music and vibe of ESSC that he went every month for years. "It was my favorite thing in the world," he says. While Weingarden, aka Mr. Fine Wine, had been collecting soul and funk 45s for years by that point, Empire State Soul Club became the jumping-off point for his own storied career in New York nightlife. The Empress recalls a young, studious Fine Wine sitting on the side of the stage with a pen and paper, noting his favorite records and labels to add to his growing collection. Fine Wine first got behind the mic across the Hudson at New Jersey community radio station WFMU in 1994, as the host of an hour-long soul 45 show called *Downtown Soulville*. Then, in 1996, he started his own soul DJ night at Botanica, a basement bar on Houston Street in SoHo that had previously housed the famed venue the Knitting Factory. When Connie The Empress moved back South in 1995, Warren Lee and Jeff The Chef asked Fine Wine to take her place behind the decks at ESSC.

★ ★ ★ ★ ★ ★

"Back then, the Empire State Soul Club was the only thing in town, and the only place you can go to hear 60s soul 45s, one Thursday a month," he says, with an air of cool pride. "It wasn't like every bar had turntables, or every night of the week you could hear a DJ. There's nothing like that going on. Soul Kitchen was attracting b-boys and people who were into music for the samples and stuff. Whereas the ESSC was more of like rock'n'rollers and mods, there was no hip-hop feel to it at all. And no 70s funk feel."

ESSC's dedication to 60s sounds drew a handful of notables, including Rufus & Carla, The Uptown Horns (a horn section that backed Big Joe Turner, The Neville Brothers, Ronnie Spector, and David Johannsen, among others) to Tramps, one of the Soul Club's original locations—as well as Stax native Eddie Floyd. "Big Bird" himself would show up, often unannounced, and ESSC DJs would scramble to find Floyd's records among their deep 45 boxes so the singer would have tracks to croon over. "Eddie brought [singer] Maxine Brown. And one of my friends said she was hustling guys who were playing pool before she got up there," Francis remembers, cackling at the thought of an R&B legend working over patrons at North River Bar.

While Giant Step and Soul Kitchen attracted heavy hitters and up-and-comers in the evolutionary funk scene of the mid-90s, and Empire State Soul Club brought living legends to the stage, New York remained a majority collector culture when it came to funk and soul born between the late 60s and mid-70s. Independent record stores catered to every possible genre of music, and a collector could spend a full day roaming from store to store below 14th Street. A savvy funk and soul fiend might take the train to West 4th Street/Washington Square and start digging at Golden Disc (later Bleeker Street Records, which boasted a massive basement of dollar bins), head around the corner and down half a flight of stairs to Subterranean Records, then grab a slice before strolling over to Second Coming just south of the park. St. Marks Place in the East Village, once a punk epicenter, was home to Sounds and Venus records, both of which

★ ★ ★ ★ ★ ★

were a short walk from A-1 Record Shop, Academy, and Tompkins Square Books & Records. Anyone willing to leave the Village could head to Downtown Music Exchange in Two Bridges or up to East 12th to check out Footlight Records—a storied home for lovers of musical theater that also carried serious soul and jazz albums.

Record fairs and flea markets also played a huge role in the development of NYC's crates. Located a world away from the Village collecting scene on the Upper East Side, the Roosevelt Record Convention was an important nexus for funk fanatics and hip-hop heads (everyone from Pete Rock to Q-Tip) looking to dig for fresh beats and breaks. Meanwhile, the monthly fair at the Holiday Inn on West 57th and the flea on 6th Avenue and West 24th drew similarly passionate collectors. Yet just running a simple errand could net a great record; the streets were lined with wax. DJ and journalist Jeff "Chairman" Mao developed his own funky universe through Bumpshop—a fabled party at APT, where Weingarden and members of the Daptone family would coalesce in the early 2000s—and on Columbia University's legendary soul radio show *Across 110th Street*. But when he first moved to New York in the 80s, Mao recalled, "It was pre-Giuliani, and the 'quality of life' crackdown on street vending hadn't happened yet, basically all you had to do was walk out the door to find records."[6]

Elsewhere in the city, Miriam Lima and Billy Miller were digging for obscurities to release through their reissue label Norton Records. The couple were cornerstones of New York's punk community: she used to drum for legendary post-punk/proto goth rock'n'rollers The Cramps; he sold records for decades, in addition to singing for a number of garage groups; and they had published punk fanzine *Kicks* since 1987. Norton created compilations based on the catalogues of a handful of greasy rock singers, kickin' R&B, and country artists hitherto forgotten by time and taste. Rockabilly singer and simultaneous multi-instrumentalist Hasil Adkins, reverb-rocking guitarist Link Wray, and screaming pianist Esquerita (from whom Little Richard is directly descended) all received the Norton reissue/preservation treatment. The label also put out comps with

★ ★ ★ ★ ★ ★

funk and soul artists such as singer Bobby Powell, Texas sweet soul group Sunny & The Sunliners, singer The Mighty Hannibal, and lesser-known tracks from Little Richard. They began releasing bootleg and "semi-official" compilations with titles *All Night Soul Stomp! Dancefloor Boogaloo Romp!* and *Whip It On 'Em* in the early 90s, echoing earlier rock and soul compilation work from Germany by way of New York label Crypt Records and that of English reissuers like Charly Records and Soul Supply. Norton's compilation LPs and CDs—a result of decades of digging—turned punks, rockers, and other primed earholes onto soulful obscurities, paving the way for multiple generations of vinyl addicts, as well as a handful of DJ nights and live music events in the city.

Operating within this network of flea-goers, street vendors, storefronts, and preservationists was an international contingent of record collectors dealing in rare funk and soul 45s. Among these fanatic collectors was Phillip Lehman, a late-twentysomething from a pedigreed French family whose previous vocations included catacombs exploration and graffiti art (he achieved a level of fame bombing under the tag Bando), as well as obscure funk collector and distributor.[7] Although he played drums, his reputation as a respectable but eccentric dude far exceeded and outlasted his musical rep. He often spoke softly but firmly through his teeth, probably an attempt to disguise his French accent, and had a decisively punk rock, fairly cavalier attitude that was foreign to many of the people he encountered in the world of records.

"Phillip lived in, like, an amazing mansion on the Upper East Side with his Oscar-winning dad, who is a filmmaker," recalls Weingarden, still mystified by Lehman's roots decades later. "I sold Phillip some record once. It was my first time being at the house, and I just remember Phillip saying, *Dad, what time's our reservation at the Four Seasons?* or something like that. And he runs to the ATM and is peeling off hundred-dollar bills to pay for the record, whatever it was, and then going back to go have this fancy dinner with his dad."

Roth adds, "His dad owned this huge building on, like, 82nd Street, and I think had an agreement with the Met or something where they would insure his art collection in their basement if he agreed to let them display ten percent of it at any given time. It was that type of family—and a real creative, productive family. His dad had cool recordings from the jungles, and all kinds of film awards."

Although deep pockets aren't a requisite for collecting rare funk singles, they certainly don't hurt. Working with partner Aldo Rosati, Lehman released deep funk compilations, reissues, and bootlegs under the Pure Records imprint—and Roth, who had since dived headfirst into the funky abyss, bought them up. By the time Roth was a junior at NYU, he was collecting funk and soul records and playing in a Gap Band–esque group called Dine-o-matic, while making moves toward becoming a math teacher. "I was studying music technology, which was a little bit of a bullshit major just because I wanted to teach high school, and to teach high school all you need is a bachelor's degree in anything, really. So I just kind of looked through the book, and picked a major that sounded like it had cool classes."

The music theory and history were important, but perhaps not as much as Roth's classes on acoustics, electronics, and music recording. Lehman wanted to make funk records in the style of those he was collecting, and word of Roth's recording skills reached his ears. A friend "told Phillip that I knew how to make records, which I didn't, really," says Roth, then relatively fresh faced and without his trademark Fu Manchu mustache. "I was engineering, and I didn't know what the fuck I was doing either. But I was just trying to make really rough records, so I didn't really give a shit." Ever the punk-rocker, Lehman didn't give a shit either; the two bonded over their shared taste in tough funk from the early to mid-70s and obscure soul while hanging out at Lehman's loft.

"The night I met Phillip, he introduced me to The Poets Of Rhythm," Roth recalls, referring to the troop of German James Browns who had been creating funk from the same well of inspiration, thousands of miles away in Munich.[8] Working under the name Bus People Express, the Poets released a 45 called "Augusta, Georgia," effectively fooling Roth and other

★ ★ ★ ★ ★ ★

in-the-know fans about the tune's origins. "I thought it was some old band from Georgia. So I was like, *What the fuck*, and that kind of blew my mind. Partly because it was so good and because I'd been fooled, but also because it gave me the idea that, like, you could actually still make records like this."

Not too long after their shared brain-dump, Lehman and Roth started a band. Roth's friend Mike Wagner, a horn player and guitarist who also played in Din-o-matic, joined as a multi-instrumentalist; Lehman, true to form, would be the group's "weird, cool" drummer; and Roth bought a bass at a pawn shop for $90. "We would just make records on a four-track or whatever, as rough as we could," he says. While the band didn't yet have a name, they had a vibe, and they wore their inspirations on their sleeves: pre–"Hollywood Swingin'" Kool & The Gang, the Poets, and rare funk 45s from the likes of James Brown, Eddie Bo, and Hank Carbo. Because of the acid-fueled dominance of groups like Parliament, Roth and Lehman had a difficult time finding other musicians who understood the groovy simplicity of their foundational bands. "At that time, it was all about the breakbeats, like Bread and heavy stuff like that," Roth says. "Everything was kind of slick and all the musicians in New York at the time were playing six strings, slapping and popping everything. I couldn't find anyone who wanted to play simple."

That simplicity became the key to Lehman and Roth's funky kingdom—a guiding principle for their developing ensemble that favored serving the whole rather than the chops of any single player. Slowly but surely, they met likeminded musicians, among them percussionist Fernando "Bugaloo" Velez and baritone saxman Martín Perna. While drinking at DJ Franc'o's "sleazy listening" gig Vampyros Lesbos—a twice-weekly event featuring topless go-go dancers, projections from films made between 1965 to 1972, and a soundtrack of French pop, organ-combo funk, and porno-film bow-chicka-wow instrumentals—Roth was introduced to a guitarist and bartender from Milwaukee named Frank Stribling, who, for the next twenty-plus years, would be known as Binky Griptite.[9]

★ ★ ★ ★ ★ ★

"We just started talking about music, and we were just on the same page," says Griptite, who, when he met Roth, was coming out of a multi-year performance hiatus to unlearn some bad habits. "It's a syndrome—good guitar players will have a tendency to want to show how good they are and play a lot. I was just like, *Yeah, I have nothing to prove. I just want to play rhythm.*"

When Griptite came by for an audition a few weeks later, Roth and Lehman had planned a test. They fired up James Brown's swinging 1970 hit "Give It Up, Turn It Loose" with the intention of seeing "how long he'll play the same thing without fucking around," as Roth puts it. The three of them settled into the rhythm of the popular break. "Five minutes, ten minutes go by, and we're just playing it. Didn't call the change or anything, and Binky leans back, and he starts to fall asleep. He fell asleep and he was still playing it," Roth says excitedly. "And Phillip and I were like, *Yeah, man, this dude's in!*"

CHAPTER TWO LET A MAN DO WHAT HE WANNA DO: DESCO RECORDS DIGS

Gabe Roth was raised by two civil rights and discrimination lawyers who exposed their kids to a wide variety of people—activists, judges, people accused of murder that they were defending. When he was thirteen, Roth's parents took in a Guatemalan teenager whose mother was battling cancer; his sister's friend, a young Black man who went by the name T.T., moved in a few years later to escape a troubled home.[1] The additions continued over the years as space and need dictated, laying a foundation for the "family you choose" mindset Roth would champion as a musician.

With a growing clan of players that included Fernando on congas, Mike Wagner on guitar and trombone, and saxophonist Joe Hrbek, Lehman and Roth began rehearsing at Phillip's Union Square loft in 1995. The following year, they established Desco Records—named after a vacuum supply store a short walk away from Lehman's apartment on 14th Street, near 8th Avenue in the Village—and quickly began creating a record that would fool collectors in the same way The Poets Of Rhythm had gotten one over on them.

"Unfortunately, back then, people would associate funk bands with really shitty stuff," Lehman told the *Village Voice* in 2009. "There were a bunch of bands from England, but they all sucked, in my opinion, and that was it. There wasn't any good new funk being produced at all."[2]

"Phillip was always kind of a rebel, he had such a punk rock attitude," Roth says, clenching his teeth to imitate Lehman's terse speech. "He was like, *Fuck it. We're gonna record a kung fu soundtrack and we're gonna pretend it's old, a reissue. Fuck everybody, they won't know what it is.*"

★ ★ ★ ★ ★ ★

The Revenge Of Mister Mopoji was recorded at a basement studio on Ludlow Street in the Lower East Side and released exclusively on vinyl into an unsuspecting world in 1996. Credited to Mike Jackson & The Soul Providers, Desco billed the record as a "100 percent guaranteed classic funk soundtrack" to a 1974 kung fu picture directed by the fictional Sam Lung and marketed with a painted cover in 70s-does-the-40s style featuring guns, cars, and a woman with knowing eyes (modeled on Lehman's then girlfriend) hiding behind a fan. Tracks like "The Wisdom Of Master Shen" and "Unstoppable Oldsmobile" made up enough of a plot, and the "reissue" sold five or six thousand copies—most of which were hocked by pounding the pavement at record stores in New York, Philly, and Boston.

"People were bullshitting us, like, *Oh, I got the original. My cousin's got the movie on Betamax*," Roth recalls, smug at his ability to pull one over on the community of record collectors lusting after the same rare funk 45s as he and Lehman did. "I didn't really take any of it that seriously because I didn't think of it as a career path, you know?" he continues, though Roth, Lehman, and Wagner put significant effort into cutting their records live in a room, and overdubbing horns, vocals and percussion only when needed. "Not that I wasn't trying—I was trying really hard, but I didn't have ambitions to be successful in the music industry the way that a lot of people do, and I think that really makes people very timid. They don't take the same kind of risks and do the same kind of crazy shit. And Phillip was out of his mind."

Studio space comes and goes, and for whatever reason the space on Ludlow stopped being a viable spot for Desco's crew. They started venturing out to the Long Island suburb of Deer Park to record at a heavy-metal space called Dare Studios. Roth and Lehman were still flying by the seat of their pants: "Phillip would pick me up and just tell me what we were doing. One day he's like, 'Oh, we're gonna do a sitar funk record with James Brown and The Meters covers.' I was like, 'Okay, great. Who's gonna play sitar?' 'You're gonna play sitar.' I'm like, 'That's a classical Indian instrument, I don't know how to play it.' Phillip's like, 'I rented one, it's in the back.' I look in the back and, sure enough, there's a sitar."

★ ★ ★ ★ ★ ★

Desco duly released a couple of funky sitar singles under the name Ravi Harris & The Prophets, using a Dare Studios employee with long hair and a hippie-ish outfit to play the role of Ravi Harris on the record's picture sleeve. "The funny thing is, because he had curly black hair, everybody thinks it's me," Roth says, adding that *Funky Sitar Man* was licensed to BBE and was one of the first records Desco released in England. "Okay, that one kind of backfired on me."

As Desco's house band, The Soul Providers began recording their real debut, *Gimme The Paw* (also released as *Soul Tequila*, with most of the same songs but in a different sequence). The album was an early exploration of Roth's prolific songwriting abilities, and many of its songs drew directly from life experience. "The Landlord," for example, was written when Roth and Martín Perna were getting evicted from their apartment in the Lower East Side; for good measure, Roth penned another tune, "Mr. Kesselman," to make sure the landlord's name would be all over the record.

Released with a photo of a cute dog as the cover in what hindsight would describe as a particularly 90s aesthetic, *Gimme* was a flop. While collectors clamored for the *Mister Mopoji* "reissue," Desco couldn't sell *Gimme The Paw*—even though both were recorded with the same band.

"We were like, 'Surprise! That was us, we're The Soul Providers, this is our new record.' We couldn't even give that thing away, man. Nobody wanted that record; still, man, nobody wants that record," Roth says ruefully. Groovy as they were, The Soul Providers were still downwind from popular taste. "At the time, if somebody said, 'There's this funk band playing,' or 'There's this record,' even any of us at Desco would just write it off. Nobody was thinking, like, *Oh, this is going to be good*, or *That's gonna be rough*. There wasn't really any context to put out music like that."

Although *Gimme The Paw* didn't do much to give Desco acclaim, mainstream cred, or cash, it did put the label on a collision course with one of its heroes. "We're out in Long Island recording a track and are like, *Man, we should get somebody to sing on this*. Then Phillip's talking about Lee Fields," Roth recounts, still surprised or impressed that his

★ ★ ★ ★ ★ ★

partner would have the gall to suggest simply calling up a soul legend. Fields had performed with Kool & The Gang, O.V. Wright, Betty Wright (no relation), and Darrell Banks, among many other fabled acts, and was sometimes referred to as "Little JB" for his vocal and physical resemblance to the Godfather Of Soul. As an independent performer, Fields released wickedly rough singles in the exact vein of Roth's taste, including "She's A Love Maker" (1973) and "Funky Screw" (1975), the latter on his own Angle 3 Records. But the rise of disco and DJ culture pushed Fields, like many of his contemporaries, to the margins of taste. By the early 80s, he was working (successfully) in real estate. "I didn't abandon music completely, but I was buying properties and renting them out. But my mind was always on music. Thank God in the 90s things opened up for me," he later told the UK's *Daily Express* newspaper.[3]

"I didn't even know if he was alive. I was like, *You can't just call Lee Fields*," Roth says, recalling his incredulity that Fields would deign to do a session. "But nothing was really impossible for Phillip." Lehman, ever determined in his quest for funk greatness but operating in a world that hadn't yet experienced the power of Google, contacted music publishing and royalty company BMI and got a contact number for Fields who, fatefully, lived not too far away, in Plainfield, New Jersey. "A couple days later, he'd offered Lee Fields some cash, and he was in Dare Studios."

Stunned and slightly intimidated by the prospect of recording with a living legend, Roth quickly wrote two tunes for Fields: "Steam Train" and "Let A Man Do What He Wanna Do." Fields—a consummate professional with a Southerner's polite, classy attitude, and the cool you'd expect from an OG funk musician—"came in and just crushed it."

"Let A Man" was a fairly simple, early 70s-style funk tune with emphasis on drums and rhythm guitar. Fields's voice comes in sweet, talking about a friend who's having lady trouble. Fields adds hints of James Brown, wailing as he encourages his friend's woman, "*Baby*, let your man do what he wanna do" on top of punchy backup vocals offering the same refrain.

"I barely remember even having him in there. I just remember him

★ ★ ★ ★ ★ ★

opening his mouth and my jaw dropping, because I don't think anybody sings like him," Roth says. "That was one of those first moments for me. Hearing something I wrote come out of his mouth, and realizing something I did—not because I did something extraordinary, but almost the opposite, because I did something kind of mediocre but structurally sound—in the hands of a real artist, it just became something so beautiful. It was really a rush."

Lee Fields and The Soul Providers were onto something, and Fields himself knew it. "I felt like these guys had an idea, but at the time they were a bit green," Fields reflected, telling *Relix* magazine that the young Desco musicians had more ambition than skill. But what the journeyman singer did hear was glorious. "I could understand later why they found me—because we had so much in common. They were the new generation of musicians, but they had the same vision I had—they wanted to make what they *like*, and I think that's what still keeps everything tight."[4]

At the start of his 1998 Desco debut LP *Let's Get A Groove On*, Fields puts the call out to listeners with the smooth ramble of a well-respected neighborhood hustler or an ultra-cool uncle. Speaking to the young bloods, old cats, those in the know, and others who might be dropping the needle on some super heavy funk for the first time, he declares:

> The Soul Providers and I put this little record together to remind some of you about how soul music used to be back in the day—before synthesizers and samplers and drum machines. I'm talking about way back before disco, when it was all rough. Yeah. And nasty and genuine. There's a lot of folks out there making music nowadays who seem to have forgotten what the word funk used to mean—and lord knows there are too many who never knew. But that ain't nothing because here at Desco Records, we believe we got enough to go around. Oh yeah! We got plenty. So if you're listening to this record at a club, a bar, a block party, a barbecue, a family reunion, or even if you're in a cabin somewhere with nothing but your two feet and a record player, I want you to hear me when I tell you it's time to get up! Get down! I mean c'mon! Let's get a groove on.

★ ★ ★ ★ ★ ★

The introductory manifesto was written almost entirely by Roth and Lehman, and while Fields sells it, it doesn't sound entirely natural. "Not sure he was on board with all of it, but he was a good sport," Roth remembers, an ode to Fields's consummate professionalism. On its release, an *AV Club* critic questioned the manifesto's dismissal of decades of music, "but if *Let's Get A Groove On* is meant to provide evidence of the old school's continued viability, he makes a pretty convincing case."[5]

The Fields session was a huge musical step, and Desco cut a single of "Let A Man Do What He Wanna Do" along with the raw, brassy strength of "Steam Train;" Roth considered it the best record the label had done. He and Lehman hopped in Phillip's Jeep and hit their usual distribution channels with a box of Lee Field's first funk tune in decades. "It was a monster," Roth says. "I was so proud. Anybody who's into that kind of music, I don't see why they wouldn't love it." But, just as with *Gimme The Paw*, "we couldn't give them away." The Desco heads sold a few singles for two dollars each and were beginning to hit a wall when Lehman had an idea: they needed to tap back into that rare groove collector mentality. "Phillip, being the way he is, went home and got a bunch of copies and scratched them up. And, like, rubbed the labels with newspaper, so they looked faded and went from mint condition to VG-. We would go into record stores with one of them and sell them for, like, $50 or $100."

But perhaps the most important and soulful kismet connection in Desco's storied history came in the form of those backup vocals kicking up Lee Fields's message on "Let A Man Do What He Wanna Do." Enter Sharon Jones, a five-foot nothing, forty-something, sharp-tongued, powerful-lunged singer with a wide smile and a dime-sized mole above her left eye, from Brooklyn by way of North Augusta, South Carolina. At the time, Jones was dating sax player Joe Hrbek, who had told Lehman and Roth that he could bring three women to the studio to record backing vocals. The next day, Jones showed up alone.

★ ★ ★ ★ ★ ★

"I'm like, 'Yo, where're your friends?' And she said, 'Why pay three when you could pay me?' and she links up all three parts of the harmonies," Roth recounts, with a mix of humor and astonishment. No stranger to hustle—Sharon Jones spent much of her life trying to break into the music business, working club gigs in a wedding band, as an armored truck driver, and even as a guard at New York's infamous Riker's Island jail—she turned a $50 gig into a $150 opportunity through skill and finely applied pressure. The whole crew was taken with her, and when a buddy of Lehman approached the label to do a *Blowfly*-esque comedy rap about getting out of jail, Roth knew the tune would need some background vocals.

Drawing from memories of Blaxploitation flicks, Jones flipped out some harmonies of the word *switchblade*. "What the hell is this song about?" she asked pointedly, and Roth and Lehman broke down the as-yet-unrecorded concept album. "She just started talking shit and had us rolling instantly, because she was way funnier than Phil's friend. And right off the top of her head, she's all, 'I'm gon' slit you where the good lord split you!' Sharon could talk shit like that forever." Roth sped up the tape machine so Sharon's voice would sound lower, her expert melding of camp and funk running point on "Switchblade's" funky, simple guitar melody and three-part horn section.

While Roth recalls Sharon's first sessions through slightly rose-colored lenses—a slight deviation from the dark shades he's consistently sported on and offstage for the past decade and a half, the result of a car accident that left the bassist with severe ocular damage—the singer was initially skeptical of the twenty-one-year-old kid mixing her vocals. "I remember thinking, *What the hell does this little white boy know about funk?*" she recounted in 2008. "But Gabe knew what he was doing. We finished the session that day, and I remember walking out of the studio thinking that that boy was reincarnated—he was a fifty-five-year-old Black man in a little Jewish boy's body."[6]

"Switchblade," the first of many songs Sharon Jones would sing lead on, also made it onto *Gimme The Paw*. But her presence—a mixture of

★ ★ ★ ★ ★ ★

tough-as-nails attitude and a gut-level relationship with soul music, the foundation of which was laid in church and a lifetime spent idolizing James Brown and Tina Turner—would prove anchoring to Desco and The Soul Providers. Sharon, who in later years would be introduced by Binky Griptite to adoring crowds as a "super soul sister with that magnetic je ne sais quoi," was hungry to work, and she quickly became entrenched in the Desco family. Roth had been writing copious amounts of music for Desco's various studio projects, but now, with a budding diva to belt out his lyrics, Sharon and company laid to waste a handful of singles that, finally, were being accepted in funk collector circles.

The crew left Long Island to return to their roots in the Lower East Side, renting a studio from an old Jewish couple on Orchard Street and Grand, and immediately outfitting it with thick carpeting to muffle the impending funky sonic boom. In the week or so before the couple kicked Desco out, the crew managed to record several killer singles: "Damn It's Hot" (a tribute to the lack of AC in the studio, where nearly a dozen musicians were cutting everything live to tape), "Bump N Touch" b/w "Hook And Sling Meets The Funky Superfly." New Lee Fields singles were recorded at Orchard Street as well, including "Hey, Sallie Mae (Get Off My Feet)," a tribute to Roth's mountain of student loan debt and the bill collectors who regularly hounded him.

Even with Lee Fields and Sharon Jones embedded in Desco's growing clan of musicians, the label continued to experiment with concept albums and phony reissues. Drunk on the genius of Nigerian bandleader Fela Kuti—a musical pioneer who developed Afrobeat in the 70s by mixing Yoruba rhythms with American soul and jazz—Lehman and Roth decided to record an Afrobeat album under the name The Daktaris (Swahili for "doctors") at Dare Studios. Although the music of Fela and his contemporaries drew interest from funk and soul legends of the era, Afrobeat was certainly outside of popular taste and still fairly uncommon among collectors in 1997. *Soul Explosion* was a masterclass in Afro-inspired funk, with covers of Desco favorite James Brown and Fela, Ethiopian

★ ★ ★ ★ ★ ★

rarities, and enough legit-sounding originals with seemingly African names—including "Eltsuhg Ibal Lasiti," which, critically, is "It is all a big hustle" spelled backward.

Soul Explosion was released in 1998, following Fela Kuti's death and a renewed interest in the music he made a global phenomenon. The album design was intentionally misleading, with a low-res safari scene on the cover and a proclamation that it was produced in Nigeria, not forty miles from Midtown Manhattan. Liner notes by a "Peter Franklin" of the nonexistent Abidjan Musique declared, "The Daktaris is a well-disciplined army of two hundred African Bull Elephants marching relentlessly up your business to the beat from Funky Drummer." In reality, the players were still The Soul Providers and friends, though all the musicians credited on *Soul Explosion* used fake names (with the exception of Joe Hrbek and trombonist Neal Pawley) made up by Tunde Adebimpe, a singer of Nigerian descent who would go on to front Bowie-loving alt-rockers TV On The Radio, who at various times lived with Mike Wagner, Pern, and Roth.

"*Soul Explosion* is scratchy and raw to the point of total distortion, old-school to the point of being crude," Ezra Gale wrote in the *Village Voice*. "Drums claw like they were recorded on a cheap cassette player, guitars practically scrape the insides of your speakers, and the horn section sounds like it's blasting out of a loudspeaker at the other end of a parade ground... like James Brown recording in Lagos, or Fela in Memphis."[7]

Many people assumed The Daktaris were, indeed, a long-lost African group—a perturbing trend among Desco's faux-reissues. "We had an ethnomusicologist in LA tell us that he had other Daktari records!" Roth later told engineering publication *Sound On Sound*. The rough recording and attention paid to faking out listeners—who, at the time, relied on message boards and insight into Desco's operation to learn that the album wasn't a genuine artifact from 1970s Nigeria—netted a few thousand sales. More importantly, it was influential aural honey for some key musicians.

Martín Perna, who played saxophone on *Soul Explosion* as well as a number of other Desco recordings (and also happened to be Roth's roommate in South Williamsburg), was mesmerized with music The Daktaris produced and the originals that inspired the band. "After we did that record, he really wanted to take The Daktaris on the road. And Phillip was like, *Nah I don't want to do it*," Roth says. "So, Martin started his own band called The Conjunto Antibalas," who would reintroduce Afrobeat to a new generation over a twenty-year career.

"The transmission is clear," Wagner told the *Voice*. "Phillip to the Daktaris, because he introduced us to all that Afrobeat and Afro-funk stuff. The Daktaris to Antibalas. Antibalas to everyone else."

Soul Explosion was also mind-blowing to organ player Victor Axelrod, a native of Brooklyn's Park Slope neighborhood who would go on to be an integral part of the Desco/Daptone family as a musician and producer. A serious, studied, and fairly soft-spoken player who's "not quick to just go around and introduce myself or get in people's faces," Axelrod first came into contact with Desco while recording with another band at a Manhattan studio. He had been eyeing a cassette credited to The Other Side—a jazz-funk project that would put out one album, *(Don't Look Back) Behind The Shack*—on a table at the studio, and, when he eventually pressed play, "It was all clearly James Brown–inspired instrumentals. And I could tell that it was new. But clearly it was made with this direct inspiration and direct aesthetic. It was just made with the discipline that I really yearned for in my life."

While Axelrod may have craved musical discipline, he was already operating a tight ship in his twenties. He attended some Giant Step parties and played at Soul Kitchen once or twice, but he was "so clear on the fact that if I was going to be any good at this, I needed to be practicing." Much like Roth and Lehman, Axelrod hadn't met many other musicians who loved the basic goodness of James Brown. "I just never met people who are going to, like, sit on one chord and make that work," he says from his quiet apartment/home studio in Gowanus, Brooklyn. "I always wanted to experience playing a simple part with a bunch of other people who are playing simple parts. I was hearing that on this tape, and I

★ ★ ★ ★ ★ ★

was kind of blown away. I rarely ever had that feeling of, like, *Who's that? I need to know them.*"

Axelrod started hanging out with Roth and Lehman, turning each other on to records and listening to Desco demos, and made his label debut in 1998. While the record didn't claim to be a reissue, Desco enlisted the eponymous help of a French musician and electronic pop pioneer for their next release: Nino Nardini & The Pop Riveria Group's *Rotonde Musique*. The LP's liner notes promised "copious amounts of greased-out Hammond and flood-pounding break beats" for a wicked record that melded jazz with funk and psychedelia—continuing Desco's tradition of confusing collectors and piquing the interest of those in the know. "At the time, I didn't even know where it was all headed. I was just happy to make the connection and Gabe had albums worth of stuff that needed organ on it, so I just worked with him for two days and plowed through all these songs," Axelrod says.

In 1998, Desco had its own Stax-eqsue explosion, putting out jazz-tinged funk and soul with some help from a Boston transplant and sax man who moved to the city in 1991. Neal Sugarman came up in Boston's punk scene and headed south to play jazz, but he found his musical lane by performing bluesy R&B in the vein of tenor saxophonists Gene Ammons and Stanley Turrentine. While Sugarman was hip to the acid jazz scene burbling in the city and across the pond in the UK, he wanted to play something edgier. He founded The Sugarman 3—which, contrary to its name, was a four piece—and the group offered up soul and boogaloo with a heavy dose of swing (itself experiencing a mini resurgence in the mid-90s) at gigs in the East Village. After hitting it off with Gabe Roth at a Soul Kitchen gig, Sugarman brought a demo to Lehman's Fifth Avenue loft, and the sound was an immediate hit. "They were just like, *Okay, when can you record?* They were super excited about it," recalls Sugarman, a tallish, unassuming player with short brown hair that would eventually recede into a shock of blonde as the years and tour miles went on.

★ ★ ★ ★ ★ ★

Sugar's Boogaloo was the first album recorded at 440 West 41st Street, Desco's new Manhattan home base. Lehman, Roth, and crew built out a studio in the basement of a ten-story brick building on the corner of Dyer Avenue overlooking the entrance to the Lincoln Tunnel, with a dollar bill stuck between the windowpanes that separated the control and live rooms. The studio was in a particularly convenient location for Sugarman 3 co-founder and organist Adam Scone, who happened to live five floors up in the same building. Scone loaded his Hammond B3 in the elevator to attend Sugarman 3 recording sessions, but also just found himself hanging out in the nondescript and often smoke-filled space, which saw constant activity. Lee Fields and Sharon Jones popped in and out—the latter recorded several smokin' funk 45s there, including a cover of James Brown's "I Got The Feeling"—and even Joe Williams, 440's doorman, left his post to make a vocal cameo on the *Let's Get A Groove On* track "Bad, Bad, Bad." At the time, Williams was involved in a patent dispute with an English company over a combination rattle/pacifier that was being marketed under the name "Binky Griptight."

The studio buzzed with horn players, at least two organists, percussionists and axemen, and a few guest stars, some of whom would plant their roots with the Desco family. Among them was Joseph Henry, a soul and gospel singer living in Bed-Stuy, Brooklyn, who used to perform with 50s novelty group The Coasters. After a short stint with Roth in a group called the Eastside Soul Congregation—the result of an ad Roth took out in the *Village Voice* circa '94—Henry busted out two songs with The Soul Providers: "Who's The King (You Know That's Me)" and "I Feel Right," which gave the label its first real taste of acceptance and respect from the international funk scene.

Around this time, Fred Thomas of J.B.'s fame—who played bass on many of Desco's favorite hard funk tunes and was an idol of Roth's—came by for a session. When Roth later went to see the bassist perform at a dive bar in the Village called Nightingales, Thomas was backed up by a blind pianist named Cliff Driver who played "in a sturdy style, completely

★ ★ ★ ★ ★ ★

devoid of the self-conscious artiness that Roth disliked in indie rock."[8] Roth became Driver's apprentice of sorts, a young twentysomething Jew filling in on bass for gigs at storefront churches in Harlem, East New York and occasionally the far reaches of Allentown, Pennsylvania.

"Cliff didn't bullshit anybody," Roth says, "and he won't tell you that you're doing something right. But he'll tell you if you're doing something wrong. So the idea that he kept me around and he liked me playing with him was huge for me. It helped me figure out just how to play that shit. It's cliché, but when you're going through that shit, it's fun and it's cool. But it's not till years later when you look back on it that it seems more extraordinary. I was very fortunate to be able to play with all those guys, man. It's crazy to me." But Roth also pushed his own style, and the two would regularly argue and debate; Driver later told the *New York Times* that the young producer-engineer was "an old traditional type" enthralled with a sound the then-septuagenarian would have been content to leave in the 70s.

Equally important to their dynamic was the introduction of Naomi Davis, a gospel and soul singer originally from Alabama who made her living cleaning houses. At night, Davis fronted The Gospel Queens, a group with four singers and the J.B.'s Fred Thomas on bass, led by Cliff Driver—whom Davis first met in 1963 while gigging at the Night Cap on Flatbush Ave. in Brooklyn. Scratchy-throated in the vein of Wilson Pickett, Davis recorded her own midtempo funk singles, "Wind Your Clock" ("their first record, I think, that became rare and expensive," recalls avid 45 collector Fine Wine), "Good Thing," and a vampy track with The Knights Of 41st Street that became an anthem of Desco's 440 era: "41st Street Breakdowne."

In 1998, Roth and Lehman connected once again with The Poets Of Rhythm—the German group that truly kickstarted the funk revival in the early 90s. Poets JJ and Max Whitefield headed to New York at Desco's behest to record as The Whitefield Brothers, playing a band's worth of instruments between them, from organ to vocals and bass. With assistance from Roth, Sugarman, and a teenager named Leon Michels (who wrote

★ ★ ★ ★ ★ ★

horn arrangements and played sax and flute), the German duo created a psychedelic funk record with heavy African influence. Although the sound predates similar output from Roth and company, the recording session was marked by creative differences and changing tastes among The Whitefield's production team. The resulting record, later called *In The Raw*, was deemed too ethereal and trippy for the raw funk-focused Desco.

Across town at Friends Seminary—a Quaker day school in the East Village—drummer Homer Steinweiss, bassist Nick Movshon, guitarist Sean Solomon, and saxophonist/organ player Michels were moving away from the standards and licks they were learning in their school jazz band and getting psyched out on 70s funk. "The seniors, when we were in eighth grade, were really into Parliament Funkadelic, and we thought those guys were the coolest guys in the world. So we're like, *Let's start learning about Parliament*," says Steinweiss, also a curly haired Jewish musician with a thick brow. They formed Poly Six & The Cacalactic Quartet, a Funkadelic-inspired group in both name and sound, and performed at a few pay-to-play venues in Manhattan as teens. However, the young band's break came not at a show but at the house of a sax student of Leon's—possibly the actress Jemima Kirke, who was just a couple of years younger than Michels, and whose father was the drummer in the 70s rock bands Bad Company and Free. Steinweiss recounts that Kirke's father was friends with Phillip Lehman, and when Lehman and Michels happened to be at the Kirke residence together, Desco eventually came up.

"He was like, *We love funk music but we hate 70s funk music; we hate Parliament Funkadelic, we hate Stevie Wonder*. We're like, *How is that possible, that's the best music ever*," Steinweiss says. But Lehman had given Michels a mixtape of deep funk singles as inspiration, so Poly Six made a Meters- and James Brown–inspired demo, were renamed The Mighty Imperials, and sent it over to 440 West 41st. The Mighty Imperials had hit Desco's vibe right on the head: as teenagers, they embodied the unpolished, excitable edge Roth and Lehman were enamored with, and they harbored a deep curiosity about 45s.

★ ★ ★ ★ ★ ★

Among The Mighty Imperials, taking the opportunity to make a record with a group of cooler older guys was a no-brainer. "There was a punk rock element to it," Steinweiss says. Gabe was very DIY, and Desco as a whole didn't "really give a fuck about" who they were making music for—though anyone involved had to have serious chops. Steinweiss continues, "You also have to know what you're doing—even if you can play an instrument, you have to, like, know all the records." Like many teenagers exposed to the musical taste of older, cooler friends (to say nothing of those under the tutelage of a scene's leading producers and musicians), Steinweiss recalls becoming almost embarrassingly obsessed with the style of funk Lehman put on that initial mixtape. "I think in order to have a bit of a vision, you have to shut a lot of things out. I actually shut everything out."

The Mighty Imperials were also beginning to engage with the notion of simplicity in a city where most musicians wanted to show off their chops. "Back then, it was like anyone who could play really fast was the guy who was getting all the gigs," Steinweiss says, while preparing cups of extra-strong pour-over coffee—the drummer's good taste in food and drink the result of years on the road (though, as a teen, he wasn't there yet). "Not showing off was a big deal—because even in school it's like, *Okay, now it's your turn to solo*. I never really wanted to do a flashy solo. So Desco's musical foundation really spoke to me."

Roth would buy the Imperials pizza with prosciutto and arugula during recording sessions, "and we would go home and be like, *Yeah, we're recording with this record label and they give us as much pizza as we want!* And our parents were like, *Okay, red flag. Kids working for pizza and making creative content*," Steinweiss remembers, noting that both his parents were classically trained pianists and songwriters. Eventually, all the families got together for a dinner with Lehman and Roth to establish some level of trust.

"Gabe was really smooth-talking and, like, he's the nicest guy; everyone loves Gabe. But his partner felt super shady. And my parents kept asking, 'How are you guys doing this?' and Phil's like, *Super simple, super simple, you just, like, just publish it, and then you do it*. Our parents were like, *This doesn't sound super simple.* They're all very sketched out," the drummer, who was fifteen or sixteen at the time, says. "But they're also, like, *What are you going to do?* Their kids are fifteen and you're going to put out their record. *How do we stop that?* So eventually they just kind of went with it."

In the early summer of 1999, The Mighty Imperials played hooky from Friends Seminary to record tracks for a couple of 45s and what would become their first and only LP, *Thunder Chicken.* While the majority of the Imperial's recordings were grooving, organ-heavy instrumentals in the style of The Meters, Joseph Henry also sang on three of the tracks. "When he first walked in, the guys were already messing around on some groove, waiting for him," Roth recounted. "He threw off his coat and walked straight to the mic. 'Keep it just where it is,' he commanded. He had already started singing by the time I got across the control room to the record button. Later, we added some horns and put it on the record as 'Soul Buster.'" The band would also back Henry on his own release, "I've Never Found A Girl" b/w "The Matador."

As dedicated music students—both in the traditional scholastic sense and in their excitement to learn by recording at Desco—the Imperials honed their taste and imperfect skills, setting the stage for Homer and Leon to become Desco session players and find themselves deep in the family fold. The young band started playing gigs around the city along with the rest of the Desco crew—including at Franc'o's Vampyros Lesbos party (which they were well underage to attend), and shocked attendees with their technique and knowledge of a genre solidified long before they were born. "I was impressed by them, seeing these kids who were so good and looked so young," recounts Mr. Fine Wine, who attended an Imperials show at Franc'o's night in the Meatpacking District. "It was an eye-opener—I walked out of there thinking, *Goddamn.*"

Desco eventually won over the record collectors and DJs who worshipped the sounds of decades prior. "If it's a new record, they're listening with a more critical ear … [but] they liked it before they realized we were new, and once they realized they liked it, they couldn't not like

★ ★ ★ ★ ★ ★

it. And it really opened things up for funk bands and gave it legitimacy," said Sugarman, who was a regular session player on many Desco releases and already cooking up his second eponymous record. But while Desco's distinct sound might have been a breath of fresh air or at least a strong whiff from the 440 basement, funk never truly disappeared from popular consciousness. "Different sounds come in and out of fashion. Disco came and all that stuff; R&B got slick, and drum machines and all that might change people's ears a little bit," Roth says. "Eventually, more and more people got into our sound, because when people heard it, it would blow their mind. It didn't sound like anything, especially if you weren't digging those old records, you know?"

Desco's reputation was growing far beyond New York. English promoters visiting the city came by the 41st Street studio to hear sessions and test pressings from Sharon Jones and company. But when they weren't producing, engineering, or playing in the heaviest funk bands in the northern hemisphere, Lehman and Roth would show off their digs on Columbia University's WKCR. Initially guests of station manager Brian Linde circa '98, the Desco heads eventually ran not one but two programs: the long-running and influential soul radio show *Across 110th Street* (Saturdays, noon to 2pm) and *Night Train* (Wednesdays, 1–5am). At one point they did a forty-eight-hour soul festival, playing records in shifts and interviewing soul legends such as Marva Whitney, Eddie Bo, Bobby Byrd, and James Brown on air.

"The night before I interviewed James Brown, I thought so hard about the questions I wanted to ask him," Roth recounts, ever studious about his fandom. "Questions about his music and where he was influenced from, and his take on bands that took from him or that he took from, and Fela and Dyke and The Blazers. But he just talked about his new record. It was not dissimilar to that interview where he's probably on PCP and he just keeps screaming names of his songs."

"Just in terms of exerting influence, there's definitely stuff that I heard for the first time listening to WKCR as a young adult," Victor Axelrod observes.

★ ★ ★ ★ ★ ★

"People were much more about breaks at that time. The bag that Phillip and Gabe were drawing from was much more of this, like, collector vibe. I'd go around them and hear all kinds of stuff that I'd never heard before."

WKCR had pull far beyond its 1,350 watts, and the Desco-programmed radio shows had serious fans on the north shore of Staten Island. There, a scene of five or so groups, mostly made up of guys in their teens or early 20s, were brewing up soul and Afrobeat-influenced instrumentals as Schlitz 36 and Fast Breaking Classics—which, in 2000, somehow connected with the Los Angeles band The Breakestra for a show at community arts venue Rubulad, forming early links in a bicoastal funk brotherhood.

"Staten Island is referred to many times as the forgotten borough," saxophonist Jared Tankel reflected. "It's the most removed out of any of the five boroughs. We relish in that. We can do whatever we want in our little studio on the north shore of Staten Island and people leave us alone." Yet their outer borough funk scene was in thrall to Desco's catalogue.

"We loved this Desco shit, especially The Daktaris' record, which had a really big influence on us because we didn't have any soul singers where we were in the 'burbs," multi-instrumentalist Tommy "TNT" Brenneck effuses. "So, when we heard The Daktaris, and it was instrumental, it was kind of like, *Yeah, we can do something like this*. We missed the mark, but isn't that how all great things come to be?"

CHAPTER THREE GOT TO BE THE WAY IT IS: SUBCULTURE, COLLECTORS, AND DJS KEEP THE LOVE OF SOUL BURNING

At the dawn of the new millennium, Desco was more preoccupied with laying down wax than any impending Y2K paranoia. They were readying The Sugarman 3's second LP, a stripped-down album that leaned into funk and away from more traditional jazz solos called *Soul Donkey*. But unlike other jazz projects that might've taken themselves too seriously, Desco rarely shied away from taking the piss.

"Rupert, the Soul Donkey, was reared on a farm in South Carolina. From the tender age of 15, he carted loads of getdown across the Southern Donkeyway out to Mississippi," the liner notes read. "Along the way he learned about hard work, perseverance and how to do the Broadway Combination without spilling his oats. Now he's a full-grown Soul Donkey, way past 21. He can strut his Donkey stuff and he ain't no jive!" The group's take on "Turtle Walk," a 1969 Blue Note tune by saxman Lou Donaldson, was released as a B-side but became one of Desco's most popular 45s for its danceable tempo and frantic organ.

The label had cemented its roster of session players and bands, with The Soul Providers backing Lee Fields, Sharon Jones, Naomi Davis, and Joseph Henry. The crew reconfigured to perform Afrobeat as The Daktaris (who would soon evolve into Antibalas with the addition of a couple of new musicians, including a British-Nigerian frontman and community activist

★ ★ ★ ★ ★ ★

named Duke Amayo); then slimmed down to play organ-forward soul-jazz as The Sugarman 3. Finally, with help from a few underage kids, the instrumental The Mighty Imperials rounded out Desco's canon. Following in the cool custom of soul families large and small, Desco regularly held revues for a growing and devoted audience. The Desco Soul Revue found homes at lower Manhattan venues like Baby Jupiter, Wetlands, the Knitting Factory, and the Mercury Lounge.

"I remember doing a show at Wetlands with Lee—it was such a big deal for Gabe to back up Lee Fields, whereas I never heard of Lee Fields before I met Gabe," says Victor Axelrod, who became a founding member of Antibalas, playing keys, but occasionally sat in with other acts. At the end of the night, he still hadn't gotten paid. "After the gig, I was asking Gabe what was up with the money, like, *Is Gabe taking me for a sucker right now?* And he was just riding so high. It only took a few more gigs, then he was just kind of like, *Oh, yeah, I need to consider making sure everybody goes home with something.*"

Desco artists also performed at NoMoore, a bar on the small strip of North Moore Street in Lower Manhattan that would eventually be forced to close due to numerous noise complaints. Packed shoulder to shoulder and stepping in time behind Lee or Sharon—who, invariably, would stomp and sweat something fierce—the crew could feel the crowd's heat from the stage. The mercury would only increase if the revue, or any single Desco artist, was performing alongside a DJ at a mod night.

"People would just be losing their minds, going for hours," recalls organist Adam Scone, adding that most rooms the soul revues performed in were small and could barely contain the energy of a studied performer like Fields or the ever-energizing Jones. The band, almost always dressed for the occasion, would sweat through their polyester-blend suit jackets. "That was a real family-building situation. It was all about supporting each other's bands and going down there to be the opening band or just check it out."

Sharon Jones and Lee Fields shared a deep mutual respect. They

★ ★ ★ ★ ★ ★

loved singing with each other—a result of their early encounters at Dare Studios—and created an electric vibe onstage. Fields, Roth notes, was particularly moved by Jones's showmanship and ability to command an audience with her evocative singing and innate ability to work a crowd with stage banter and serious dance skills. Jones possessed a raw dynamism, and while "Lee is arguably the best singer alive, he was never as comfortable onstage as Sharon," Roth contends.

The pull was irresistible for Tom Brenneck, a tall, long-haired guitarist still in his late teens who would schlep across the Verrazano Bridge from Staten Island and sneak in through the venue's kitchen for a chance to rub elbows with Roth and Lehman, and to have his mind blown by Desco bands. "Not only were they playing this music on the radio, but there was a burgeoning scene. And we started going to these shows," says Brenneck, who founded a funk and soul band called The Bullets out on Staten Island in the early 2000s. "Our percussion player in the band at one point was selling fucking drugs to Antibalas, so that helped us get into the door and then we had our demo CDs, and we just gave everybody in the band one."

While Desco was actively filling a void for live musicians among New York funk and soul fans, the scene supporting those sounds was small, and well-paid gigs few and far between. Although the meager pay was partially the result of having to split miniscule show profits among a large number of musicians (a typical problem for any band with more than four members), it was also an issue of popular taste. "Soul never went away; there's always bands playing soul music. But nobody believed it was commercially viable," says Binky Griptite, who by 1998 was well entrenched in the Desco family as a session player, and still rocking shoulder-length locks.

Crammed into a van, The Soul Providers would do small tours of the East Coast and Southern California with Sharon Jones and sometimes Lee Fields, hustling to feed a musical need people didn't know they had. Audience appreciation for Desco's dedication to hard funk and performance grew with each gig, and records disappeared from merch tables, though love for the label remained seriously underground in the

States. As with other independent labels dealing in similar sounds—including Los Angeles's Ubiquity Records and the influential hip-hop label Stones Throw—Desco's reach was limited to deep funk fiends who were initially fooled into purchasing the label's "reissues" and came to favor Desco's "vintage" aesthetic, or were simply stunned by a modern band's commitment to rawness. In any case, Desco had been slowly amassing a cadre of collectors, DJs, journalists, and fellow musicians who would further the label's cause. They shared an aesthetic and the sensibility that the acid jazz and neo-soul scenes were too smooth and inauthentic; that the best shit was done with sincerity and an ear finely tuned to the imperfections of 60s and 70s records.

Chief among these early champions was the UK's Keb Darge, an influential DJ and producer who is credited with originating the term "deep funk," and who operated a massively popular Friday night residency called Legendary Deep Funk at the London strip club turned music venue Madame JoJo's. Darge—along with colleagues Snowboy, Pete Issac of Jelly Jazz, and a handful of other early adopters—spent years building successful funk DJ nights with dedicated soundtracks, hammering tunes like "Hook And Sling" by New Orleans' Eddie Bo, obscurities from Cross Bronx Expressway, and a way funkier take on "Blueberry Hill" from Joe Washington to eager dancers.

Although there was a sonic and subcultural precedent for Desco's funk in New York City and other parts of the US, Britain proved to be much more fertile and receptive ground because of the country's unique club culture and soul history. As with many of his contemporaries, Darge came up in the northern soul scene—a musical subculture that's more descriptive of a regional taste than a particular sound. A foundational piece of youth culture among mods, soulies, and suedeheads (former anti-racist skinheads who had "moved on" from the culture), northern soul song lyrics cum slogans like "Keep The Faith" and "It'll Never Be Over For Me" became tribal banners. Supporters were dedicated to clubs and specific venues—chief among them the Wigan Casino, a club located between

★ ★ ★ ★ ★ ★

Liverpool and Manchester, where Keb Darge danced—and kids would make pilgrimages to dance to and dig for their favorite tunes from Tamla Motown, Ric Tic, and countless other smaller American labels, as well as singles from UK labels slinging reissues.

Twenty-something years later, the culture of northern soul had been enveloped into UK musical history and deeply influenced the acid jazz and funk scene of the 90s. "It was really the deep funk scene that Desco was birthed into; that's why Desco kind of worked," Roth muses, adding that deep funk scenes had popped up in France and elsewhere in Europe. "There was context for the love for funk and stuff like James Brown. There's much more respect for that, culturally, once you get out of United States. People here always kind of looked at it as this retro thing, whereas other places people look at it a little deeper. I guess we take it for granted."

Darge and company were the first to lend their support when Desco started pressing 45s—the preferred medium of northern soul, deep funk, and other vintage sound collectors—in 1997. "The stuff recorded today on these marvelous digital studios, to me, is piss," Darge told a London TV program in 2002. "But you listen to this nice warm analog sound which existed in '67 to '72, '74, is just pure from-the-guts music."[1]

Of course, Desco's sound existed in the pocket of that specific era. "*Yo, your 45s are crazy*," Roth remembers British DJs saying. "Keb would play Joseph Henry's 'Who's The King' two or three times at night. The Sharon Jones 'Damn It's Hot' too."

Desco expanded its network of likeminded, hip folks across the Atlantic, connecting with the likes of Adrian Gibson, who booked Camden's legendary Jazz Café (an important venue for soul and jazz, and a haunt of budding chanteuse Amy Winehouse, who in 1998 was still a teenager). The label gigged across Europe, with all of Desco's groups taking flight except The Daktaris. Lee Fields did one weeklong Euro tour in those early days but, as an established musician, had more extensive touring requirements and a larger fee. "He knew he could just afford to say no," Griptite notes, "but Sharon was down to roll, so Gabe started doing more stuff with her."

★ ★ ★ ★ ★ ★

With support from Darge and others, Sharon Jones and The Soul Providers had a built-in British audience that far exceeded the band's hometown crowd. As The Soul Providers readied themselves to take the cabaret-sized stage at Madame JoJo's, Keb Darge amped up the crowd, big-upping the band without a hint of insincerity. "Nobody's doing this," Darge bellowed in his pleasing Scottish accent. "This is the best band you'll ever see, fucking pay attention! I play their records every night, you know."

"We could only get twenty, thirty people down at the Pyramid or the Mercury Lounge, but when we went to England we were playing for like hundreds of people," Roth recalls. "People knew the words to the songs." In May 1999, when the band travelled across the country to Plymouth—the British disembarking point for the Mayflower, and the site of famed club Jelly Jazz—the band were suddenly performing to a thousand-seat ballroom. "People were dancing and singing along, and like wanting autographs—it was crazy."

Interviewed with Lehman the morning after their show and looking remarkably awake for someone who had stayed out until 6am, Roth said he mistook the screaming crowd for guitar feedback. Discussing the New York versus European scene from behind huge aviator glasses and characteristically clenched teeth, Lehman reflected on the party atmosphere of Jelly Jazz. "It's just a whole bunch of people having fun, not giving a shit. In New York, it's all about attitude and this and that."[2]

Although he was just sixteen at the time, Leon Michels told seminal blog *Flea Market Funk* that the Plymouth gig was the most memorable he's ever played. "There were five hundred people in the room and when we hit the stage they looked totally possessed.... I just figured that we were wildly popular in England but later found out it was essentially a rave and the entire audience was on ecstasy."[3]

On that same tour—during which Roth and Jones would swear they saw the Queen at a ghetto motel above a gay bar and massage parlor in the Welsh seaside town of Swansea—The Soul Providers opened for J.B.'s sax

★ ★ ★ ★ ★ ★

man Maceo Parker at the O2 Forum in Kentish Town. "It was the most amazing thing when we got there," Jones said in 2001 from a Williamsburg basement. "There were so many people there. I came on, right, and if I would've said, 'Everyone take off your clothes and get naked,' they would've gotten naked. When Maceo came on I was standing at the back of the stage and they're like, 'Maceo, call Sharon up.' That was amazing. I was like, 'Get out of here!'"[4]

The Sugarman 3 also hopped around the UK, performing at Jazz Café, in Leeds at the Yardbird Suite, zipping to Manchester and then over to Jelly Jazz. While in Belgium during those early years, the quartet performed a last-minute show at an Antwerp jail after another gig was canceled. The money was good, but "no one wanted to hear boogaloo," Scone remembers, laughing. At the time, the Ohio native was fresh out of jazz school. "They all wanted to hear black metal!" With their parents' blessing, Roth chaperoned The Mighty Imperials on a European tour where, Steinweiss recalls, "there's this huge reception for these, like, fifteen-year-olds playing organ funk, which wasn't really happening in New York."

If the New York scene for raw funk was limited to Desco and its affiliates—the city, by the late 90s, seemed more interested in hip-hop from the likes of Jay-Z and Nas, and was on the cusp of a reinvigorated indie-rock scene that would spawn LCD Soundsystem, Interpol, and others—a handful of bands around the world were picking up on a similar soulful vibe. Among them were The New Mastersounds (a British band associated with Keb Darge that a handful of Desco folks relegated to the acid-jazz scene and were generally unimpressed by) and Japanese funk orchestra Osaka Monaurail, who headlined a bimonthly funk and soul party called Shout! starting in '98 and toured with J.B.'s disciple Marva Whitney. In a desolate Finnish suburb, a funk group called Calypso King and The Soul Investigators formed in 1997 and released a couple of seven-inches on their homemade Jive label. In Melbourne, Australia, New Zealand–born producer/guitarist/songwriter Lance Ferguson formed an instrumental funk group called The Bamboos based on the same Meters/

★ ★ ★ ★ ★ ★

J.B.'s influences. The group grabbed the ear of Darge, Snowboy, and UK musician-producer-DJ Quantic, who himself would develop funk and soul projects around the world.

Thousands of miles away, a distinctly West Coast fascination with funk and soul was unfolding along the sun-bleached highways of Los Angeles. Youth who were invested in the area's mod, Britpop, ska, and northern soul subcultures had been championing 60s soul as collectors and dancers since at least the early 80s, eventually gravitating toward DJ nights like Good Foot in Long Beach and Funky Sole in LA (two long-running vinyl-only DJ nights, which were founded about a year apart), as well as gigs around downtown and western Los Angeles. While northern soul parties held under the Golden State Soul Society banner were sonically strict, 90s mod- and Britpop-focused soul events put garage bands next to songs from Motown, Stax, and Chess records; it wasn't uncommon to hear verified dancefloor crushers like James Brown's "Sex Machine" next to British R&B/rock band The Spencer Davis Group.

Grown in subculture and fueled by its inherent danceability, soul music had had a place in Southern California nightlife for at least two generations. "LA's 'underground' was always really, really big," says DJ Clifton Weaver, an impeccably dressed mod from Long Beach and longtime Funky Sole resident who cut his teeth (and a number of rugs) among the college crowd attending early Good Foot parties. "I feel like there were enough people who were into unique sounds that allowed unique nights to really spring up and stay successful for a very long time."

Southern California had long dabbled in commercial versions of funk. Between 80s soul-influenced subculture and prior to the next generation of DJs picking up the mantel, LA had been home to the wildly popular Red Hot Chili Peppers, who specialized in funk rock (a hybrid sound no one knew they wanted) and attempted some deeper cred by collaborating with P-Funk's George Clinton and covering Stevie Wonder songs on their

★ ★ ★ ★ ★ ★

1989 breakthrough *Mother's Milk*. By the time RHCP released *Blood Sugar Sex Magik* in 1991, they were signed to Warner Bros and making funk-punk-rock that, according to a *PopMatters* critic, "in one funked-out, fucked up, diabolical swoop ... reconfigured my relationship to music, to myself, to my culture and identity, to my race and class."[5] But while critics lavished accolades upon the biggest "funk" band of the 90s and the album cock-rocketed up the *Billboard* charts, no one involved in SoCal's funk and soul communities (or elsewhere, for that matter) took the band seriously.

Absent the kind of live band that was truly committed to funk music, Los Angeles and beyond were primarily engaged in collector culture; hard funk didn't have the same subcultural ties that 60s soul did. But just as New York was living through the golden age of hip-hop in the 90s, so too was Los Angeles, and many area musicians, collectors, and DJs were finding their way back to funk through samples. This fascination with funk had been underway as early as 1991, stemming from a strictly hip-hop party called Peace Pipe. "I was fresh out of high school and it was exactly everything I wanted—a place where I could see if the music that I liked to listen to works in a dance setting," says Cut Chemist, aka Lucas MacFadden, a famed LA-based turntablist who performed with funk-influenced groups Ozomatli and Jurassic 5. Chemist was raised in Hollywood, started DJing at eleven, and had been producing hip-hop for a few years by the time he arrived at Peace Pipe. The party offered a unique—and hitherto nonexistent—space to share music and knowledge. "It was just a hodgepodge of musicians and DJs kind of getting together going, 'Hey, do you know this one? No? What about this one?' And we all had something to share with each other."

Years later, Peace Pipe evolved into a fabled hip-hop meets turntablism meets funk jam called The Breaks. Held every Tuesday night at a bi-level coffee shop and a handful of other locations, The Breaks was the jumping-off point for Los Angeles's funk scene, drawing heads and musicians interested in the songs sampled for hip-hop breakbeats. Musicians would bring their own equipment, form an ad-hoc band for the night, and play

★ ★ ★ ★ ★ ★

breaks while an MC or singer riffed on top, then a DJ would play the original cut. After a year or so, Miles Tackett, a tall, lanky bassist whose father was in rock band Little Feat, invited The Breaks' most regular players to form a house band called The Breakestra.

"The concept was funk performed live from the perspective of a hip-hop DJ keeping a groove," Tackett says quietly, his voice awash in the dull roar of a Highland Park restaurant—a part of LA not yet hip when The Breakeastra formed in 1997. "We would just kind of freestyle it and I would be playing these breaks. I think 99 percent of it in the beginning was all stuff I knew from hip-hop." The group performed covers of popular breaks in a revue style and eventually graduated to original compositions, releasing the seven-inch "Getcho Soul Togetha" with friends at Stones Throw Records in 1999.

While The Breakeastra were the only game in town performing hard funk in a similar style to Desco, other bands operated in the same stratosphere—Weapon Of Choice performed later 70s funk à la Parliament; Orange County's 00 Soul performed originals in a 60s soul style; mostly instrumental boogie group Orgone performed instrumental funky disco from the San Fernando Valley; Ozomatli (who predate Breakestra by a few years) melded funk with hip-hop and Latin flavor. Whereas Desco was often characterized as a collection of funk purists and could get away with being fanatical about a specific era with audiences in New York and the UK, popular taste in Los Angeles required less specificity. A band that wanted to grow beyond scene fandom or the approval of diggers needed to add extra ingredients to make their sound more palatable to a wider range of listener.

"There wasn't anybody immediately connecting hip-hop to the funk like Breakestra was, or in the way Ozomatli was," Tackett muses in between bites of an heirloom tomato, grown in his garden nearby and occasionally given as gifts to local restaurants or visiting journalists. "If they were not doing covers, they were doing music that referenced funk while referencing hip-hop as well. To my knowledge, the funk revivalists at Desco would just go and straight reference the source of deep funk—

★ ★ ★ ★ ★ ★

60s to early 70s music. And, obviously, with The Daktaris and Antibalas, African and world funk."

Trumpeter Todd Simon, who played with bands on both coasts but moved to New York after seeing The Soul Providers live, drew a distinction between influential West and East Coast scenes. "The musicality was completely different. There's some Breakestra breaks that the New York guys would play, but they were nailing the sound and the imperfections. LA is known for perfection and gloss, and the show-off kind of thing." With the New York funk scene jumping off, Tackett found an opening and more of an ear, Cut Chemist posits. "He was then, and still is, the only guy holding it down for the funk scene hard like that—ride or die."

Cut Chemist is but one (though a very prominent one) of a generations-deep community of crate diggers and DJs in Southern California—a lineage he traces to Skatemaster Tate, a skateboarder and collector who was fascinated with the A-sides of the ballads his friends collected in the mid-80s. Tate started collecting, and, the following decade, sold heavy records at Pasadena City College swap meets. "People get talking," Cut says, "and the word gets out. Tate's collection was kind of ground zero for LA collectors."

Some of those early Tate records would influence a mixtape Cut developed with partner DJ Shadow, and help spread the deep funk movement. *Brainfreeze*, the duo's live 1999 mixtape, was recorded in San Francisco that February and provided fifty-five minutes of funk and soul 45s, scratching, and radio clips that were both familiar to hip-hop fans and relegated mostly to the deep crates of Desco-like collectors. *Brainfreeze* offered expert mixes of Marlena Shaw's state hymn "California Soul" into The Vibrette's harmonic and break-ready "Humpty Dump (Part 1)," and followed up by Gabe Roth and Keb Darge favorite Eddie Bo, both sating collectors and offering a well of obscurities for new funk fiends to tap into. Initially a limited-edition CD (one estimate has two thousand copies pressed total), *Brainfreeze* was first available only at shows and then at boutique record stores like San Francisco's Groove Merchant and the influential hip-hop store Fat Beats, but was quickly bootlegged and sold on eBay.[6] Just as the famed *Nuggets* compilations brought 60s garage rock into a new era, or the Empire State Soul Club-inspired set *The Complete Stax / Volt Singles: 1959–1968* reinvigorated love for the southern soul label in 1991, *Brainfreeze* "made it cool to get into old funk records," Sugarman told a Boston newspaper in 2003. "That opened lots of doors for us."[7] Two years later, Stones Throw heads Egon and Peanut Butter Wolf released *Funky 16 Corners*, a hugely popular compilation of deep and dusty funk gems with detailed liner notes.

"Whether it's old Black people or young white people, or mixtures in between, there's always some musician that wants to play the music they want to play," Binky Griptite theorizes from his ground floor apartment in Bed-Stuy. "But what happens is, the business, whether it's real or imagined, will just sort of make people think that they're not wanted. A lot of people just never made it out of the basement for that reason. The pendulum has to swing, and shit has to go out of style and be out of style for long enough for people to call it new. It just started to crest at that time—'98, '99. You'd go out to a dance club and see like, sexy people sweating with each other listening to fucking thirty-year-old records."

Desco and the deep funk scene were in full bloom by the late 90s, existing in parallel to an increasingly popular world of neo soul and hip-hop acts who also wore their inspirations on their sleeves. Artists like D'Angelo, artist-producers like Raphael Saadiq (himself a product of Oakland 80s funk group Tony! Toni! Toné!), and Philly hip-hop group The Roots were just as indebted to rap legends like J Dilla and A Tribe Called Quest as they were Sade, drummer Max Roach, and Stevie Wonder. Members of The Roots, in particular, were diggers, dedicated to paying tribute to the musicians who informed the depth of their sound with a unique jazz-meets-hip-hop sensibility and live instrumentation.

As Desco reached a crescendo in 1999, The Roots' breakthrough *Things Fall Apart* offered a stark contrast to and a seriously soulful take

★ ★ ★ ★ ★ ★

on contemporary hip-hop. *Mojo* magazine praised the album for its uniqueness in a "world dominated by well-worn pop samples and rap rewrites of 80s chart hits" and encouraged listeners to cherish the band's risk-taking.[8] Drummer Homer Steinweiss considers The Roots (founded by fellow drummer Questlove, aka Ahmir Khalib Thompson) and their Solquarian colleagues to be a more mainstream version of the Desco-Daptone universe. "Those guys, like, know their soul music and brought that live musicianship to so many records in the 90s. But that's like totally different than what we're doing."

On both sides of the radio dial, in the mainstream and the underground, live musicianship in R&B and soul music were reemerging to excited audiences. "There's a lot of grown-ass people that don't remember a world without samplers and drum machines," Griptite says. "Whether they realize it or not, I think a lot of people want to understand what they're looking at, and you get that with soul bands." With the help of DJs and collectors, college radio programmers, and a growing dedicated fan base, the next century would certainly be more funky than the last.

Onlookers who hadn't come up in a subculture, or weren't hip to the way a good record's influence spans time and space, often incorrectly correlated Desco's success with a larger interest in nostalgia. "How can you be nostalgic about something that you haven't experienced? In Antibalas, we're not nostalgic for 70s Lagos," Victor Axelrod states. The organist and producer contends that Desco and their contemporaries are *romantics*—people who conjured images and feelings from reading liner notes or listening to a sultry horn part that evoked a rainy Havana afternoon on a Celia Cruz record. Speaking to the *Village Voice* in 2010, Sugarman said, "We proved that what we're doing has a place in modern times. We were never thinking about whether that sound is old. We know what we're going for, and it's focused."[9]

CHAPTER FOUR YOU BETTER THINK TWICE: DEATH OF DESCO, BIRTH OF DAPTONE

Desco continued to pile on the touring miles and studio hours, bringing new folks into its fold—but always through a network of known entities. The label's publicist and contact at Caroline Distribution were friends; their new marketing and promotions hire, also a friend of a friend, encouraged Lehman and Roth to make CDs as an appeal to their non-record collecting listeners.[1] Without operating on a basis of outright "you can't sit with us" exclusivity, Desco had long recognized the necessity of working with people who "got it." If the business end of the label relied upon a network of agreeable people, the musical flip was all about the hang and how a player fit into the family. Rather than combing through New York's top talent, Roth in particular cherry-picked musicians who may not have been the most proficient but were cool and shared the same goals and taste.

Steinweiss—still a teenager and grappling with the idea of doing music as a capital-C career—often wondered how he managed to become The Soul Providers' drummer. "I'm not very good, but there's not a lot of drummers with an understanding of the tradition," he muses. Back then, he was positive that the first decent sub the band auditioned would replace him. A more proficient drummer, especially one trained in the style of later 70s and 80s funk, might play the hi-hat with both hands, or add in extra cymbals and drums to focus on embellishment instead of simply the kick, snare, and backbeat. "Other drummers probably could have held the tempo better, but they would have been playing all this fancy stuff; they would be getting a lot more shit from Gabe and Victor. But I was doing all the right things, just like not really, technically there."

Even if the part itself wasn't complicated or only involved a few notes, many players would get overly focused on simplicity. "Where it gets complex is everybody fitting themselves around each other to get the right interaction so that the shit feels right. That's hard, and you need the right people to do that," Axelrod proposes, reflecting on an interview Gabe Roth gave once about maintaining a band with so many musicians. "He said something to the effect of there was some little crack in the universe, in the universal fabric, which allowed this to happen. Like this sort of defies logic."

But while the family grew and Desco continued to add album masters to the shelf, the cracks in Phil Lehman and Gabe Roth's relationship were starting to grow. Both had strong personalities, which they exercised in different ways—Lehman with a no-holds-barred punk-rock attitude and creative drive that didn't consider limits, Roth with a highly attuned musical sensibility that, while operating outside traditional lines, may have been more practical. "Phillip was kind of the visionary creative guy that had a lot of ideas. And Gabe was also very creative and visionary, but also, like, really good at executing," Steinweiss opines. Lehman, Roth later said, was "a real unique individual, and at some point it just couldn't hold anymore."[2]

With records from The Mighty Imperials and The Whitefield Brothers and a third album from The Sugarman 3 in the can, Roth and Lehman's differences came to a breaking point. Although Lehman never spoke publicly about the reasons behind Desco's demise, Roth says their partnership ended because of inevitable "business differences—money and shit."

"So we went our own ways," the bassist-producer continues. "We had all these albums kind of ready to go, and touring was going good; everything's going really well. So it's kind of a shitty time. Some shit went foul, and I didn't want to do it anymore. So I told Phillip, 'This is done.'"

★ ★ ★ ★ ★ ★

The Soul Providers were fresh off the road, where they rang in the new millennium in Aspen, Colorado, with legendary New Orleanian pianist Dr. John, a funky nightcrawler himself, and fellow Crescent City residents The Wild Magnolias. "That New Year's gig, that topped it too," Jones said during a 2001 interview. Seated at a keyboard in Roth's basement, she recounted how "everyone's all like, 'The world is ending, we're all gonna die,' and I was like, 'Let me die singing, baby.'"[3]

The Aspen show is marked in Sugarman's memory as the point where the scene and sound grown from Desco started to feel real and accepted. "I was super bummed when Gabe told me that Desco had folded because I felt like it was a real home; it was like a family. It was a scene of musicians and when we were touring, you could say, *I'm on Desco Records*."

The Mighty Imperials' debut LP was also lost in the Desco closure. "It was kind of a good lesson, like, right away, how the music business is so sketchy," Steinweiss says, adding that while he was disappointed, he was also just happy to have made a record before going to college. "I was also like, *I don't want to do music full time. This is just for fun*, so I wasn't that serious about it. I was serious about the music itself, but I wasn't serious that music was going to be my life, that I was going to be a funk and soul drummer twenty years later." Steinweiss did enroll in college, where he studied philosophy, but it wasn't long before Lehman and Leon Michels would put up the funky bat signal for the young drummer.

In late 2000, Lehman partnered with DJ Jeff Silverman to form Soul Fire Records, bringing Michels along for the ride too. Soul Fire was still operating in the same auricular field as Desco, but with slightly different support—many of the original Desco musicians would continue to do sessions with both Lehman and Roth—creating, in Steinweiss's view, fewer classic, focused, and fully envisioned albums.

"When they split up, Gabe was like, *I can just execute all my own ideas*, and Phillip was like, *I kind of need someone else, like another Gabe, to execute*," says Steinweiss, who played drums on a number of Soul Fire releases, including as part of the label's house band. "Phil was like, *Oh,*

★ ★ ★ ★ ★ ★

this kid Leon basically can play everything. He had Leon play all the other instruments instead of Gabe, and Leon was like a machine."

Soul Fire used Desco's growing recognition and Lehman's own international ties, releasing The Whitefield Brothers' record from the Desco session, Finland's Soul Investigators, and a handful of seven-inches and LPs from previously unheard, non-Desco affiliated groups, including experimental psych-funk group J.D. & The Evil's Dynamite Band. Just as he did during the Desco days, Lehman cut raw funk singles—some of which were recorded in Homer's parents' attic to a vintage four-track—and pretended that they were classic finds from a dig. Soul Fire pressed singles from nonexistent bands like The Soul Diggers and The Explorers, creating a phony Soul Side label and issuing singles without catalogue numbers and crossed-out dead-wax markings. Steinweiss recalls Lehman selling The Explorers' "Countdown To Soul" single (the first thing the young musician did with Soul Fire) on eBay for $200. Although the label only pressed about a hundred copies, making them rare regardless of whether they were recorded in 2001 or 1971, "Leon says that people found out and got really pissed.

"I remember going to Staten Island, the first time I met Tommy Brenneck and all those guys, and they're like, 'Have you heard this Soul Diggers record, it's the craziest record ever.' I was like, 'I played drums on that music.' Tom was like, 'No you didn't. Fuck you man,'" Steinweiss remembers, laughing. "To me, it was such validation of what we're doing, because it was like this whole other scene that was doing the same shit, geeking out on random records. I had basically tricked them into thinking that that was some authentic record." Lehman had also retained Lee Fields in the Desco split, and Fields recorded his follow-up to *Let's Get A Groove On* in "Phil's dad's apartment or something that, like, wasn't a real studio," with Michels playing most of the instruments. That album, *Problems*, mixed the heavy funk of Fields's previous release with softer ballads, including a timeless lover's croon called "Honey Dove."

Roth had come a long way from being a nervous songwriter agog at Lee Fields's performance and didn't take it personally when the singer followed

★ ★ ★ ★ ★ ★

Lehman to his new venture. "Lee's old school, you know?" Roth says. "You want him to show up and sing, you give him some cash and he'll sing. He would have done a record with me if I would've had the money to pay him to come in to do it, but I didn't. I was kind of newlywed, and my wife was pissed off because we were broke and couldn't pay the rent and stuff. Meanwhile, Phillip just kind of kept going; he started Soul Fire Records right away, and right away started working with Leon and Homer, and a lot of people who worked with us. So I was kind of super bummed about that. Of course, he started recording with Lee Fields, which really, really hurt for me."

Although Roth credits Lehman with much of his trajectory and aesthetic fearlessness, he looks back somewhat suspiciously on the debt and maxed out credit cards under his name post-Desco. "It was weird because obviously Phillip had so much money. So when Desco went under, I was super bummed, because I wanted to get something going; I was just broke and had a lot of pressure." Roth enrolled with a temp agency and, ironically, was sent to Sony Records' distribution arm—the "last fucking place I wanted to be right after my completely independent, really rough label just, like, fell apart." Week after week, Roth did his best and most evasive work at Sony, playing his two bosses off each other while he made long-distance calls and doodled logos for his next musical venture.

Sometime after Sony patted Roth on the back for his hard work and offered up a full-time gig (which the musician summarily rejected before walking off the job), Roth hooked up with See Through Records, a label part-owned by a European company called Play It Again Sam. Roth and See Through shook on a sweetheart deal, which would allow the twenty-ish producer to manage an imprint where he could get paid a dollar rate, as opposed to a percentage of each record, and "just make records and they put them out. They'd give me a shit ton of money and I'd do whatever the fuck I wanted."

For an increasingly jaded creative genius, the deal was almost too good to be true, but Roth ran with it and started setting up his first post-Desco

★ ★ ★ ★ ★ ★

session. He called up Sharon Jones and paid her in cash, then hired Griptite, Steinweiss, Axelrod, and Michels to start recording a Soul Providers–type album under the name Sharon Jones & The Dap-Kings. But with Desco's West 41st Street basement studio a thing of the past, he needed a new place to record.

A couple of years prior, Roth and Antibalas co-founder Martín Perna were walking through their South Williamsburg neighborhood and happened upon the Afro Spot, a storefront on a soon-to-be gentrified stretch of Grand Street where Nigerian kung fu *sifu*, percussionist, singer, and designer Duke Amayo had an apartment and community space—a two-story building with a basement he had fixed up in exchange for discounted rent. Crucially, the Lagos native also knew the music of Fela Kuti, and Perna and Roth were eager to bring him into their Afrobeat project. Amayo, on the other hand, saw two new members he could recruit to his dojo.

Perna's Conjunto Antibalas were officially performing as Antibalas by 1998, with many members of The Soul Providers (including Roth, who also wrote and produced; Axelrod; Griptite, performing as Del Stribling; percussionist Fernando "Bugaloo" Velez; and Anda Szilagyi on trumpet) and gigging around town. Both groups had "powerful, domineering band leaders that influenced each other," says Griptite, who played bass rather than guitar, noting, "It's just playing the same songs and flipping the beat around."

The following year, Antibalas had its own weekly residency at NoMoore called Africalia!—which ran for eighteen months and usually featured three seventy-five- to ninety-minute sweat-soaked sets—toured Europe, then released their debut, *Liberation Afrobeat Vol. 1*, in the summer of 2000. Antibalas's dedication to the Afrobeat form, and particular New York sensibility for recreating it, earned the band nods from Fela Kuti percussionist Tony Allen (who would later perform with the band during a gig outside of Paris), trumpet player Tunde Williams, and Fela's right hand man, J.K. Braimah, who told the group, "I thought this music

★ ★ ★ ★ ★ ★

was going to die after Fela died." Perna recalled during a performance on Seattle radio station KEXP, "That blessing is not something we talk about, but there were a couple key people who could've just been, like, *This is not for you*, but there was that encouragement. And that gave us the confidence."[4]

Antibalas—perhaps even more so than locals Kokolo, a project of singer Ray Lugo who lent recording space to Desco in its early days—were bringing Afrobeat to new ears, spearheading a revival related to the deep funk scene with earthier resonance. "One time I went to watch the band play, and they were playing some Afrobeat, but they didn't have Afrobeat drumming. It wasn't authentic, but the vibe and the intention was authentic," Amayo recalls, adding that joining Antibalas was not part of his plan for community building through kung fu. But after watching Antibalas with drummer Jojo Kuo, who had played with Fela Kuti, and another shekere musician who had a proper groove, Amayo was impressed. He officially joined Antibalas shortly after subbing in for a percussionist who had been selling mushrooms to put himself through college but hastily quit the band after receiving a disconcerting call from the FBI. Speaking to documentarian Jeff Broadway, Perna recounted how he "called Amayo and said something like, 'I know not all African people play percussion, but do you have any skills?'"[5]

"That period, to me, represents a thin film where creativity is at its height," Amayo continues, with a measured, British-Nigerian inflection. "At the millennium, there was energy around that was about to go down. I was feeling the need to do something, to participate in something, to make a shift." It didn't hurt that Amayo also had a T-shirt printing business and could now print Antibalas's merch. "To me, the key word here is community. I guess the gateway to entering this community was Gabe. His vibe, his personality was right on. He's quick, easy, a smooth operator. He's got the groove and people that play bass and drums got some spirit about them. They carry with them the rhythm of life," Amayo says. "You had a lot of tough gongs [in Antibalas], but Gabe was the nucleus and the shield. He was always working on something! We could get a song going in a day, because Gabe is that quick. He's one of my favorite collaborators because he has no ego. He's very generous, ready to move on."

Life in New York City was evolving at a clip, the Giuliani administration having spurred population changes by depressing some of the city's more visceral and traditionally seedy characteristics through crime control and "urban renewal." Artists and musicians followed by moving from the Lower East Side and elsewhere in Manhattan to industrial, semi-industrial, and immigrant or minority neighborhoods—early steps in a decades-long gentrification of the outer boroughs. Brooklyn neighborhoods like Williamsburg, Bushwick, and Bedford-Stuyvesant boasted larger spaces and cheaper rent for growing creative communities, which were dealing with the forced closure of many popular bars and venues (including NoMoore in April 2001) as the mayor cracked down on clubs and cabarets. Amayo's Afro Spot studio was already the nexus for an underground arts scene and party called Organic Grooves (which he promoted and did security for), and it also became Antibalas's rehearsal space toward the end of the Desco era. "Propelled by burly saxophones, fierce percussion, and righteous anger," the *New York Times* decreed, as well as Amayo's tendency to operate on a more astral plane of consciousness, the band were among the first musicians to perform in Manhattan after the terrorist attacks of September 11, 2001.[6] Just three days after two planes felled the Twin Towers, Antibalas took the stage at midtown club B.B. Kings, proving that they, and by extension New York, were as strong as their name—Antibalas translates to bulletproof in Spanish.

That same year, Amayo opened Afro Spot to fellow bulletproof musician Roth, who started building a basement recording studio for his new venture: Daptone Records. Working in advance of his check from See Through Records, Roth purchased an eight-track Otari recording machine, soundproofing for the basement's six-foot ceilings and stone walls, as well as a variety of gear, creating the next iteration of a funky basement. There, Roth, Sharon Jones and seven other musicians (more than half of whom

★ ★ ★ ★ ★ ★

were already using the basement to record as Antibalas) pounded out *Dap-Dippin' With The Dap-Kings*. The rough but affectionate album featured ten originals and a funkified cover of Janet Jackson's "What Have You Done For Me Lately," made even greater with Jones's vamping, plus an introduction from the booming but jolly Binky Griptite, who took his MC duties from the stage to wax.

While *Dap-Dippin'* would fit just fine in Desco's catalogue of raw funk, it pulled no fake-outs by pretending to be a reissue, and it held nothing back in its adoration of late-60s James Brown or dance records. The album's first forty-five seconds namedrop a handful of Jones-created dances from Desco singles, including the bump'n'touch and the dap dip—all of which would become important parts of their live show. The recording burst with the live energy of those Baby Jupiter and NoMoore shows, with Jones front and center for a full twelve inches of "the funky and dynamic sister exciting dancefloors across the nation."

But just as the majority of musicians have been bent over by labels, so too was Daptone's fate. Roth recalls a See Through rep who was also an engineer coming by the Afro Spot and lavishing praise upon the record, even lending a homemade compressor for recording. Shortly after Roth delivered *Dap-Dippin'*, however, See Through said it didn't like the record and wouldn't be paying up.

With his head just barely above water from his Desco debt, Roth was once again drowning—he had borrowed money from everyone in his life to build the Afro Spot studio and pay his friends. "I was like, *That doesn't make any sense, because if you like Desco shit, how could you not like this record?* I've made some mediocre records, you know? But that record was a good record, and it was exactly what I had been doing, but better."

A couple of weeks later, Roth learned that Play It Again Sam had pulled out of the See Through partnership—one of a number of seismic changes happening in the music industry as CDs evolved into the MP3 age and downloading platforms like Napster and LimeWire fundamentally transformed how people consumed music. Broke and royally pissed off,

★ ★ ★ ★ ★ ★

Roth left the deal with little beyond a new album and See Through's compressor—which he still refuses to return, decades later.

Just as news of his crippling, $45,000-plus debt began to hit, Roth hooked up with Spanish club owner-promoters Mas i Mas—a long-running company dedicated to highlighting music with Black roots—and landed a monthlong residency in the summer of 2001 at a Barcelona club called La Boite.[7] Although, by Roth's admission, The Dap-Kings were barely a band, the chance to play a new record for receptive European audiences who were already familiar with Sharon Jones was an opportunity—even if it didn't pay much. "They told me everybody who plays sells shit-tons of merch—you gotta bring lots of merch. So I made T-shirts and I made LPs and I made 45s," Roth recalls, adding that pressed copies of *Dap-Dippin'* were so new they had plain white jackets instead of the low-res image of Sharon Jones later pressings would have. "So I went over there with all this fucking merch, and we didn't sell much of any of it. We ended up bringing almost all of it all the way back across the Atlantic to New York."

Tucked away on a quiet square in Barcelona's Diagonal neighborhood, La Boite was a 150-ish-capacity jazz club and a proper intimate space Sharon and The Dap-Kings could blow out. Nine or ten Dap-Kings—whoever was available, including Leon Michels and Homer Steinweiss, who were on summer break from college—performed for an hour at 11pm or midnight, Tuesday through Saturday. The city already had a strong appreciation for soul music and a flourishing mod subculture—which had evolved from scooter rallies and bands like Brighton 64 in the 1980s, to soul parties such as Floorshaker by 1994, and, later, Movin' On and Straighten' Up, as well as soul girl group Blackcelona. Barcelona also had DJs who were hip to Desco Records, and a few had gigged alongside Keb Darge. Some of those soul fans and collectors saw the band perform at La Boite over a dozen times.

"It was that trip where we really became a band, because we were playing every night," Roth says. Griptite, out of his element MCing in another language, opened each show by mouthing along to a Catalan version of his band introduction—a rapid fire, *Good evening ladies and gentlemen, how's everybody doing tonight? We want to welcome you to the Daptone Super Soul Revue and we are The Dap-Kings. Right now we wanna introduce to you the woman we call the brightest star in the soul universe... Miss! Sharon! Jones!*—much to the delight of audiences. The Dap-Kings warmed up with an instrumental, often played a half-step quicker, building anticipation for the "110 pounds of soul dynamite" that would soon launch onstage to belt out one of the band's hits.

Sharon Jones was never a covers artist, and anyone on or off the stage would be far out of line to call her an impersonator—even if she certainly paid homage to the greats. But as Roth observes, "That was the first time Sharon really started coming into her own, natural." Enlivened by the vibe in the crowded club, the singer was a ball of energy, working dances like the camel walk, the boogaloo, and her very own dap dip into the set.

Axelrod, who wasn't playing organ during the residency and soon joined Antibalas full-time, gets chills thinking about The Dap-Kings' show. "If it was at least an hour set, The Dap-Kings would use a song and then fall into a one-chord James Brown–style vamp. They would just sit right there, and then Sharon would get into her zone. Then the band would get really loud and then bring it right back down. That was my favorite shit."

The band also picked up a few tricks of the trade. "We always made sure that at the very beginning and at the very end of the show was super tight and complicated," Roth would later note. "Then everyone has the impression that you're real tight, that you don't make any mistakes, and as long as everything in between there kind of grooves, you're okay."[8]

While Steinweiss was feeling more secure about his ability to keep the beat of the band, the Barcelona tour provided a serious learning experience, particularly in keeping tempo. "Sharon would just be stomping at me, everyone would be looking at me all the time—*Speed up, slow down, you're going too fast*—night after night," he reminisces. "That's the best teacher you're gonna get. You could sit in your room and practice every night, but until you get out there and get behind something like that, you don't really

★ ★ ★ ★ ★ ★

know what it takes to keep everything moving along at the right pace. Sharon's gotta entertain and you gotta keep it going for her."

Sharon, too, was still figuring out how to manage her combustible stage presence while also remembering lyrics. "In Spain, they didn't understand English," she recalled, "and girl, I'm singing this slow song... then the band starts going and I said, 'Your man go out, and he tells you he was gonna go out with the fellas and then he goes out to the club and you don't understand a damn word I'm saying right now,' and they were all like, 'Yeeaaahh!' It was so funny, but they loved me. Those people were mesmerized. They were talking stuff in Spanish, saying it was a gift and they had never seen someone with so much energy."[9]

The Dap-Kings stayed at apartments that the promoters owned, ate at their restaurant, and DJed after-parties with local mods. Steinweiss remembers the tour as a weird paid vacation, and "one of the best months of my life. We lived in this funny little flat and we just went to this place two blocks away every night and played with The Dap-Kings. And then, like, just partied until four in the morning with the bartenders at the club. It was heaven, you know? And I was like, *Okay, this is dope. I could do this; this might be a career.*"

"Yo, I'll give Gabe props man. Gabe can get anything he wants to hear from me for getting me that trip," Jones said, reflecting on one of her first "star-making" moments. "That was great. They had TV shows, newspaper articles, they hooked us all up. These guys had posters of me singing up outside of the club that were taller than me, and I'm four-eleven."[10]

Eduardo Domingo Martín—a local DJ and radio show host who spun at Madame JoJo's during the height of the venue's deep funk days and knew The Sugarman 3 from previous tours—was enamored of Sharon Jones & The Dap-Kings, and invited the singer for a broadcast interview during the La Boite residency. Employing some of her newly minted onstage dancing skills, Jones hopped up on the studio table and boogalooed to The Vibrettes' "Humpty Dump," one of the prized songs from *Brainfreeze*, which the DJs may or may not have been playing on air. "There was a big

★ ★ ★ ★ ★ ★

family feeling; you could see they were super at ease," Martín reflects. "The last day of their Boite residency, we all brought them a big bunch of roses and some champagne bottles as a thank you. It was that special."

Sharon Jones & The Dap-Kings, as well as Lee Fields and Antibalas, would return to Spain many times over the years to larger audiences, and some of those original Boite attendees would make an appearance or set up DJ gigs for The Dap-Kings who collected. But even as the band flew back stateside in the summer of 2001, feeling high off a successful month's run and under the sway of a new sense of camaraderie, the reality of Sharon Jones & The Dap-Kings' future would smack Roth in the face just like the smell of hot garbage baking along the New York City streets.

In between tours, The Sugarman 3 had also convened at the Afro Spot to record their third album, *Pure Cane Sugar*, which happily featured Lee Fields on multiple tracks alongside Naomi Shelton (nee Davis) and a James Brown impersonator named Charles Bradley. Sugarman was in talks with the newly launched Velour Recordings—a local label that later released New Orleans–influenced jazz funk from Boston-based Lettuce in 2002—but he ultimately wasn't satisfied with the offer and, in true collector form, considered the rest of its roster to be corny imitators. "We were both collectively taking meetings," Sugarman says. "Gabe was trying to figure out how to find another label to build a subsidiary. It's a vulnerable time for the music industry, and people were telling us whatever we wanted to hear. Ultimately, I remember talking to different labels and we hated all the other records on the label."

Still smarting from the Desco fallout, and up to his ears in debt, Roth was wary of starting a new business—it would be easier, more fun, and probably more fulfilling to produce and engineer records, even if it meant working through someone with less taste. Sugarman, on the other hand, saw an opportunity to pick up where Desco left off as the partner of the label's most visionary (and more dedicated) man. Together, they could start

★ ★ ★ ★ ★ ★

a new label based on Desco's card catalogue, distribution network, and connections, as well as two well-traveled house bands. Sugarman liked the business end of music; he had been self-managing his eponymous group since 1996, while noting the ways Desco could've improved promotion. He proposed a "you make them, I'll sling them" business plan.

"I wasn't thinking of it as an opportunity as much as, like, *How can I save this relationship, which I felt really good about?*" Sugarman says. "I loved hanging out at the Desco office, and I was kind of itching to get deeper into the business, but that was Phillip and Gabe's thing. And in some ways, I was kind of letting things run their course with Phillip until it was, like, *Hey, I can do this.*" The two agreed that their new label should spend wisely, pay musicians well, and follow their guts. "It was never about money. It was just kind of, *How do we keep this thing together and cool?* Because, ultimately, that's what we were giving up by handing our records over to some other label that was not that cool. In our eyes, they were making all kinds of different records like what we were doing, but it wasn't, like, as intense as we were."

Daptone Records—the name perhaps a nod to the 1972 classic feel-good "Dap Walk" by New Orleans funk group Ernie & The Top Notes—officially released its "old" sound into the new century in 2001, alternately operating from Roth's Williamsburg digs and Sugarman's Lower East Side apartment, as well as the Afro Spot. "Gabe would come by after I'd been up drinking coffee—it's twelve o'clock and I'm still in my underwear, selling 45s to all these different distributors and record shops," Sugarman later recounted.[11]

Dap-Dippin' With The Dap-Kings became Daptone's first official release in 2002. *Pure Cane Sugar* came next, followed by The Mighty Imperials' *Thunder Chicken*, though the teenage group had long since outgrown that name—they were now founding members at both Soul Fire and Daptone.

CHAPTER FIVE DAP-DIPPING: CREATING THE HOUSE OF SOUL

With a proper release (including on CD) and distribution to influential DJs and journalists who were hip to Desco's history, *Dap-Dippin'* made for a successful label debut. Popular UK hip-hop and funk quarterly magazine *Big Daddy* praised the record as "a major triumph" and proclaimed that "a new standard has been set."[1] *Big Daddy*—which previously featured pieces on Keb Darge and Desco—lauded Gabe Roth as "one of the best analogue producers there is" and invited the Daptone head to write a recording manifesto. Published in issues no. 4 and 5, Roth's "Shitty Is Pretty" explained in great attitudinal detail the tenets and recording processes that informed the gritty sounds coming from Desco through to Daptone:

> The first thing to understand is that if you are trying to make a Heavy Funky 45, you are NOT trying to make a "professional" record by today's standards. Funk 45's are rough because they were made rough. They were made in basements or garages or lo-fi studios by bands that played barbecues on Saturday afternoons. Many people come at Funk with this bullshit acid-jazz, smooth R&B methods. Everything comes out all clean and happy and nice. They called it professionalism. I call it bullshit. If your [sic] going to try to record Funk, you got to have enough balls to make it rough. . . .
>
> SHITTY IS PRETTY. By this I mean that in whatever you're doing, whether writing a horn line, getting some drum sounds, or designing a label, you got to be shitty, the shittier the better. The more you let go of the professional musician/engineer/producer bullshit that creeps into your head

★ ★ ★ ★ ★ ★

> while holed up in a studio, the more you will be able to let yourself record the kind of rough-ass shit that you want to hear when you're out on the dance floor tryin' to get into your karate boogaloo.[2]

The rebellious attitude and commitment to feeling over "professional" technique laid bare in "Shitty Is Pretty" wasn't new to Roth or Sugarman. Desco Records shared the same ethos—perhaps less intentionally, given the reckless, DIY nature of its beginnings—but making a statement about *exactly* how a Daptone record would be created and the intention behind the label's sound was important. "Labels today don't necessarily have a brand the same way that, when you pulled out a Motown record, or Brunswick or Dynamo or All Platinum, it meant something," Sugarman emphasizes. "That's important to us, you know? So when you see the Daptone label, it means something."

While the manifesto broke down heavy funk recording into digestible column inches, explaining Roth's philosophy on finding players ("beware of studio musicians"), melody (which should be generally restricted to horns and maybe organ), harmony, rhythm ("has got to be 99 percent of the arrangement"), and changes (the main purpose of which is to take a band out of the groove briefly, only to come back "twice as bad"), Daptone's success was about an indefinable feeling—even before the label became successful.

"I was actually never down with shitty is pretty; it was one of our first arguments. I was just, like, *All my favorite records were really well recorded*," says Binky Griptite, who grew up listening to a variety of artists but was a huge fan of Parliament Funkadelic. "Gabe ultimately came around to that, using nice microphones and actually making it sound good."

Roth, too, came to slightly regret the hardline philosophy behind his "shitty" manifesto, ultimately favoring a vibe over a specific set of techniques or lack thereof. "There's nothing pragmatic about music," he says. "It's not supposed to do anything. It's just supposed to make you feel good. I feel like the nuance, the feeling of a record, got diminished. We

★ ★ ★ ★ ★ ★

can talk about history, we can talk about rhythm, and we can talk about technology. But at the end of it, shit just feels good. That's the whole story," he adds, resigned after decades of explaining and backpedaling a philosophy he developed at age twenty-five.

Feelgood music is subjective; the ability to create music that stirs the soul and packs the dance floor is a subtle art. Yet pop consensus never entirely mattered to Daptone, which was still unconcerned with making radio hits or much money, so long as bills were paid and folks could eat. Without a real long-term strategy that would allow Daptone to outlast Desco, doubling down on the collective, cohesive taste of the label's players and staff became its major curatorial and marketing approach. If Roth and Sugarman dug it, surely other people would too.

"Gabe is really specific about the sound on every level," explains Victor Axelrod, who by 2002 was experimenting with his own productions and had put out two solo roots reggae records (one under the name Ticklah). "So, if Gabe is going to make a record that he wants to listen to, there's a whole bunch of things involved." He's quick to point out that it's not about having all vintage equipment; vibe starts with the musicians. "So he's going to be particular about who he keeps around. These are elusive things; you can hear a particular chemistry between musicians."

Daptone Records released twelve singles and three albums in its first two years, a testament to the energy and familial feeling among the label's players—half of whom were holding down day jobs or taking other gigs in between sessions and shows. And whether it was the experience of that Barcelona residency, the shared obsession with collecting records, or simply the fact that the sound was cool, Daptone amassed a proper corps of musicians who acted as the label's house band and would support Sharon Jones on the road.

Initially, The Dap-Kings rhythm section consisted of Roth (as Bosco Mann, a pseudonym he employed just in case any debt collectors began eying the label) on bass, and writing most of the SJDK songs; Steinweiss on drums; Axelrod playing keys under the name Earl Maxton; Fernando

★ ★ ★ ★ ★ ★

Velez on percussion; Leon Michels on sax; Griptite on guitar; and, about a year into the label, Tom Brenneck playing rhythm guitar.[3] Neal Sugarman later led the horn section on tenor sax, performing alongside trumpet player Dave Guy. The Daptone family expanded to include semi-regular players in studio and onstage, including saxophonist Ian Hendrickson-Smith, as well as frequent collaborators like bassist Nick Movshon, Lee Fields, Naomi Shelton, and Cliff Driver. Sharon Jones, of course, provided leading-lady energy and a gravitational pull for the band and label, though she didn't write the empowered and love-laced lyrics she belted on *Dap-Dippin'*. As if the band wouldn't have enough of a difficult time coordinating schedules, piling into a van, or simply finding a table big enough to share a meal together, a chunk of The Dap-Kings were also performing with Antibalas, who released a double LP on Rope A Dope Records in 2004 with vinyl support from Daptone.

Much like the great funk and soul labels of yesteryear and their infamous house bands—including Motown's Funk Brothers, Stax Records' Booker T. & The MG's, and the Muscle Shoals Rhythm Section (aka The Swampers) across the river at FAME Studios—Daptone's foundation was The Dap-Kings. Although Roth and Sugarman co-owned the label, the idea of it being collectively run (and certainly a collaborative creative process) was a selling point for fans who wanted to support musicians directly. Unlike most labels, Daptone was seen as embodying the best of their genre's tradition without economically exploiting its players.[4] Yet even if there wasn't a ton of money to be made, some of the cash flowing into Daptone's coffers came with publishing and songwriting credits—and a majority of those credits went to Gabe Roth. Percentages of those royalties, which musicians could earn by fine-tuning songs, were often hard-won and miniscule. Over time, this disparity in income sowed seeds of discontent.

Regardless, Daptone became a sort of college of musical knowledge: musicians would come and go—trumpeter Anda Szilagyi left and was replaced by California transplant Todd Simon, who, when he went to work with Antibalas, was supplanted by Dave Guy, while others like Michels

★ ★ ★ ★ ★ ★

would play baritone sax instead of tenor as the music and lineup dictated—but everyone could always return to Brooklyn and be welcomed. While a family home might have generations of photos lining the walls, Daptone lined the halls of its studio with framed album covers, show posters, and a forever replenishing number of boxes.

"There's a sound to this crew, this bunch of guys," Roth effused in a video commissioned for the label's anniversary. "Man, that's our number one resource here. I think that's the biggest thing, to have a crew of musicians ... that know how to make a record, know how to make a sound, know how to play together as a group." Sugarman added, "It's really a group of musicians that really are deep inside the genre and the sound of the records, and know how to play in this particular studio and make this stuff come to life."[5]

After years of sneaking into Desco revues and handing out demos for his Staten Island–based crew of instrumental Afro-funk and soul musicians, Tom Brenneck came into the fold early in Daptone's run. "I came home from one of these nights and there's a message on my parents' answering machine from Gabe Roth asking me if I could play keyboards on a gig for Sharon," he recalls over beers. Initially, Brenneck was more of a guitarist who played a little trombone; at the time, he was playing in a horn-free, less percussive, proto-Budos Band group called Dirt Rifle & The Funky Bullets. Their first Daptone recording was a single featuring a then-unknown Charles Bradley, whose vocal style was stuck somewhere between his James Brown impersonations and own heartaches and pain.

Credited to Charles Bradley & The Bullets, "Now That I'm Gone Look How You're Crying" (2004) and "This Love Ain't Big Enough For The Both Of Us" (2006) were solid enough in their J.B.'s-style vocals and were breakbeat ready, but they didn't take off. Sharon Jones & The Dap-Kings, on the other hand, were hustling on a funk express. "And then, once I started playing with them, I was just like, *I'm a way better guitar player; maybe we should just have two guitars*," Brenneck continues. "Eventually I just became the main rhythm guitar player in The Dap-Kings for many

★ ★ ★ ★ ★ ★

years, which was just an amazing fucking position to be in in that band." True to form and the tradition of this being a family affair, future Budos saxophonist and bandleader Jared Tankel earlier interned with Daptone.

If the music flowed easily, getting a distribution network to push those tunes out of the Daptone offices and into the world was more of a challenge (unlike the way records were distributed during Desco's early days, Sugarman and Roth didn't have time to hand distribute around the Northeast). Through Caroline Distribution—which worked with Desco and was also key to encouraging the label to make CDs—Daptone made a deal with a label consolidator/management organization Shelter Music Group. Shelter had promised the fledgling indie that it could expect $40,000 in royalties from that first year or so in sales, and the windfall couldn't have come at a better time. Duke Amayo had received an ominous letter from the Afro Spot's landlord while touring with Antibalas in California, effectively ending his tenancy and pulling the plug on Daptone's rehearsal/recording space.

The Afro Spot's closure was one of many changes happening in rapidly gentrifying Williamsburg, which was experiencing the beginnings of what would become a highly publicized and satirized wave of young, hip types moving into what had previously been considered an undesirable part of the borough. Neal Sugarman had also moved from the Lower East Side to an apartment on Havermeyer Street with a view of the elevated J/M line, where he and Roth mixed a few early releases. But Daptone's operations were quickly growing beyond what a New York City apartment could accommodate. With royalties on the brain, the Daptone founders scouted the far reaches of Bushwick and Williamsburg for an appropriate HQ, landing at 115 Troutman Street, a two-story brick building owned by an older Italian man named Joe Siragusa, who Roth describes as "a real scumlord."

Sugarman was uncertain about the two-family home, which sat on a

★ ★ ★ ★ ★ ★

quiet street next to an auto repair and across from a vacant lot that blossomed into a summertime homeless encampment—but Roth immediately had a feeling that the house could become something great, or at least decent enough to practice in. "They were real pioneers in Bushwick at the time," says DJ Matt Weingarden. "They were the first hipsters over there, not that they were hipsters, but the first kind of people like me venturing into Bushwick." Nightlife in lower Manhattan had changed following 9/11, he adds, while the city's 2003 smoking ban further dampened the fun. "I remember the first time I went there, it was super, super desolate, and I didn't know where I was."

Daptone signed a seven-year lease with the promise of cheap rent. Sharon Jones was skeptical and, upon seeing the rundown building, asked incredulously, "Are you gonna make this a studio?"[6] With characteristic aplomb, Jones was down to roll, calking old wood and learning how to install wiring and electrical sockets on the spot.

It takes a village to build a soul studio, and the whole Daptone crew contributed over five or six months—some of the roughest of Roth's life, he later recalled. Amayo stripped the Afro Spot of building materials and transferred them to Troutman Street, where he helped with the building's out-of-date electrics. Artist manager Alex Kadvan (who had known Gabe since his Din-o-matic days) painted and plastered. Charles Bradley was a handyman, and he was called in to repair the radiators and rebuild the stairs to the second floor, where two offices, a storeroom, a bathroom, and hybrid kitchen/merch storage would live. They rerouted gas lines, employed members of the developing Budos Band to knock down walls, realized some of those were loadbearing walls, then jacked them back up using a jack from Sugarman's car, and brought the garbage across the Verrazano to a friendly dump in Staten Island. "All I remember is just, like, carrying out trash bags full of broken wall," Brenneck later said.[7]

The crew combined the downstairs kitchen and dining room to create a large live studio overlooking an unkempt backyard; Roth repurposed the gas pipelines as curtain rods and sent heavy blue velvet—purchased at a

★ ★ ★ ★ ★ ★

discount from a local theater company—to his mother in California, who sewed sound-dampening curtains. The most enterprising musicians fanned out across the borough in search of car tires to create the foundation of the studio's isolation room, then stuffed the tires with old rags and clothes.

Floating a few rubber inches above the house, in between the live room and the shelf-lined stray couch strewn control room at the front of the building, the well-isolated room is one of the crowning achievements of Daptone's House Of Soul. "There's nothing too magical about that place as far as sitting there and playing music," Brenneck said, absentmindedly picking on a guitar on a control room couch. "It's kind of dusty and raggedy and you're kind of like, *Get me the hell out of here*. But you know, it sounds like magic."[8]

Daptone's "magic sound" quickly became the stuff of legend—due in no small part to Roth's "Shitty Is Pretty" manifesto, which was soon taken as gospel by adoring producers the world over—and the studio was filled with a variety of vintage analog equipment, cheap Radioshack microphones and whatever the hell else the label could get its hands on. Daptone's sound is drum-heavy, and the producer learned a lot about miking and the sound of a room from recording in a basement. Speaking with *Tape Op* magazine, Roth said he learned "to kind of let instruments blend themselves as much as possible," using a single mic for a horn section and usually just one or two for drums. "You can get a much more natural sound, but it's also much more challenging in a room that doesn't sound good."[9]

If Roth and crew built the studio to spec, the control room would also have to be just right. The studio started with the half-inch eight-track Otari (later graduating to a one-inch Tascam sixteen-track tape machine and eventually an eight-track Ampex gifted by DJ/producer Kenny Dope in advance of future session work), and Daptone got busy recording to tape. "We spend a lot of time on the arrangements, and getting the sound we want, before we record," chief tape operator Wayne Gordon told CNET years later. "Then we do a couple of takes, more than anything it's just a matter of what feels right."[10]

★ ★ ★ ★ ★ ★

After a session, Gordon and Roth would literally cut and splice until the sound grooved perfectly. Mr. Fine Wine, whose record collection numbers in the tens of thousands (though he refuses to count), notes that "when you buy old records, there can be drastic sonic differences from record to record, even within the same label. Some will have a muffled sound; some will be too trebly; you've got to really work the EQ. That's not true of Daptone records; they all sound really good." Roth would later tell WNYC, "You can't roll a joint on an MP3."[11]

Various members of the label had borrowed money and purchased black-market Home Depot gift cards, engaging in a properly rock'n'roll level of by-the-bootstraps financial shadiness, when they heard the news: Shelter had gone belly-up and was in debt to Caroline. Caroline, in turn, wouldn't be paying out the consolidator's royalties. "So we're just left fucking ass out. It was, like, sink or swim," Roth says, the lingering dismay of yet another deal gone wrong still audible in his voice. "We were already deeply invested; we were fucking really upside down for a long time. Little by little, record by record we kind of made it back and paid off most of the debt."

During that first year or so, Daptone released several singles from *Dap-Dippin'*, because that's all it could afford. "We could pay for the pressing, sell the records, and pay for the next pressing," Sugarman says. "I would set these little goals like, *Okay, I need to make fifty bucks today for the label before I can leave the house*. I was calling the UK and trying to convince this distributor to take a few more records. It really started small."

The first recording at the House Of Soul was a cover of Bettye LaVette's 1968 cut "(Just Dropped In) To See What Condition My Condition Was In"—made popular and originally recorded by Kenny Rodgers & The First Edition the year prior—for a Kentucky Fried Chicken commercial that never materialized. Floating atop the now unseen tires in the isolation room, Sharon Jones flipped LaVette's slightly nasal vocal for a more bassy, gravely condition; Rodgers's psychedelic vibe became a midtempo funk with heavy saxophone and trumpet lines, and barely there background vocals.

Antibalas's third LP which, according to *Pitchfork*, provided a more

★ ★ ★ ★ ★ ★

"galvanized and urgent righteous noise" that demonstrated "the American Afrobeat awakening is in full effect"—was the first album recorded at Troutman.[12] *Who Is This America?* was an epic record of long arrangements and concepts, and Roth recalls engineering every possible studio trick around Antibalas's eight or nine members, all of whom were recording live in a room that was once a kitchen. From that session, Amayo points to "Big Man" as exemplary of how "an Afrobeat song behaves; how it's written, how it speaks the subject matter, and how it's simple and it grooves." Binky Griptite recalls writing the tune and presenting it to the band unfinished, while Amayo remembers writing together in studio, drawing on their collective experience in the workplace.

Although there were and would always be different rehearsal spaces, having a local label headquarters where the vibe was as productive as it was chill brought the connectivity at Daptone to a higher plane on wax and onstage. Musicians and friends could walk from the elevated Central Avenue M or the Dekalb L to Troutman and find folks hanging out, drinking beers and listening to records, eating together in the purple kitchen or Homer, Leon and Tommy working out a song downstairs.

"The way people live and the cost of living here doesn't give you a lot of time to practice," says Griptite, who for years would commute to rehearsals in Brooklyn from 116th Street in Harlem before moving to Clinton Hill, Brooklyn. "You got to be able to swim and do your gig with minimal rehearsing. And, as a bandleader, that presents a difficulty because it's hard to have a band; a lot of time you're just hiring people for gigs and it affects what you're able to do and how you can do it. Those economics force a different type of attitude from New York musicians. Being able to do gigs like that is a specific skill and it's hard to get an ensemble vibe, like a true band vibe."

Well-engineered, vibey records were already becoming a Daptone hallmark, but live gigs were where the label really shined. Daptone continued to do label revues and play locally at Frank's Lounge, Southpaw (where the label held the majority of its album release parties), and the

★ ★ ★ ★ ★ ★

Brooklyn Academy Of Music, before hitting the road hard with Sharon Jones & The Dap-Kings as its headlining act. The eight-piece band propelled Sharon—whose commanding presence cast a shadow far taller than her short frame—through a set of up-tempo funk and late-60s soul made for dancing, as well as an occasional ballad thrown in to cool down the place. With the horn section stepping in time, percussion and drums holding tempo and two guitars driving the tune, Sharon physicalized the music—working her feet, knees, arms, and head first separately and then in glorious, outta-sight collective intensity on songs like "Got To Be The Way It Is." She occasionally brought up members of the audience—usually a man she could sing a love song to or castigate for his bad behavior. Each lucky fan quickly learned whether they had the chops to keep up with a fast footed diva with a locomotive energy. "I think Gabe saw, from the very beginning, that Sharon had the power," Steinweiss recalls. "If she can get in front of people, we were going to get people coming back to see us."

Daptone bands gigged regularly at the Lucky Cat in Manhattan (where Binky had a weekly DJ night) and across the East River at legendary bar Frank's Lounge. They also held a few larger gigs at Park Slope's Southpaw, yet there was no big soul or funk scene in the States at the time. And while audiences were always enthusiastic, fans were hard won. The band would pack into a fifteen-passenger van and spend weeks driving from New York to South Carolina, then to Austin, Texas, and back across the Midwest, playing the occasional festival and small clubs like San Francisco's Elbo Room and La Cita in Los Angeles for $50 to $100 apiece each a night—which Steinweiss assumes often came out of Bosco Mann's pocket. "They would be shitty clubs, but every time that we played a show Sharon would just own it. And so, the next time you go to that town, someone told their friends, and it's very organic growth," he remembers.

The band's shared musical aesthetic continued to grow organically as well. Although Apple had already unleashed its iPod onto the world and would fundamentally change how people listened to music, personal MP3 players were financially out of reach for most of the band (which was

★ ★ ★ ★ ★ ★

already embedded in a more analog musical view). SJDK spent van hours listening to classic funk and soul mixes, as well as albums like The Isley Brothers' *Get Into Something* (1970) and The Ohio Players 1977 self-titled LP, with Roth manning the CD player most of the time. "Not even that many people had Walkmans," Griptite says. "We were mostly all listening to the same stuff, just all classics. They help keep everybody in the right frame of mind to do the shows, because that's just the world we're living in. Conversely, with Antibalas, it was all Fela all day, so you're just, like, in that vocabulary, and you don't have to think about it. It just comes out," Griptite says, adding, "we'd get in the van, light a blunt and ..."[13]

While few women would want to be stuck in a van with a gaggle of men a decade younger, Sharon Jones rarely complained about these rough early tours or the energy required to lead a funk band—especially in front of a small crowd. She didn't psych herself up prior to a show, instead just enjoying a little tequila (she and the rest of the band preferred to save the party till after the show) before getting "in a state of mind." Later, Jones described how she was no longer herself onstage. "I'm like down to earth Sharon Jones here, but once I come onstage, I just go out. I lose my focus, but I don't lose my focus on the music. It's not about me. It's not about being a star. ... I'm gonna give you 120 percent. I'm going out. You came to see me and this is my job, to please you."[14]

Jones and The Dap-Kings helped each other, in the studio and at gigs. "God sent them to me because I'm able to do my stuff and be myself," she stated.[15] After a good gig, Griptite says, the band would typically "go to somebody's soul DJ night, or somebody in the band would be the DJ, and we'd go dance to soul records. And like half the time we'd be out on the dance floor, just dancing with each other."

Those great gigs and hangs helped even out rough tours, where everyone was forced to manage stress, boredom, and the irksome nature of being stuck with the same people day in and day out in a small van. But life at home wasn't always the respite the musicians needed. In the winter of 2004, Roth was heading home from Troutman Street with Homer Steinweiss

★ ★ ★ ★ ★ ★

when the drummer drove into a pothole; the car airbag exploded and lacerated Roth's eyes. He spent nearly two weeks in the hospital and went temporarily blind, unable to get around on his own for months and forced to cover his sensitive eyes with dark glasses for the rest of his life. Roth and his wife—who had long borne the burden of being married to a traveling musician with extensive debt and little income, in addition to their untold, behind-closed-doors issues—split up shortly after; the musician moved into Daptone's studio and slept on one of its used couches. That first winter, the House Of Soul studio had no heat. It would still be years before Roth and Sugarman could draw a salary from Daptone; for now, each made a living from gigs with The Sugarman 3, SJDK, weddings, and club dates while hoping their sweat equity in the label paid off.

It wasn't all highs and lows, however. Between performances, SJDK ate well (or tried, depending on how out of the way a venue was) and dug for funk and soul 45s at local record stores, which they'd listen to on tour and spin at gigs back home. When the band toured the West Coast, or Roth went home to visit his folks in Riverside, he would shop at Chandler's Wind-Up in San Bernadino—a jukebox seller with a stash of records who Roth would pay $10–$20 for a dig. "I would go back with my Fisher-Price record player and just spend days and days listening to thousands and thousands of records and come out with a stack. He'd charge me twenty-five cents, fifty cents for records. A big part of my record collection is from Chandler's," Roth says, joking that he was only willing to give up the name of his favorite non-record store treasure trove after Chandler's closed.

Bosco Mann brought the vinyl back to New York and also gave Duke Amayo money to buy Afrobeat records whenever he went home to Nigeria. "We would all spin at fucking bars on the weekends, when we weren't touring, or on weeknights, or whenever," Brenneck says, adding that the Daptone circle continued to expand to DJs who worked in record stores and collected. "There was Jared Boxx and Young Chris, and [future Daptone marketing manager] Nydia Ines Davila. They were playing, like, crazy deep ballads and just all sorts of just fun. All the musicians would love

★ ★ ★ ★ ★ ★

to go listen to them spin records on a Tuesday night at Savalas on South Fourth Street in Williamsburg for all the 2000s. We all went there and just were blown away by their fucking records; it had a huge effect on us."

Back on Troutman Street, those ballads and soul tunes were indeed having an effect on the House Of Soul studios' output. Daptone certainly released funk in 2003 and 2004, including a reissue of The Daktaris' *Soul Explosion* and a Sharon Jones 45, "What If We All Stopped Paying Taxes"—a direct critique of the Iraq war, released just before the 2004 election, on which Binky Griptite encourages, "Ladies and gentlemen, children of America, it's up to you! Let mister politician man know how you feel. Stop paying taxes. Stop paying for corruption and injustice." But the collective was also developing more soul songs in the style of Gladys Knight, Archie Bell, and Wilson Pickett.

Sharon's "How Long Do I Have To Wait For You?," a 2004 midtempo love song, would become characteristic of Daptone's mid-60s-style soul output: tunes about love always written from the perspective of an empowered woman with distinctive horn lines and drums. Over the years, songwriting evolved from a bottom-up, groove-before-lyrics method to a process where Roth developed lyrics first, then a melody and chords with input from the players. "I think Gabe is an alien and he's in disguise, man, he's been around a loooong time," Jones said jokingly. "I don't know if he writes stuff for me because whatever he writes, it fits like a glove."[16]

If Roth's songs fit Sharon like a glove, there were some growing pains felt elsewhere in the label. Around 2003, demanding and often conflicting touring schedules forced The Dap-Kings and Antibalas to form separate lineups. The members the bands had in common (Griptite, Velez, Axelrod, Perna, Roth, trumpeters Jordan McLean and Anda Szilagyi) now had to choose the path of Afrobeat or funky soul. There was no competition or hard feelings, and everyone remained close.

"When both bands started getting more offers, it was just like you had to choose," Griptite notes. "I kind of didn't choose; I think I was chosen. Sharon was always really dependent on the vibe of the band; she also really

★ ★ ★ ★ ★ ★

did enjoy my guitar playing. It wasn't any of our habits to just be blowing compliments up each other's asses, but for a few gigs that I would ever miss, she would be the one that would miss me the most."

Leon Michels was also splitting time, doing sessions at Daptone while acting as Phillip Lehman's partner and right-hand man at Soul Fire Records. By around 2004, Lehman was getting tired of the business. "I feel like Phillip was not about the business at all, just, like, *I'm fucking rich, let's just put out some stupid records*," Homer Steinweiss suggests. Lehman packed his bags for Costa Rica, where he'd try professional surfing, leaving the studio and label to Michels and Jeff Silverman. Together, they'd pull back the needle on Soul Fire to create their own project, Truth & Soul Records. "Phillip kind of brought them in to this recording situation where they could just, like, get high and fuck around and have fun making records," Victor Axelrod says. "He just, like, left the label to them, and they were actually able to take it and run with it. That's just an extraordinary situation."

At the time, Michels was performing with The Dap-Kings and getting ready to release his debut LP as El Michels Affair, a mostly instrumental "cinematic soul" record he had been working on for two years in his childhood bedroom. *Sounding Out The City* was an emotional record and an early example of sophisticated horn arrangements in the New York soul scene, though positive reception was limited to that same niche community. "Even though it was instrumental, all the songs had really strong moods, and it felt like they had a sort of narrative even without lyrics," Michels told *Wax Poetics*.[17] The album was slated for release on Daptone and recorded with Nick Movshon, Steinweiss, and Sean Solomon (all Mighty Imperials), as well as Brenneck, trumpet player Michael Leonhart, and a few additional Dap-Kings on a Tascam 388 quarter-inch reel-to-reel eight-track recorder he borrowed from Antibalas's Luke O'Malley. According to Steinweiss, "There was some, like, little moment of nervousness, and Leon pulled the record and put it out on his own label, which was the beginning of Truth & Soul." Like The Dap-Kings, El Michels Affair became Truth & Soul's studio band.

★ ★ ★ ★ ★ ★

If there was any saltiness on the part of Daptone—which was busy working on a more soul-centered effort for SJDK's sophomore album, while also readying a debut from The Budos Band, an Afrobeat group so metal they would come to have their own brand of booze and funk-fueled mayhem—it didn't show. Instead, the younger generation of Desco/Daptone musicians (Movshon, Brenneck, Steinweiss, Michels, and Dave Guy) formed a tight-knit group who, according to Brenneck, played "on all of the records that were being produced around New York City," including Daptone, Soul Fire, Truth & Soul, and even productions from Mark Ronson—who at the time was mixing and developing mixtapes for Jay-Z's Rock-a-Fella Records while working on his second solo album, *Versions*. Because of their years-long performance history and shared taste, the group developed an unspoken, almost extrasensory, understanding of musical phrasing and how to finesse imperfections.

"The Dap-Kings had this gap in the age of the group," Brenneck reflects, standing behind a small bar in the lounge of a Hollywood recording studio. "I was around nineteen, and Homer and Leon were nineteen, and they'd already been in the band for three or four years. Leon quit after I was in the band for a year or two, which was so, so sad. When I joined Sharon, we all started playing together on the regular, toured together and were making records in between tours. And that unit was just incredible."

Neal Sugarman contends that The Dap-Kings was a breeding ground for studio bands and the wider soul revival. From The Budos Band to El Michels Affair to Tom Brenneck's developing Menahan Street Band and everything Leon Michels would create at Truth & Soul and beyond, "whether they admit it or not, those concepts kind of came out of working in The Dap-Kings," the Daptone head states. "I also think that's what made The Dap-Kings great, because you had a group full of leaders and in most cases, that can be a catastrophe where everyone wants to do their own thing. But in this case, it worked perfectly because everyone knew how to make good music. And it was never about one person—it was always about the band and the way the band sounded together."

CHAPTER SIX FISH IN MY DISH: SHARON JONES GETS HER SHINE

As the younger generation of Dap-Kings were forming their own musical unit that would appear on records inside and out of the soul scene, Sharon Jones was coming into her own as the matriarch of Daptone's universe—a funky galaxy that was continuously sucking new fans, musicians, and tastemakers into its orbit. In between tours, SJDK settled back into their Bushwick digs to record *Naturally*, Daptone's fourth LP, which would further propel the singer into the limelight as a soul superstar.

Naturally pulled from a wider musical tradition than *Dap-Dippin'*. The album offered a modern take on lovelorn ballads in the vein of Gladys Knight, with "You're Gonna Get It" and the Lee Fields duet "Stranded In Your Love"; meanwhile, Sharon called out lovers everywhere with the speed of James Brown on tracks like "Your Thing Is A Drag" and "My Man Is A Mean Man." Few know whether Sharon was drawing on personal experience to perform such familiar but never clichéd love songs—Roth penned almost the entire album; Jones was single for the majority of SJDK's run, and occasionally had to dismiss assumptions that she was gay. Jones certainly looked to divas past, drawing swagger and inspiration from the likes of Aretha, Ann Peebles, and Lynn Collins for her excited but controlled vocal stylings. Roth wrote for the force of a woman he imagined Jones to be in private, and for the easygoing friend he spent weeks with on the road—"Fish In My Dish" was written in tribute to Jones's favorite pastime, which occasionally provided respite from long days on a tour bus.

The resulting album was more technically proficient than its predecessor

★ ★ ★ ★ ★ ★

but also showcased more developed arrangements and a broad range of influence. "*Naturally* is a testament to how much was lost in R&B over the past decade," *Pitchfork* decreed, adding that Daptone "may seem arcane if not retro, but there is an undeniable substance in a tradition bled dry from so many Boyz II Men, Mariah, and Babyface records."[1]

Sharon Jones & The Dap-Kings had come a long way from the basement sessions for *Dap-Dippin'*, a record created while the band was on the verge. By the time they assembled in Troutman to record *Naturally*, Jones told writer Andy Tennille, "Everything was more organized and everyone was contributing. Gabe would have some of the charts written out with what he wanted, but somewhere along the way the guys started adding their own stuff too because they were feeling it. We were all feeling it."[2]

The sophomore effort also includes a righteous take on Woodie Guthrie's anthem "This Land Is Your Land," reimagining the iconic folk song, with its 1944 political lyrics reinserted in a funk context, then pressed into a seven-inch vinyl single on a red, white, and blue label emblazoned with the words *Vote Early! Vote Often!* Unlike "How Do I Let A Good Man Down?"—"If I had a good man, I wouldn't let him down!" Jones once told *Fresh Air*'s Terry Gross—here Jones is audibly emotional, perhaps pulling form her own lived experience as she belts verses about inequity and insecurity:

One bright sunny morning in the shadow of a steeple
Down by the welfare office I saw my people
They stood hungry
I stood wondering
I was wondering
If this land was made for you and me.

Although the singer was lauded for her humble, humorous spirit and perseverance, by the time she stepped into the isolation booth to lay down vocals for the tune, Jones was defiant: she had long been told that the music business was decidedly *not* made for her. In an oft-quoted refrain—which would later become a reminder of all of her achievement—she was "too Black, too fat, and too old" to make it.

Sharon Lafaye Jones had spent a lifetime laser-focused on her dreams, very early declaring that she wanted to be a singer and become successful enough to buy her mother, Ella Mae Price Jones—a mom of six of whom Sharon was the youngest, and who was also raising her sister's kids—a house in North Augusta, South Carolina. One James Brown grew up just across the river in Augusta, Georgia, and Jones family lore has it that a young Ella Mae used to play with Soul Brother No. 1. Sharon was born into a world where James Brown & The Famous Flames' simmering "Please, Please, Please" was climbing the charts and becoming a signature hit; her own musical journey would be a similarly slow burn, a decades-long plea that never took "no" for an answer.

Ella Mae moved her family to Brooklyn's Bedford-Stuyvesant neighborhood in 1960 to escape an abusive marriage, and Sharon, like many soul singers, began singing in church. Sharon's faith was as strong as her vocal cords, and at age fourteen she joined the Universal Church Of God on Rockaway Avenue under the direction of Pastor Elijah Fields. Sharon's precociousness and talent—as well as her obsession with both gospel and secular soul music—advanced her to the role of church music director, where she used her divine instrument to compose and sing gospel funk as E.L. Fields & The Gospel Wonders. Recorded when she was just seventeen, still small but with a sizeable afro and a lit-up smile, "Heaven Bound" b/w "Keys To The Kingdom" were early through lines between Jones's dedication to her roots, powerful Pentecostal faith, and devotion to the groovy sounds that played on her radio and home television. "Heaven Bound," in particular, bears a resemblance to Chic's 1979 smash "Le Freak"—a song that lacks much of the spiritual uplift appropriate for a church choir.[3]

Jones had a natural musicality and never took voice or piano lessons, instead following the bassist and guitarist in her church band and playing piano with two fingers. "A voice just came to me and said go play the piano in church," she told Terry Gross in 2007, adding that Aretha Franklin was her biggest inspiration. "And when I saw her on the *Amazing Grace* album and she had that dashiki on and she did this song 'Mary, Don't You Weep' ... I said, *I'm going to play this piano.*"[4]

That dogged determination and passion would serve Sharon well as the leading lady in the soul revolution, but in the twenty-something years leading up to that first meeting with Gabe Roth at Dare Studios, she hustled. Jones entered talent contests supporting local funk and soul bands upon graduating from Thomas Jefferson High School, her singing abilities soaring beyond the church but never leaving it behind. She also enrolled at Brooklyn College, becoming the first person in her family to enter higher education. Jones would be loath to call herself the family matriarch—she had a deep love and respect for her mother—but the baby of the household was on her way to being the driving force in pushing the Jones family forward, caring for the rest of the clan.

Driven as she was—and stubborn as all get out—the recording business was not interested in a barely five-foot woman with a sturdy build, dark skin, and a bluesy inflection in her voice. Jones herself was beginning to internalize the negative comments about her appearance, viewing ugliness when she gazed in the mirror rather than the glow of pride and recognition that swelled in her chest as a young woman after first hearing James Brown's "Say It Loud (I'm Black And I'm Proud)." Absent a record deal, Jones did a brief stint touring as a backup singer with a Long Island R&B group called The Magic Touch in the late 70s, but by the mid-to-late 80s, R&B favored the sounds of Teena Marie, Sade, Bobby Brown, and the new jack swing of New Edition. In New York and on the airwaves, hip-hop was exploding with catchy and critical messages from Run DMC, Public Enemy, and, later, Queen Latifah. Now in her early thirties—an age by which, presumably, a singer would have found success if success was to be had—Jones was well out of step with pop sensibilities.

She spent some time working customer service at Macy's and did session

★ ★ ★ ★ ★ ★

work as a backing vocalist on house records, often credited as Miss Lafaye Jones, while singing in church choirs. To pay the bills, Jones harnessed her sass and take-no-mess attitude while working as an armored car guard for Wells Fargo in Red Hook (where she shot rats with a pellet gun for fun) and, in 1988, to the Rikers Island Prison Complex, where she was employed as a corrections officer. Although a series of injuries put her out of commission for months at a time, Jones worked at Rikers for two years and learned how to keep control while holding attention—a professional application of her childhood toughness, back when it was rare for Sharon to back down from a fight and she began to show a characteristic strong will.

"Let me tell you, it's the look in my eyes," she recounted to Gross. "You may have like eighty inmates to maybe three officers or two officers. You could not show fear. … I got the respect from them right there, and they knew that I didn't take stuff. I wasn't scared." Jones mused that the fearlessness she summoned during run-ins with inmates at Rikers carried onto the stage. "I don't show fear there, either," she reflected twenty years later.[5]

By the early 1990s, Sharon Jones was regularly wowing audiences, though her crowd usually consisted of overdressed children and extended families in various states of intoxication. She was now singing lead in Good 'N' Plenty, a wedding band helmed by Staten Island–based music store owner John Castellano. Jones was one of the first Black wedding singers in an Italian band, performing covers of Aretha Franklin, Whitney Houston, Donna Summer, and Motown oldies, while the band jammed to era-appropriate hits. In 1991, she was joined by singers Starr Duncan-Lowe and Saundra Williams (now the "Good 'N' Plenty girls"), an early auditory connection that would bear fruit decades later at Daptone. Speaking to Sharon Jones biographer Donald Brackett, Williams said she enjoyed watching Jones interact "with the audience, with the band. Every show was wonderful with her, just watching her be herself, and she gave a thousand percent of herself on every stage." Despite her explosive stage persona and kind heart, Jones was never naïve about the world she lived

★ ★ ★ ★ ★ ★

in—the former prison guard tucked a .22 caliber pistol into her fanny pack for over a decade.

At every age and stage, it seemed impossible that such a small and, by industry standards, old package could radiate so much energy. Whether it was the wedding band, which taught Jones how to appeal to a varied crowd; the day jobs that required her to be tough as nails; or her intrinsic spunk and ability to lead, the singer's star power should've been apparent to anyone who came into her orbit. But when boyfriend Joe Hrbek brought Jones into Desco's studio to record backing vocals, Gabe Roth and Phillip Lehman were appropriately skeptical of the woman whose hard stare would melt into a big smile. Jones lacked the obsessive, almost fetishistic appreciation of funk and soul that Desco embodied, and she had spent much of her adult life trying to appeal to the pop audiences Roth and Lehman so loathed. She was forty years old and about to sing for her supper in front of a bunch of twenty- and thirtysomethings way the hell out in Long Island. But, like a true professional, Jones didn't flinch or belie any doubt—she sang the hell out of the backing vocals for "Let A Man Do What He Wanna Do" before vamping on her own track. Then, she recalled, "They started bringing out stuff that I hadn't even heard, stuff that my mother and them used to play." Her jaw dropped "when these guys started writing those songs like 'Soul Tequila.' I was like, *Damn!* It was amazing. They have some kind of soul roots in them. I loved them from then."[6]

Desco, and later Daptone, quickly fell in love with Sharon, who became the glue and much of the momentum behind their developing melodious empire. The difference in age and background was irrelevant, race a nonissue (while SJDK's audiences often had less melanin, the band had Black, white, Jewish, Indigenous, and Latino members over the years), a passion for and shared appreciation for roots music mattering above all else. And Sharon could hang—a most important quality when assessing a new member of a tight-knit musical family. She liked to smoke weed and cigars when fishing in the Delaware River Water Gap. ("I used to smoke with the band for

★ ★ ★ ★ ★ ★

pleasure every three hours," she later told *New York Magazine*. "On tour I'd make sure we'd have the weed when we got there."[7])

Jones was positive and playful, though sometimes crude and often impish, with an inclination to tease or mess with the people she loved most—though never in a malicious way. She was kind, and she had nicknames for everybody, but she was prone to calling people whose names she had forgotten "boobadoo." Austen Holman, her later-career day manager, describes Sharon's energy as almost childlike. "She was a performer. I mean, that was what she did all the time. She wanted to get you laughing. She wants to be the loudest person in the room; she wanted you to look at her. She wanted to, like, put on a show."

Jones spoke incessantly, her firecracker energy ready to explode at a moment's notice—an episode some of her band would refer to as "crazy time." "Tour vehicles do not always survive these episodes intact," Roth jokingly told Saki Knafo of the *New York Times*. "There's been a lot of chair-throwing in our band in the last few years."[8] The singer was rarely quiet about what was bothering her—be it bad sound at a show, a bandmate who was being annoying, or just not being in the mood to sing. But when she was on, Steinweiss recalls, "Sharon was like the ultimate entertainer. I've never worked with an artist who can just basically hold the audience in the palm of her hand and command them. It's like she's preaching."

Once Jones—affectionately referred to as Shern by her friends and bandmates—got in front of audiences with The Soul Providers, that inherent showmanship came out full force. She had a way of making a member of a crowded audience feel enraptured, as if they were the only person in the room and the sole beneficiary of the band's collective energy. Even casual fans of funk—those who hadn't been digging for obscurities or waiting with bated breath for a return of the mack(tress)—became obsessed after attending a live show.

"Sharon had a certain confidence onstage and, in some ways, she was more comfortable and stronger and kind of her best person on the stage," Roth says. Jones was always ready early, having laid out her dress and shoes

★ ★ ★ ★ ★ ★

(or, on the occasion of a Halloween show, a Wonder Woman costume complete with cape) ahead of time, affording herself the ability to get into the zone and ride the waves of excitement and fear, her body often shaking just before she launched onstage. "If you were watching before she hit the stage," he adds, "she would just be real concentrated and kind of quiet, and you could just kind of see the energy building up in her. It was kind of like a fighter before a fight; even the way she walked onto the stage always seemed like she was walking into the ring. It was really intense."

Jones's intensity often came from a very real, very emotional place. "Twenty-four family members and close friends of mine have died from one year to another," she told the *Sydney Morning Herald*, showing a hint of vulnerability in her otherwise unflappable performance armor. She recalled learning, just hours before a show, that her brother had passed away. "I'm behind the stage and I could see my brother and the tears are fallin' down my face and I'm tellin' myself, 'Don't cry, don't cry' ... [then, onstage] people are like, 'We love you, Sharon' ... those tears dried up, and I did my show."[9]

Like the Stax and Motown artists they so admired, Sharon Jones and her Dap-Kings were professionals, even if they preferred a grittier sound than Berry Gordy might approve of. The otherwise extremely casual Dap-Kings always wore suits and shined shoes while performing, Sharon in a sparkly or fringed dress (sometimes, both) and heels usually purchased at Payless—which she would typically kick off as her body shook, shimmied, and jerked across the stage, evoking her Black and Indigenous ancestors along the way. Trumpeter Todd Simon recalled a particularly profound moment playing with SJDK at a Polish community hall turned rock venue called Warsaw in Greenpoint, Brooklyn. "We travel in time through music, whether we want to or not. A bunch of kids were dressed up in suits, and we were in suits, and there were a bunch of Polish ladies making perogies in back, and I felt like we were in 1967. And it was a dream come true."[10]

By the time Daptone released *Naturally* in January 2005, Sharon Jones & The Dap-Kings were touring heavily at festivals and midsized clubs

★ ★ ★ ★ ★ ★

in the States and abroad, and had appeared on *Late Night With Conan O'Brien*. They had grown their audience steadily—due in no small part to Jones's charisma, energy, and dance moves, as well as an impeccably choreographed, though never put-on, sometimes raunchy charm.

The band had also found a balance between their electric, jam-packed shows and offstage antics. "Sharon used to do this thing to me where I'd do a guitar solo and then she'd make me get down to as low as she was," Brenneck, upon whom Jones bestowed the nickname "TNT," remembers. "Those were the best years of my life, playing fucking limbo with Sharon Jones. I have so many funny memories of her, sitting in hotel rooms in France, getting drunk. Me and Dave Guy would play 1920s Louis Armstrong music and she would just hang, and we just smoked a ton of weed together. She was a party animal, a lunatic."

Roth recounts less partying but recalls that, like everyone else, Jones loved to eat well and enjoy herself. "Sharon was always the one to order, like, a steak and a lobster, but she never ate much. We would always fight to see who could sit next to her because she would give us her food."

Although Sharon Jones & The Dap-Kings had graduated from shitty passenger vans to less run-down vehicles and buses, the road ahead remained long. The band was touring major clubs in the Netherlands, revisiting long-time supporters at the UK's Jazz Café, and slowly growing its status outside the soul collector scene on festival stages in France, Canada, and California. But despite a lack of competition from similar bands, SJDK were barely breaking even. They were making two or three thousand dollars a gig—which had to be distributed among nine people.

"We would go to Europe and come back and I would still have to go to my church: 'I need $200,'" Jones told *New York Magazine*.[11] Despite growing fame, she was still living in the projects with her mother in Far Rockaway, Queens—a forty-minute drive from Daptone's studios, past JFK Airport.

Still, it was more about the music than the money for Jones who, after a lifetime of working on the fringes of the music business, fell easily into her growing fame. Binky Griptite says that she "was never shitty about it," though Jones was quick to speak up if she felt she wasn't being treated right. She remained down to earth, humbled by her luck and late-in-life success—a twist of fate she regularly thanked God for but also relished in. "She loved fans, always loved seeing people after the show," Griptite notes.

Sharon Jones & The Dap-Kings fans fell outside of a specific target audience, age, or ethnicity, and the group was bolstered by love from college and public radio. SJDK's energy appealed to everyone, and the band's leading lady bridged a gap between nostalgia and a visceral music experience many listeners had been lacking. "There were not a lot of other acts like that around that time; it was like canned power," says Brenneck, adding that Sharon Jones was unique as neither a throwback nor a legacy act.

Perhaps a sign of age or, more likely, a particular taste culled by osmosis on tour buses and basement studio sessions, Jones dismissed much pop music, though she remained a fan of singers such as Beyoncé and Rihanna, as well as the more soulful stylings of Erykah Badu, Alicia Keys, and Jill Scott. "The new stuff out here, just after a while they don't make any sense. It all sounds the same. The new stuff don't hold my attention," she told the *New York Times*, in an interview conducted from the waiting room of her ear, nose, and throat doctor. "You don't even know what they're saying.… When you're singing you're telling a story. That's why it's so important to me when these guys bring a song, if it don't make any sense, if I can't tell a story, then I don't want to sing it."[12]

Still, other older female singers released new music around the same time, perhaps priming audiences and critics for the more roughhewn soul and propulsive energy of Sharon Jones & The Dap-Kings. In 2004, Mavis Staples of the legendary Southern soul family group The Staple Singers released *Have A Little Faith*, a gospel, blues, and soul album—her first in nearly ten years. The album was a critical smash and netted several awards, and Staples brought a distinct, if not more sophisticated, entertaining energy to the stage. In September 2005, fifty-nine-year-old soul singer Bettye LaVette—a Detroit native who had a brief career in the 60s and

70s, as well as a short stint touring with James Brown—unleashed *I've Got My Own Hell To Raise*, an album of covers by other female artists. Both LaVette and Mavis had long performance histories, and, in the case of Staples, a familiar name driving interest and appreciation, yet no one quite embodied the spirit of the early 70s or the energy of James Brown in the way Sharon Jones did.

"You aggressive like that, Sharon!" Staples told *Spin* in a joint interview with Jones. "You're the hardest working' lady—the Lady James Brown!"[13]

While Jones's enigmatic presence and cred were rarely, if ever, called into question, she and fellow Daptone artists were often dubbed as "retro soul" by well-meaning press and fans. For a group of musicians so enamored with the nuances of music past, who had managed to pay homage without imitating, slapping the label "retro" on their efforts was a watermark of misunderstanding. For Sharon, it was also an affront to her personal history. Speaking to the *New Yorker*, the singer snapped, "There's nothin' retro about me, baby. I *am* soul!"[14]

Sharon's soul was unstoppable onstage, Roth says. "She would connect to people in this very personal way where, when you went to a show, you felt like you were just partying with her all night. And that's how she felt about it, too. So it was very real and visceral, and the rhythm was unbelievable. As a live experience, I don't think there was much competing with us and that's why I think it transcended audiences."

Even if the money wasn't there just yet, Jones believed that SJDK were destined for big things, and she regularly told Roth and Neal Sugarman that she thought they could sell a million records if they pushed hard enough. A million record sales would be quite a feat, if not totally improbable, for an independent label operating on a shoestring budget in a rapidly deteriorating musical economy (in 2007, *Billboard* reported that *Naturally* had sold fifteen thousand copies).[15]

Speaking on a panel at Los Angeles's Grammy Museum, Roth added, "but it didn't really matter because she never wanted to take any shortcuts either. She was never like, 'How can we get on the radio?' or 'Can't we do a

★ ★ ★ ★ ★ ★

song that's like so and so?' She just wanted to feel it; she wanted the music to be driving and honest and soulful."

Jones, Roth, and crew believed that what comes from the heart touches the heart, and their approach made profound connections around the world. The Daptone style had already connected with Mark Ronson, who sampled Sharon Jones on his 2003 debut album, the hip-hop and contemporary soul mash-up *Here Comes The Fuzz*. "Sharon Jones had one of the most magnificent, gut-wrenching voices of anyone in recent times," he later tweeted—though by 2006, the New York–based, British-born stepson of Foreigner guitarist Mick Jones was more interested in tapping The Dap-Kings for a project with a different singer.

Just two weeks after Jones celebrated her fiftieth birthday in May 2006, the singer hit the stage at New York's Irving Plaza—a ballroom not too far from the Union Square apartment where, in 1995, Phillip Lehman and Gabe Roth had their first machinations of a funk label. The sold-out birthday celebration marked a new height for Daptone Records and for Sharon Jones, who headlined the soul revue to a thousand-strong adoring crowd. The label brought its entire roster out for the event, a constantly rotating configuration of musicians coming on and off stage as project and sound dictated: The Sugarman 3 and The Mighty Imperials (who had long since "disbanded" in favor of other studio work) performed; the string section known as the Bushwick Philharmonic was present; and Naomi Davis & The Gospel Queens brought a religious fervor to their set, with Sharon singing backup. Antibalas, fresh off tour and in between releases, performed, bringing up old members who were lost in The Dap-Kings split for a cacophonous Afro-funk riot; nine-piece psychedelic Ethiofunk group The Budos Band, who had been touring their self-titled debut from the previous year, backed up Charles Bradley—himself a rising star. For most of the people involved (at least those with a less hazy recollection) the birthday celebration was the first time they felt *noticed*—a real show of recognition by a hometown crowd who appreciated their grooviness and presence.

SJDK kept the festivities going on the road. Promoter and Daptone

★ ★ ★ ★ ★ ★

family friend DJ Pari recalled a down-home celebration in a local park while the band was touring in Germany. Sharon manned the grill all night, and "the next day I took her to do her laundry… it was a funky affair," Pari wrote on Instagram.

For her milestone birthday, Gabe Roth penned Sharon a subtle but powerful anthem. "Longer And Stronger" spoke to Jones's deep well of strength and sincerity, declaring, "Fifty years of soul gone by and fifty more to come / You think you've seen something / But, Lord, I've just begun."

Although it wasn't officially released until 2015, "Longer And Stronger" was used by Solange on her 2008 Mark Ronson–produced album, used as part of the *For Colored Girls* film soundtrack, and earnestly performed by Jones for years. Onstage, Jones reimagined the song as a lesson on self-worth from her mother, singing with the seriousness of a woman who had come so far and, as the song goes, "can stand the test of time." With strength from Ella Mae (who would pass in 2012) and sonic support from The Dap-Kings, it seemed as if Sharon Jones had finally found her stride. She had even met her idol, James Brown, just months before he passed on Christmas Day 2006. As the singer sputtered to get words of appreciation out of her mouth, Brown looked Jones square in the eyes and said, "God bless you, daughter"—a short sentence acknowledging her torch-bearing status that would remain one of the proudest moments of Jones's life.

Yet, five months after she celebrated a half century of soul, a new singer would arrive on the scene. The singer was younger, white, and became a cultural force that would require Sharon to reckon with renewed feelings of insecurity and usurped success. True to form, Sharon Jones wouldn't go down without a fight.

CHAPTER SEVEN WHAT HAVE YOU DONE FOR ME LATELY? AMY WINEHOUSE RECORD HERALDS A NEW ERA FOR DAPTONE

Mark Ronson is effortlessly cool, with a low transatlantic lilt and the look of a good-hearted frat boy or Thomas C. Howell in *The Outsiders*; his slight smirk and small, wavy brown pompadour complement an understated though highly stylish aesthetic. Ronson lacks the road-worn look of some of his musical contemporaries, and an unaware onlooker might feel more comfortable placing him in Manhattan's Murray Hill neighborhood instead of behind the mixing console, where he's produced some of the most legendary hip-hop and soul acts of the twenty-first century.

Ronson grew up in New York City and attended NYU, where—like many musicians who packed a love of raw funk and soul into their performance gear—he found a growing fascination with the link between the old school and the golden age of hip-hop. He graduated from guesting at DJ nights to running his own popular gig and spinning album release parties for Jay-Z, eventually producing for pop-soul artist Nikka Costa, playing multiple instruments on his own records, and starting a label. Ronson had developed a unique ear for samples, chopping up tracks from Lenny Kravitz, musician-poet Labi Siffre, and the Fania All Stars on his debut *Here Comes The Fuzz*, alongside performances from Mos Def, Jack White, Sean Paul, and even Weezer frontman Rivers Cuomo. Ronson came into the favor of Puffy, Pharrell (then known more for his work with

★ ★ ★ ★ ★ ★

hip-hop group The Neptunes than as a solo act or producer), and Busta Rhymes for his beat-making and DJ sets—which he'd say were "60 percent hip-hop, 30 percent funk and disco, 20 percent reggae, and 10 percent rock'n'roll," often mixing jazz-pop and rock from the likes of Steely Dan with hip-hop hits for a club crowd.[1]

This musical philosophy likely had an influence on—or, at the very least, came up alongside—producers like Kanye West and Kendrick Lamaar. It also existed concurrently with the rise and fall of Desco Records, and Daptone's early successes. And while Ronson and Daptone were operating in separate scenes, the label's musicians got around. In early 2006, Ronson was beginning to work on *Versions*, an album of covers in a throwback soul and hip-hop style, and he connected with Dap-King trumpeter Dave Guy to develop horn arrangements for demos.

Guy—who had come into the Daptone fold post–*Dap Dippin'* and replaced Todd Simon after he returned to California in 2003—arrived at Ronson's Mercer Street studio in downtown Manhattan with his own demo in hand. SJDK had just cut a cover of Stevie Wonder's 1970 Motown hit "Signed, Sealed, Delivered, I'm Yours," and when Guy pressed play on the track (which wouldn't be officially released until 2014), Ronson was blown away. "It was just so much the real deal," he later effused.[2]

When Ronson wasn't squeezing in demo sessions for his own project, he was collaborating with a young British singer named Amy Winehouse who was looking to evolve from the jazz-inflected vibe of her debut record. The two had met through a friend of Ronson at EMI Publishing, and they decided to work together after spending some time hanging out at the studio, where they bonded over soul music and 60s girl groups like The Shangri-Las. Winehouse and Ronson shared a cultural and ethnic history (both came from North London Jewish families and were, unknowingly, in the early stages of a legendary project), as well as an easy, honest musicality. Early on, Ronson had developed piano chords and a simple, reverb-drenched beat for what would become the title track of Winehouse's *Back To Black*. The twenty-three-year-old singer was so impressed that she

★ ★ ★ ★ ★ ★

stayed in New York an extra week to finish demos for her eleven-song Motown- and 60s-soul-influenced album.

Winehouse's expressive contralto vocals and intensely personal tales of love lost, addiction, and rebellion were a perfect match for Ronson's production style, but getting her rough cuts to sound both old and rhythmically engaging was a challenge. "I was probably using, you know, like, whatever computer trick I could [to] make things sound old," Ronson told NPR. Then, he put on the Sharon Jones cover Dave Guy had recently shown him. "I said, like, 'How good is this? We should get these guys to play these demos.'" When Winehouse responded with an affirmative, enthusiastic "It's the nuts!", Ronson called up Gabe Roth to set up a few days of studio time.[3]

Winehouse had already flown back across the pond by the time Ronson knocked on the door of 115 Troutman for his session with The Dap-Kings, CD-J demos and arrangements in hand. The band recorded six songs for *Back To Black* and, later, the ever-popular "Valerie" for Ronson's *Versions*. The collaboration with Ronson was natural, and probably made more seamless without Winehouse in the room; The Dap-Kings played each song just three or four times before moving on.

"I had never worked in this way, but it was pretty cool actually, because Mark could just queue her vocals as the track goes on," says Steinweiss, recalling that hearing Winehouse in his headphones was almost like having her in the room. "It's kind of at tempo, and I'd be playing along."

"That was, like, the most professional thing we'd done to date," Binky Griptite reflects. "We'd just been doing our own thing and on our own time in Gabe's studio, or were at home smoking weed and working on our own schedule. So we weren't used to having another producer being in there, like, *Okay, we gotta knock this out by five*. I mean, we'd had a taste of it, but it was still in the early days."

The Dap-Kings also developed on Ronson's arrangements, sinking into horn parts, charting chords, and adding Steinweiss's drum sound,

★ ★ ★ ★ ★ ★

which managed to meld the refinement of a jazz-educated drummer with a minimalist, almost childlike approach to playing. In an NPR interview, Ronson cited the band as the driving force behind "You Know I'm No Good," *Back To Black*'s second single: "I had always thought of it almost as ... kind of Latin, like, samba." He wasn't feeling his arrangement in the studio, so he offered it up to The Dap-Kings to interpret in their own vocabulary. Sugarman and Guy came back with horn lines, emphasizing Ian Hendrickson-Smith's baritone sax to complement Winehouse's deep voice (Ronson speculated that *Back To Black* was the first time he'd utilized that instrument), while Steinweiss and bassist Nick Movshon developed an intimidating rhythm.

"[They're] probably the most incredible rhythm section I've ever worked with," Ronson added, publicly cementing the band's torch-carrying lineage. "That was when I really discovered the magic of The Dap-Kings and ... very much like The Wrecking Crew in LA, and, you know, The Funk Brothers, like, are a special group of musicians that really just bring you something that nobody else does."[4]

While doing local promotion for *Back To Black* in October or November of that year, Winehouse finally got a chance to meet the band on her record; the songstress and The Dap-Kings hit it off immediately. Ronson observed Winehouse as she walked around Bushwick and settled into the homey vibe of the House Of Soul: "It was one of the last times I remember her just being unencumbered by any threat of drama or press or paparazzi," he later told the *Village Voice*.[5] They recorded "Valerie" the same day—unlike the originals on *Back To Black*, it was a cover of a song by the British indie-rock band The Zutons.

The Dap-Kings spent an entire day working up a slow, sweeter version, Steinweiss remembers, "But then at the end of the session, Mark was like, 'Can we just try a Motown version where it's upbeat?' That type of beat is not something we ever did; the tempo is more like The Strokes or something," he adds, matter-of-factly. The band did one final up-tempo take, which became the radio version of "Valerie." Released in 2007, the

★ ★ ★ ★ ★ ★

song was one of Winehouse's longest-lasting hits and a testament to the collaborative pop genius of Ronson and The Dap-Kings.

Back To Black was released on Island Records (Ronson's producer credit shared with the legendary Salaam Remi, who worked with Winehouse on her debut, *Frank*) in October 2006. It quickly ran up the charts in both the UK and stateside, its pop-meets-soul sensibility, Winehouse's punky Ronettes look and diaristic but insightful lyricism coming along just ahead of what pop scholar Simon Reynolds called "retromania."[6] This musical phenom lamented the lack of originality in pop music and its reliance on increasingly relevant material from the past, though such an affinity for a previous generation's aesthetic wasn't relegated to pop radio. Winehouse's music was charting at the same time that *Mad Men*, a groundbreaking and period-perfect cable television series set in the 1960s, was increasing interest in the era's fashion, design, and music. The Dap-Kings had unwittingly found themselves at the center of a cultural phenomenon—though they were still operating behind the scenes.

"Amy just had such a unique voice and lyrical vision," reflects Steinweiss, who considers *Back To Black* one of his favorite professional efforts. "I think that the production kind of fell on Mark to meet that with something as classy. That's why producers come to people like us, because they're like, *We want that classy sound and you guys are obsessed with it. So you help us make it.* That era of girl groups and soul music actually elevated her music, because no one was doing something with that type of class."

A wise producer or musician won't hijack nostalgia, Ronson explained in a 2014 TED Talk. "It leaves the listener feeling sickly. You have to take an element of those things and bring something fresh and new to it."[7]

Even though Amy Winehouse had already achieved a significant fanbase and sales in the UK—and came from the same Camden soul scene that had long supported Desco and Daptone's revivalist efforts—few at the label thought much about the session after it was over. "We didn't have a clue about her already being a star," Griptite says casually. "She probably told us that, but we were, like, *Whatever, her name ain't Marva Whitney.*

★ ★ ★ ★ ★ ★

So we did it and it was done." But the reality of Winehouse's skill and celebrity quickly became apparent—*Back To Black* had several charting singles in 2006 and 2007, and *Time* magazine dubbed "Rehab" the best song of 2007. The following year, she took home four Grammys, including "Album Of The year." Winehouse's "retro" soul sound was officially back in style.

"Soul music never went away and soul lovers never went away, but they're just kind of closeted because they didn't think it was commercially viable. Even soul fans inside of the record labels grew up with this," Griptite continues, flipping through his collection of records in his own home studio. "Then, when Amy's record hit, all the undercover soul fans are like, *I'm free*. And then that's when everybody's like, *Oh, there's money in it now*."

Tom Brenneck isn't sure why the record was such a success. Though Brenneck knew Winehouse's songs were "pretty fucking spectacular" even at the demo stage. He points to "Love Is A Losing Game," an orchestral ballad in which she compares her lover to fighting a five-story fire, as but one example of her poetic lyricism. Offering increasingly rare praise, Brenneck notes, "She's a gifted fucking songwriter and singer. I know some people don't like the affectation of her voice, but I really felt what she was writing. As a musician on the session, I was inspired and I think the parts that I played in those records reflect that."

The Winehouse session was one of the label's first real "money gigs," and it provided a solid foundation for session work to come, establishing Daptone as one of the most important recording houses in a generation. Yet *Back To Black* brought up conflicting ideas about major-label ethos and the effects of celebrity. Roth acknowledged that the album was influential in making revival soul more commercially acceptable, but said the work never brought Sharon Jones & The Dap-Kings, or Daptone Records, any new fans.

★ ★ ★ ★ ★ ★

As a songwriter whose ballads were written with an empowered, aware perspective, Roth found *Back To Black* too angst-ridden and self-involved.[8] But Griptite, who had a close working relationship with the irreverent singer he described as a "little thing who loves to curse and shoot pool" appreciated how the album was "a flying *fuck you*" to pop trends; a mainstream culling of the same punk attitude that made Daptone so unique. "Amy was so 100 percent unapologetically herself. She was on that 'zero fucks given' before that term was coined."

Sharon Jones had also been on the "zero fucks given" tip for years as an older frontwoman competing for audiences with singers half her age, only to have one of those singers swoop her support system right from under her nose. "Amy made a fucking ten-million-selling record, and we were just trying to sell, like a hundred thousand with Sharon," Brenneck notes, his frustrated acceptance still audible. During the *Back To Black* sessions, Jones looked on at Winehouse and The Dap-Kings with a sense of impending doom and lapsed loyalty—was she going to lose her band to an artist with broader appeal, deeper pockets, and a producer who recognized the canned magic of The Dap-Kings? Jones was angry and, early on, indignant. "I'm old enough to be Amy Winehouse's mother, how am I supposed to take a back seat to that child?" she questioned.[9]

Even after he left Antibalas for the West Coast, Todd Simon and Jones spoke often over the phone. "There was a point where she was, like, going to get her own manager. I'd always be like, *Sharon don't worry. You've gotta keep your composure through this. The guys gotta do what they gotta do, and think of the resources that this is gonna bring.*"

Eventually, and with significant reassurance from her fellow musicians, Jones recognized the boon Winehouse's success and a relationship with Mark Ronson could be for Daptone's wider appeal. With a little prodding, she regularly thanked both for recognizing The Dap-Kings' soul power during interviews. Jones also understood the need to put *100 Days, 100 Nights*—SJDK's third studio album, recorded in the latter half of 2006—on pause while the Winehouse business ran its course. But Brenneck

★ ★ ★ ★ ★ ★

concedes that SJDK's attempt to ride Winehouse's coattails only worked indirectly. "How could you tap into a young audience with a fucking forty-nine-year-old Sharon Jones?"

The Dap-Kings played a few gigs with Winehouse in the lead-up to her record launch, standing in for her English band when she toured the States. On January 16, 2007, the eight-piece Dap-Kings and two backup singers assembled at Joe's Pub in Manhattan's East Village to support Winehouse's post–*Back To Black* American debut. The singer was lauded for bringing soul and R&B back to pop audiences, and seemed genuinely happy performing for an adoring audience that included musical luminaries like Dr. John, Mos Def, and Jay-Z in a short black dress and trademark enormous beehive hairdo. But despite her in-studio professionalism, the singer was starting to show signs of trouble. "She sounded great but acted like she didn't believe it," Amy Linden wrote in a prescient review of the Joe's Pub show for the *Voice*. "It made me fear that Amy had the talent to be a star, but might not have the strength."[10]

Early on, Winehouse was subsumed by frenzied paparazzi who pounced on the singer's struggles with mental health, her volatile relationship with partner Blake Fielder-Civil (who allegedly introduced Winehouse to crack cocaine), and partying with "it" celebrities of the day, including Paris Hilton. But while the train wreck depicted in the press was real, and Winehouse imbibed heavily in drugs and alcohol, it was not the entirety of her personality. "She was like a real, 100 percent bona-fide musician," Griptite remembers. "There were hints and moments of her issues, but there was also a lot of getting down to business and cracking jokes and being a cool person."

Brenneck chalks up Winehouse's slow spiral to youth and a relentless press, which capitalized on the tabloid-worthy qualities of her personal life. "We were all pretty young at that time, and nothing that we were doing was dangerous. But her fucking lover was Blake and then she married him. And he was really self-destructive. And she was, like, really consumed by that."

Still, The Dap-Kings supported Winehouse on a national run that

★ ★ ★ ★ ★ ★

included a highly anticipated stop at Coachella. While audiences hungered to see the *Back To Black* singer, the *New York Times* called Winehouse's performance a drag, comparing it to "watching someone eat herself alive" (her band, however, received modest praise).[11] Winehouse and Sharon Jones had met during a 2008 SJDK performance at the Jazz Café in London, spending close to an hour talking in Jones's dressing room. In an interview with the *New Yorker*, Jones recounted seeing Winehouse in London: "I don't even want to talk about it. ... Instead of people laughin' at her, pray for her. Drugs are so horrible."[12]

The Dap-Kings' relationship with Winehouse concluded in July after a seventeen-date tour; the singer then canceled the remainder of her 2007 gigs due to the "rigors involved in touring and ... intense emotional strain."[13] Although the press began to highlight her lackluster performances and stumble-drunk behavior—a result of both addiction and a contentious relationship with fame—*Back To Black* continued to gather awards and critical praise, and spent multiple weeks atop the *Billboard* charts. Winehouse's alternative, anti-heroine vibe, combined with the timelessness of 60s soul and the big pop mixes that dominated it, were incredibly contemporary, fundamentally changing pop music to favor a "retro-influence" and live musicians. Although the family Daptone had been a serious road band for a decade and had multiple bands touring new music in 2006 and 2007, the label and its favored sounds were still underground. Through *Back To Black*, Daptone's aural obsessions were thrust into the limelight by a singer with appreciation but not the hard-won insight and ability to play it perfectly. "The sound that we had been working on for so long was now, like, a household sound—you heard that Daptone sound everywhere," says Simon, a world away from the Winehouse sessions in his Southern California home. "She was kind of the vessel for The Dap-Kings' sound to come out. It was hip, and made it cool for people to use horns again. I was getting calls for session work left and right from people who were like, *We want to sound like Amy Winehouse*."

Winehouse was cool—more identifiable for her youth, and, unfortunately,

★ ★ ★ ★ ★ ★

her whiteness. She also made relevant a sound many of her contemporaries would've previously considered to be music for their parents' generation. "Americans have never cared about their musical heritage—we rely on people from other countries to preserve our stuff," New York DJ Matt Weingarden theorizes. "Soul never died, but it was definitely lacking on the top charts for decades until the Daptone people came along."

Like many studio bands before them, The Dap-Kings got a payday (a whopping $350 per musician, per song), but they were edited out of prominent documentaries.[14] Although Sharon Jones and The Dap-Kings had long received positive press for their authenticity and exciting stage shows—and would only continue to do so—the band existed as a footnote in Winehouse's rising star. They also had to negotiate a crisis of confidence among diehard fans and hardheaded musicians.

"That whole Amy Winehouse moment was kind of difficult for our scene," says Steinweiss, who would also work with Ronson on a dozen other projects. "We were doing something that was very much more an underground, niche thing. I always believed in SJDK, but I was always really proud of *Back To Black* at the same time, and I didn't feel like one was fighting the other one." The Dap-Kings received a framed platinum record for their work on *Back To Black* (to signify over one million sales in the USA) and, with the appropriate amount of fanfare, hung it above the toilet in their upstairs bathroom. Roth casually notes, "It was the only free space we had."

The band was supposed to perform at the 2008 Grammys with Winehouse, but the singer's visa application was rejected. Notes Alex Kadvan, "They also worked with Mark on the track for the James Bond film *Quantum Of Solace*, with Amy at vocals, but the project got shelved by the film's producers due to her condition." The Dap-Kings never worked with Amy Winehouse again after that 2007 tour, though their relationship with Mark Ronson would grow plentiful fruit. Ronson employed the Dap-Kings horns on his sophomore solo record, *Versions*, and a dozen other projects. "He thought we had something special," notes Sugarman, "and

★ ★ ★ ★ ★ ★

had us in the recording studio every week. Post–Amy Winehouse, we were getting calls from other producers who were chasing what Mark made, which is cool because we were playing raw."

Those producers and musicians came to Daptone not to read charts but to help create lines—a much more interesting gig than a typical union call. "We were able to influence a lot of the music and the records we played on—we were trying to make everything sound a little bit cooler," Sugarman says. "It's incredible to watch how things unfolded."

The younger generation became Ronson's de-facto rhythm section across a variety of funk-influenced projects and straight pop acts. Various Dap-Kings appeared as session musicians or producers on tracks by Michael Bublé, Foreigner, Pharrell Williams, Kesha, and myriad others, lending a specific ear and deeply connected performance ability to more popular records than the players' modesty would allow them to cop to. Tommy Brenneck is among the players for whom *Back To Black* kickstarted a lasting production relationship. "If you're Mark Ronson or Pharrell and you're like, *I just want a sick horn part on this*, you either get Dave and Leon, or get The Dap-Kings to just put a sick horn section on it. Does he have to keep his ear to the ground and listen for other great horn sections, or just use his homeboys that he's been using for a decade?" he asks pointedly.

"That whole record was kind of based around those horns and a concept that we were deeply involved in. I'm not implying that Mark couldn't have done it without us, but that's what good producers do—they're able to pull the right people together and get the most out of those people," Sugarman concedes, choosing his words carefully. "It got a little weird after [Winehouse]. Suddenly, major labels and uncreative people were trying to copy what other people do. There were a number of sessions that we got called on because somehow people thought there was some magic. Some of it was okay, and some of it was really corny."

After Amy Winehouse died of alcohol poisoning in July 2011 at the age of twenty-seven—a coroner's inquest determined her death to be the result of "misadventure"—she was further elevated to the status of

★ ★ ★ ★ ★ ★

legendary musical genius. She's been the subject of multiple documentaries, books, articles, and museum exhibitions, as well as unrelenting questions during interviews with Daptone musicians. Homer Steinweiss speculates that, were she alive today, Winehouse might fuse soul and jazz with her renowned lyricism. "Amy Winehouse was writing these really deeply personal, intense lyrics, and I think that's probably where the differences were with SJDK," the drummer surmises. "One thing is a tradition and one thing is an artist's expression. Even though our thing was an artist's expression too, Amy was just singing her truth. That's a rare, harder thing to come by in the world of artistry."

Although the entire Daptone crew would go on to greater levels of success, the Amy Winehouse collaboration was their biggest crossover and yielded the most sales. A 2019 op-ed in the *Guardian* argued that *Back To Black* was the best album of the twenty-first century, and the inclusion of The Dap-Kings a "masterstroke."[15]

"I can't think of a more important moment or better climax in our career," Brenneck reflects, adding that the fact that Sharon subsequently managed to ride the wave of pop heights and make her own indelible impression "may be the coolest thing. Everything else seems smaller than that. Any of our pop endeavors are like little apples on a tree, and the branch is those two women in the mid-2000s."

CHAPTER EIGHT MAKE THE ROAD BY WALKING: REVIVAL SOUL STRETCHES OUT

While The Dap-Kings expanded their horizons supporting Amy Winehouse on tour, Sharon Jones was also branching out to worlds beyond Bushwick. In early 2007, she traveled to Australia to sing in Lou Reed's reimagining of his 1973 album *Berlin* at the Sydney Opera House. After a bit of an awkward start to their working relationship, she brought tears to Reed's eyes with her interpretation of "Sweet Jane," done in a classic Sharon Jones does Tina Turner style.

"He called me the magnificent, talented Sharon Jones, and said I took him to the mountain top," Jones later told *Billboard.* "Performing with him was a big deal for me, too. After we were in the dressing room, and I said, 'Me being here with you, Lou—I'm here with a big icon. I'm looking up to you like you're Stevie Wonder or James Brown.' He said, 'Wow.' And we got a hug in."[1]

Jones was set to tour *Berlin* in Europe but, much to Reed's consternation, pulled out three days before after being cast in a Denzel Washington movie. The actor was starring in and directing *The Great Debaters*—a film based on the true story of a debate team from a small Black college in Texas that competed against Harvard University in the 1930s—and needed an era-appropriate soundtrack. Sharon Jones laid down seven songs for the soundtrack at Memphis's legendary Ardent Recording Studio, working with Al Green axeman Teenie Hodges and The Carolina Chocolate Drops. Jones also appeared in the film, singing "That's What My Baby Likes," and, in a rare show of fandom, printed photos of herself and Denzel,

★ ★ ★ ★ ★ ★

which she carried in her back pocket and handed out proudly—including to total strangers on airplanes. In Sharon's book, Denzel Washington was up there with Oprah and Ellen DeGeneres.

Giving testament to her unpretentious attitude (or, perhaps, her desire to be recognized and affirmed), Jones would encourage people to Google her and her band—an action that became less and less necessary as their popularity grew on noncommercial radio, late-night TV, and festival circuits.

"Honestly, when we did *Dap-Dippin'*, we were just playing hundred-person venues," Steinweiss recalls. "When we did *Naturally*, it was a little bigger, we had a little scene going. I think if we had never made the Amy Winehouse record, we would have kept going at that pace," he posits. "Ultimately, it just propelled our band into a different stratosphere. When the next record came out, it was like we had this star power to our band. *Back To Black* took us from, like, local cool thing to a kind of world-touring stage thing, which was really great for us. I think it propelled all of our careers."

100 Days, 100 Nights, Sharon Jones & The Dap-Kings' third album, was released in October 2007 and peaked at No. 3 on *Billboard*'s "breaking and entering" Top Heatseekers music chart. The ten-track LP was another evolution in SJDK's sound, steering almost entirely away from funk in favor of rootsy R&B, late-60s Motown soul, pensive ballads, and a proper gospel number to close. Where the band's first two records had a sense of enthusiasm and naïveté, *100 Days* had the Daptone crew firing on all cylinders; they ooze hurt, passion, and certifiable soul from rhythm to phrasing, but always with a distinct style.

"Every time we made a Sharon record, I wanted to get to that Amy level—reach more and more people and break through," Steinweiss admits, adding that while he was getting burnt out on touring, he was always excited about the band's growing attention. "I think if I had produced *100 Days* and not Gabe, I would have succumbed to some pop style. Instead, Gabe was like, *Let's keep doing exactly what we do, really well.*" Bolstered by aggressive touring (the band visited three continents in as many months

★ ★ ★ ★ ★ ★

during 2008) and the limelight cast from being "Amy Winehouse's backing band," Sharon Jones & The Dap-Kings' latest sold several hundred thousand records. For the first time, Daptone started making money.

The album-release show for *100 Days* was another high-water mark for the band—the first time they would grace the stage at the legendary Apollo Theater in Harlem, a nexus for the best and hardest in music, as well as a pinnacle of Black American excellence. Speaking to *New York Magazine*, Jones said slyly, "When I first played at the Apollo, the owner didn't even know who Sharon Jones was. The Apollo had never seen so many white people coming uptown."[2] But that audience went wild from the moment Sharon bounded onstage, out of her shoes and into a series of not too choreographed dances. During their nearly two-hour show, SJDK ran through hits from *Dap-Dippin'* and their new record, paid tribute to James Brown with a heavy take on "This Is A Man's World," then brought Lee Fields up for a medley of J.B. tunes and dancing.

"Nobody, let me reiterate that point, nobody, was sitting down," Jamison Harvey, the DJ and journalist who founded *Flea Market Funk* in 2007, wrote of the show. "Nobody makes music like this anymore. Nobody entertains like this anymore. Nobody except Daptone. For twelve years they have been doing things their way, working hard and paying dues. Now they finally did it their way, at the Apollo Theater."[3]

"We were definitely not a household name," Griptite recalls, "but people that knew music knew us, and insiders knew our name. After *100 Days, 100 Nights* came out, it got to be really normal to be on TV; we did all the late-night shows except *Saturday Night Live*." The night after James Brown died, the guitarist was watching *The Late Show With David Letterman* when he caught actor Dan Aykroyd offering up his own support. "Dan Aykroyd is known as a big music fan and is a partner in House of Blues; we've always had a good relationship with them. Letterman is like, 'Such a shame losing James Brown,' and Aykroyd is like, 'Yes, and that's why we have to support Sharon Jones. Because we have to support these artists while they're still alive.'"

★ ★ ★ ★ ★ ★

But if there were audiences who *still* didn't know about Sharon Jones and The Dap-Kings, producers, music directors, and legendary musicians were certainly taking notice of Daptone Records. Guitarist Dan Auerbach had pulled inspiration from some of the same musical wells as SJDK in his own band, The Black Keys, and had caught Sharon Jones performing in Cleveland's Beachland Ballroom a couple of years prior. "That was the best soul band I ever fuckin' saw," he enthuses. "It was the tightest soul band ever; they made it so real. I had never seen it so real before." The guitarist went backstage to meet the SJDK crew (which included Leon Michels at the time), kicking off personal and professional relationships that would lead to a variety of studio work as well as a Black Keys/Sharon Jones & The Dap-Kings tour of Australia in 2006.

The Roots (and Questlove in particular) had long championed Amy Winehouse, sharing a stage and some kebab with the singer in the UK before *Back To Black* broke stateside. "The talk eventually moved over to the players and why *Back To Black* was sounding that way, and that's when I started hearing the Daptone name," says Roots guitarist Captain Kirk Douglas, recalling that Roots MC Black Thought often played SJDK backstage to amp up the band. "I remember hearing the version of 'Pick It Up (Lay It In The Cut)' and 'What Have You Done For Me Lately'—that was a real head trip, because you start wondering, *Did Janet Jackson cover this song?*" Even as a serious student of music and member of a taste-making band, "the discovery that this was actually music that was made within the past five years" was an exciting shock for Douglas.

The Dap-Kings' pitch-perfect ability to recreate an era led to early session work doing replays—a licensing workaround where a band is paid to cover a popular song that's otherwise far too expensive—and, following *100 Days*, requests to license songs from the label's catalogue increased. Daptone tunes were featured in a Ken Burns documentary, the Oscar-winning film *Up In The Air*, and commercials for Verizon, I Love NY, Chase Bank, and Tropicana.

Licensing was never part of Daptone's business plan, Sugarman asserts, suggesting that the increase in licensing agreements coincided with a larger change in how music was produced for television. "We don't make music to be licensed. We're not writing music that we think is going to entice people to use it on their soap operas; it just sometimes happens. And then it pays well enough that you can't really turn it down."

Sometimes the opportunities came organically: Daptone licensed an instrumental track to R&B singer Solange for use on her 2008 album *Sol Angel And The Hadely St. Dreams*. The instrumental was developed on the road and tacked on to the intro bars of Sharon's "Longer And Stronger." Laying on his back to tool with the underside of some piece of vintage recording equipment, Roth recalls how the band's instrumental songs "had real fucked up names. That song was something like 'Britney Spears Tit Hoss'—some weird tour shit from when we'd just been in the van too long," he says. Those songs would end up on a setlist, then played to perfection over the course of a tour. "And then we license it to Solange too and she's got our tune and just sang over it. So we have to, like, change the name of the tune so we could license it to her – our manger thought we'd get more money if we didn't call it 'Britney Spears Tit Hoss.'"

As their reputation continued to grow, The Dap-Kings snagged "sexier" sessions with Michael Bublé and CeeLo Green, whose bouncy, summertime pop-soul single "Georgia" relied heavily on Daptone horns and put the label on a path to later work with Green's songwriter: a young man named Bruno Mars. (The Bublé session netted Sharon enough money to buy her mother a house down South: "In order to be happy in the next few years, I have to concentrate on myself, and I can't do that with my mother worrying about me," she told Jambands.com.[4]) Even Rod Stewart came by for a disconnected four-song session which, "about halfway into the process, like most things in the music industry, just kind of fell apart" due to having too many cooks in the kitchen, Roth recounted.[5]

Because Daptone was a family of music-industry misfits who didn't invest too heavily in such session work, the label heads always held steadfast to their commitment to taste. Like Motown's Berry Gordy—who

★ ★ ★ ★ ★ ★

famously promoted or ditched records based on whether he'd rather spend a dollar on a hot dog or the single in question—Daptone refused to put out records that didn't live up to their standards. When guitarist/soul and blues singing legend Syl Johnson came by Troutman in 2008, "It was cool, and we had a lot of expectations. But in the words of my friend Victor Axelrod, it just smelled like bullshit after we recorded. It just didn't feel good," Sugarman states matter-of-factly.

The same thing happened when Latin jazz percussionist Bobby Matos came in to record. "We all really loved him, and we brought all these great heavy hitters in the studio and tried to make a record," the Daptone co-founder says. "We spent a lot of time and energy, and there was just something missing." The Dap-Kings brought a specific energy to the studio, he continues. "When we were making those records, we were tapping into the same thing that 60s- and 70s-era performers were; we were not bullshitting. Everyone can play really good and everyone was feeling that music and knew all the records we were referencing, and how to use the studio. Those records felt really grooving, hard, and very soulful. And we wouldn't have put them out otherwise."

Even if some of their sessions didn't bear vinyl, The Dap-Kings were regularly getting noticed and called on. The Dap-Kings horns, Roth, and drummer Steinweiss played on *Lay It Down*, a 2008 Questlove-produced, Grammy-winning album by Al Green, and were also tapped by Public Enemy producer Hank Shocklee to work on the original score for the film *American Gangster* (which coincidentally starred Jones's favorite, Denzel Washington). The Dap-Kings even served as the house band for ESPN's Espy Awards.

Meanwhile, Sharon backed Rufus Wainwright and They Might Be Giants and was featured in *Hal Willner's Doc Pomus Project*, a tribute to the late songwriter held in Brooklyn's Prospect Park. She supported Stax Records' house band/instrumental legends Booker T. & The M.G.'s in 2007, stirring up the sound of new New York soul with its Memphis inspirations. While they encountered many celebrities over the years as

★ ★ ★ ★ ★ ★

their fame grew, several Dap-Kings cite meeting Steve Cropper—the M.G.'s guitarist and Stax songwriter and producer—as one of their few starstruck moments.

In 2009, Sharon Jones, Saundra Williams (who, along with Starr Duncan-Lowe of the Good 'N' Plenty Girls, would soon join SJDK as a backup singer), and Dave Guy supported psychedelic jam band Phish at their Festival 8 in Indio, California. Phish were covering The Rolling Stones' *Exile On Main Street* and their own rarely performed single "Suzy Greenberg." While Jones was no stranger to the unique pressures of a festival set, she wasn't too familiar with *Exile* or Phish, and she had just two three-hour rehearsals to learn her parts. Even though the process was nerve-racking, Jones continued to Jambands.com that she enjoyed performing with different people. "We have a large family, but a change is coming. I gotta get prepared. The Phish thing was right up my alley. I mean, I'm looking forward to doing more stuff like that."[6]

The singer was also featured in a number of star-studded projects including *Baby Loves Jazz*, an album of kids tunes, and a compilation for AIDS research called *Dark Was The Night*. A release show for the compilation at Radio City Music Hall brought together David Byrne (who would call on Jones to sing on the soundtrack for *Here Lies Love*, a theater piece on Philippines First Lady Imelda Marcos), The National, Bon Iver, and others for a sing-along of "This Land Is Your Land." Sharon, donning a short spangled coral dress and ever ready to tear the house down, strutted onstage to turn the folk classic up in her key of funk. A writer for the *New Yorker* reminisced that this SJDK version "was so infectious it was difficult not to pity everyone standing onstage alongside her, even though they, too, were clearly in on the joke. The joke being, of course, that Sharon Jones is a better singer than anyone."[7]

As Sharon Jones upstaged and over-sang some of the most legendary musicians, and The Dap-Kings were quickly becoming sought-after session players, Daptone Records' reputation as an influential recording house continued to climb. "We had a good rep with musicians, and obviously we

★ ★ ★ ★ ★ ★

always had good press," Binky Griptite says. "Even bad reviews couldn't dis us; somebody would make some snide comment about *retro this* or the it's-been-done-ness of the band, but they couldn't say we're bad, 'cause *we bad*."

★ ★ ★

Daptone as a whole, and SJDK in particular, continued to cement their status as the dynamic undercurrent of a burgeoning revival scene—which itself was growing to include more bands, collectors, and DJ nights (among them Chairman Mao and Mr. Fine Wine's Bumpshop, which became a gathering place for Daptone family and admirers such as Q-Tip from A Tribe Called Quest). "It's one thing to have records that have that aesthetic, but I think that if it was just records, soul would have been a trend that evaporated within four or five years," theorizes Clifton Weaver, the LA-based mod and DJ who carried SJDK records in his car for years on the off chance that he could get a fellow DJ to spin a cut. "But you have performers that are going out there and supporting those records, playing shows to that same kind of level of intensity and showmanship that they had back there in the 60s and 70s. It's almost like a religious experience."

When Sharon Jones & The Dap-Kings took the stage at the 2008 Roots Picnic—on a bill that also featured Gnarls Barkley, Deerhoof, and Diplo—Kirk Douglas was watching from the wings. He was equally blown away. "People hear with their eyes a lot of time; [SJDK] really understood that. For everybody that missed out on the experience of seeing James Brown in his prime, you got to see music that was executed with the same energy, the same precision and with the same showmanship. And you got it with this female energy. They were truly original compared to other bands that were playing at the time."

But years on the road and near constant action in studio was taking its toll: Homer Steinweiss was tired of touring after years of back-to-back national and international gigs; Griptite sometimes missed rehearsals; some players felt Gabe Roth held too much creative control; Sharon was not happy with the money. In 2008–09, following festivals and club dates

★ ★ ★ ★ ★ ★

in Australia, New Zealand, Ireland, England, and a handful of hometown performances, Jones and Roth started to clash over royalties. Per Sugarman and Roth's original vision, everyone working for the musician-owned label got a cut of royalties; however, songwriting credits offered the most financial reward. According to the *New York Times*, Jones wanted publishing royalties on songs that she didn't write, arguing that interpreting Roth's songs amounted to equal creative effort.[8]

After significant debate—and against the advice of his lawyers—Roth decided that the ethical move would be paying Jones a percentage of publishing income from the past twelve years' worth of songs she sang on—a significant sum. The move likely saved their working relationship, but it wouldn't be the only sizeable chunk of change coming out of Daptone's coffers—the studio at 115 Troutman Street was robbed in February 2009, with losses amounting to over twenty thousand dollars. Burglars pried open the ground-floor studio gate and smashed the studio's front-door window, then ripped out wires from Daptone's Trident series 65 mixing board and stole mics, pre-amps, monitors, turntables, guitars and several computers. None of the items (including rare instruments) were insured, though, ironically, Roth had been shopping around for coverage earlier in the month.

"It's hard to tell if they came here because they knew Daptone was here," label manager Nydia Davila told the *Times*. "The cops were actually surprised it had never happened before."[9] In an email to friends and fans, Roth remained unfazed. "Thankfully, we all still have our health, ambition, tape machines, and sense of humor intact," he wrote. "You can slow us down, but you can't stop us. Sleep well knowing we here at Daptone will continue to keep putting soul up."[10]

Through robberies, relentless touring, and the occasional personnel change, Daptone hadn't stopped. Instead, the label continued to make good on the promise of its motto to keep putting soul up by championing underdogs inside and out of the House Of Soul. Daptone released a second album from The Budos Band in 2007—the scorpion gracing its cover a

★ ★ ★ ★ ★ ★

sinister warning of their dangerous interpretations of Mulatu Astake's Ethio jazz, and dark, rhythmic inversion of the Temptation's "My Girl." The Budos—a riotous band with all the intensity you'd expect of Staten Island metalheads who'd soundtracked their decades-long friendship with Cymande and Sabbath—were perhaps the most direct expression of Daptone's punk attitude and their shows a hardcore flip of SJDK's studied showmanship.

They were a confounding machine of a band with a grooving but abrasive wall of horns, irresistibly moody melodies, and a vibe that engendered (if not outright demanded) a party on and off the stage. The Budos made themselves known at breweries and bars across the country, downing beers and spewing bullshit in a gregarious but occasionally shocking clip. "Watching The Budos Band get fucked up is not fun," says soul singer Jason Joshua, who followed the Budos on tour before he began his own soul career. "They are like their concert: it's in your face, it's loud, you're gonna get some sweat if you're close. Like, you might get bit bro." Translated onstage, it seemed as if the Budos were having so much fun that the pent-up chaos would tear them apart and no one would even mind. Before an encore, one of the musicians—usually trumpeter Andrew Greene, holding a beer and slathering spit onto someone else's mic—would encourage the audience to demand the band back onstage with a Staten Island-friendly call, "Hey! Fuckin' Budos! *Get the fuck out here!*"

Daptone tapped its Afrobeat vein throughout 2007, first shepherding the vinyl distribution of a double LP from Antibalas (then on Anti Records) called *Security*. While the band had been racking up an average of fifty shows a year at clubs and festivals around the globe, *Security* wasn't a commercial success (though few of Daptone's records would constitute such a metric). Still, Antibalas's euphoric performances and militantly pacifist but still highly danceable message was recognized by the creators of *Fela!*, an off-Broadway musical celebrating the life of Fela Kuti.[11] In 2008, several of Antibalas's members arranged, music-directed, and performed in the musical—which would go on to win three Tony Awards—while others

★ ★ ★ ★ ★ ★

lent their horns to Grammy-winning world music records and performed with the likes of Paul Simon, Allen Toussaint, Amadou & Mariam, and Fela's son, Femi Kuti. Antibalas had also caught the ear of The Roots, who invited the band to join them in a live version of Public Enemy's *It Takes A Nation Of Millions To Hold Us Back* at the 2009 Roots Picnic.

Following up on growing interest in Afrobeat, Daptone had previously rereleased The Daktaris' *Soul Explosion*—Desco's influential fake reissue, which masqueraded as a lost 1970s Nigerian masterpiece—and, in 2009, reissued a real Afrobeat record by Pax Nicholas & The Nettey Family. Led by Nicholas Addo-Nettey, a percussionist and singer in Fela Kuti's Africa 70 band (itself a musical family with many branches), *Na Teef Know The Road Of Teef* (1973) was so quietly intense and hard-driving that a threatened Fela forbid the album from being played. As such, the record was essentially shelved for thirty-six years until an enterprising collector tracked down Nicholas in Berlin, then connected the performer with Daptone. Though released with relatively little fanfare via Voodoo Funk Records, *Na Teef* reflected the roots of both Antibalas and The Budos Band while reminding students of Daptone's catalogue that the label was still invested in the sound that drew James Brown, Ginger Baker, and Stevie Wonder to Lagos in the 70s. Several years later, Daptone again joined forces with Voodoo Funk to release an anthology of 60s and 70s hits from El Rego—a soul legend from the West African country of Benin whose breadth of influence was equal to that of Fela Kuti—along with a twenty-page book about his life and music.

Gabe Roth's funky origins came full circle during this period of post-Winehouse recognition and Stax Explosion–like creative output. The label reissued The Poets Of Rhythm's 1994 album *Practice What You Preach*, and would later compile an anthology spanning the group's output from 1992–2003. In 2008, Daptone launched a reissue imprint called Ever-Soul Records, bringing back to sound systems a handful of forgotten soul singles from Hank Mullen (a singer from Buffalo, New York, who died of a heart attack in his mid-twenties), northern soul favorite Darrell

★ ★ ★ ★ ★ ★

Banks, and Phoenix duo Eddie & Ernie. The latter's "You Make My Life A Sunny Day"—an alternate B-side, with huge orchestration, to the more popular "Bullets Don't Have Eyes"—was sampled ten years later by Jay-Z & Beyoncé for The Carters' "Lovehappy." Although not on Ever-Soul, Daptone put out two pressings of Bob & Gene's *If This World Were Mine*, a previously uncompiled album of sweet soul tracks recorded between 1967 and 1971 for Buffalo's MoDo label. The record was a hit with discerning listeners who dug excitable brilliance as much as the sadness on ballads such as "I Can Be Cool," which would later get a reggae treatment by Ticklah.

But while Daptone's reissues were popular among collectors, they were largely a difficult sale. "The reissue game is tough. They were all great records that we loved, but it was never like putting out a band," Sugarman says. "It just goes to show that people do want something that is breathing; that's not just a concept, whether it's cool or not. If you have to guess at the story too much, it's always going to be a little bit niche."

Daptone's sound was already considered niche to pop audiences, and the label was also relatively late to the reissue game. In the world of independent labels, operations like Madrid's Vampisoul, Seattle's Light In The Attic Records, Stones Throw subsidiary Now Again, and Numero Group in Chicago had all been doing important archival and reissue work since the early 2000s. Although no one was making massive money, their efforts (and those of reissuers prior) to unearth rare and forgotten tunes from little-known labels and one-off artists complemented Daptone's championing of in-the-flesh funk.

Between *100 Days* and the release of Sharon Jones & The Dap-Kings' fourth studio LP, *I Learned The Hard Way*, in 2010, Daptone also dabbled in various forms of gospel. Previously relegated to the private life of Sharon (who remained a devout churchgoer when she wasn't on the road) and Roth's history of gigging with pianist Cliff Driver at storefront churches a decade prior, Daptone actively mined the roots of soul music in the rural town of Como, Mississippi. The label placed ads in local papers and on the radio, inviting singers to record traditional and original a cappella

★ ★ ★ ★ ★ ★

gospel at Mt. Mariah Church. Recorded in 2006 and released in 2008, the sixteen tracks on *Como Now* blur the lines between ethnographic study and roots primer, and eventually led to The Como Mamas (whose musical knowledge can be traced directly to legendary bluesman Mississippi Fred McDowell) releasing their own record on Daptone. Como Mama Della Daniels recounted to a Daptone documentarian that she wasn't sure if a secular audience would accept their music. "I thank God for Daptone; I thank God for Gabe opening his heart up when he heard us and to take us on as a cappella singers ... Daptone wasn't gonna leave Jesus out!"[12]

The following year, Naomi Shelton & The Gospel Queens released a more contemporary take on praise songs with their gospel-funk *What Have You Done, My Brother?*, cut while they were performing weekly at jazz bar/pool hall the Fat Cat in Manhattan. The record featured J.B.'s bassist Fred Thomas (who first introduced Gabe Roth to Shelton and Driver in the 90s) and hit no. 41 on the *Billboard* gospel charts—a potent reminder of the direct link between gospel and the hard stuff Daptone dealt in with Sharon Jones and its other acts. At age sixty-six, Shelton's hard voice and messages of love and faith deftly ripped through the soul. *What Have You Done* and Shelton's long road to releasing her first record inspired many, including a suicidal public radio caller who said the record gave her something to live for. Speaking on WBUR Boston in 2009, Shelton said, "My whole thing was if I could just reach out and touch peoples. ... Then that is money in my pocket already."[13] The success of the Gospel Queens in particular proved true Roth's belief that, for Daptone, releasing a gospel record was more punk rock than actually releasing a punk record.

"Gabe doesn't give a shit—he does what he does and he doesn't care about a review, and we've all gravitated to it, because it's what we like as well," says Mikey "Custodian Of Soul" Post, who first encountered the world of Daptone as a DJ in the early 2000s. Like many who came into the label's circle, Post was also a musician, down for the hang, and was at the ready when Roth asked him to sub in for The Gospel Queens' drummer during a gig. Post would drum with Shelton and the Queens for years,

and he also started working for the label as an intern before becoming Daptone's production manager (among the many other hats that come with working at a small label). "We have a team of people that are all on the same page. We all kind of know each other's tastes and that makes things come together much, much easier."

★ ★ ★

A fifteen-minute walk from Daptone Records along Myrtle Avenue, under the elevated J/M train, Tommy Brenneck had set up an ad-hoc studio in the bedroom of his apartment at 250 Menahan Street. His apartment wasn't big, even by New York standards, but he still managed to fit a half-inch eight-track tape machine, a piano, drum set, organ, and a small amplifier around his bed—then invited the younger Daptone/Truth & Soul crew over to record instrumentals for a tune called "Make The Road By Walking" as Menahan Street Band.

First released in 2006 as a vibey, wah-wah pedal heavy single on Brenneck's own Dunham Records imprint, "Make The Road" caught the ear of Sean "Diddy" Combs, who was among a number of producers working on a Jay-Z concept album called *American Gangster* (inspired by the Denzel film). Diddy's production team, The Hitmen, came upon the single while digging for sample-worthy albums in the East Village at Big City Records—a hole-in-the-wall shop on East 12th Street renowned by DJs and producers. Co-owner Jared Boxx (whose previous vinyl vocations included A-1 Records and Sound Library, which sold Dr. Dre David McCallum's *Music: A Bit More Of Me* to sample on "The Next Episode") was a Bumpshop DJ and long-time Daptone affiliate.[14] Boxx added the MSB single to the pile of records he pulled for The Hitmen.

The record struck a chord with Jay-Z, who, coincidentally, grew up not too far from Menahan Street in Bushwick's Marcy projects. Menahan Street Band's revelrous horn arrangements would be a cornerstone of Jay-Z's 2007 single "Roc Boys (And The Winner Is . . .)." The rapper's team invited Brenneck and the Daptone heads to a Midtown recording studio

★ ★ ★ ★ ★ ★

to "play music for him to see if there was anything else worth taking," Sugarman recalls. Although Jay-Z was already a hip-hop superstar, he was easygoing and respectful; he was also familiar with Sharon Jones. Jay-Z was "really feeling it," Sugarman adds, as he, Roth, and Brenneck listened to Hova rap over his newly constructed track—which, to the musicians' delight, hadn't cut up MSB's horns. "I think Tommy said, *Hey, I think it's cool, but can you give us a shout out on the rap?* Jay-Z was just like, *You wish*," Sugarman says, laughing at the memory of such bravado.

Speaking to *Now Toronto*, Brenneck said, "It was a crazy situation, not only having something I recorded in my bedroom being used in Jay-Z's next single, but having to approve Jay-Z's lyrics as part of the clearance requirements."[15] *American Gangster* topped several *Billboard* charts and was nominated for a Grammy in 2008; yet in an album built on soul samples from Marvin Gaye, The Isley Brothers, and Barry White, "Roc Boys" stood out for its use of material by a twenty-first century band. Menahan's distinctive tempest of horns would blast out of car radios for months—a marvel for the unsuspecting crew who recorded a hit in a bedroom.

The sample netted a platinum plaque and decent money for Menahan Street Band's songwriters. It was also just the first of several collaborations with Jay-Z. "We can thank a lot of our heroes who got ripped off for making that happen," Brenneck later said during an in-studio performance at Los Angeles NPR affiliate KCRW. "In the 80s and 90s, when James Brown and Syl Johnson and The Meters and all these bands were being sampled, they had to fight for it." But by the time Menahan Street Band and its ilk were being sampled, the industry had changed. "Jay-Z and Roc-a-Fella Records reached out to us."[16]

Over the next several years, and between tours with Amy Winehouse, SJDK, and The Budos Band, Menahan Street Band convened in Brenneck's apartment to record *Make The Road By Walking*. Named after a nearby nonprofit for social and economic justice, the 2008 debut album featured essentially the same lineup as El Michels Affair, and it followed much of that record's playbook in creating a moody, lushly atmospheric

★ ★ ★ ★ ★ ★

instrumental vibe that was laced with Mulatu Astatke–style Ethio jazz. Although developed by Brenneck, who cites Curtis Mayfield as one of his biggest inspirations (a common enough refrain among soul musicians, though few truly share Mayfield's feel), *Make The Road*'s ethereal city-soundtrack quality is made most visceral by horn players Dave Guy, Michels, trombonist Aaron Johnson, and Cochemea Gastelum (who played flute on the album and soon joined The Dap-Kings as a saxophonist). The record grooves easily between the exuberance of "Home Again!" and "Birds," then meanders into darker, sometimes brutally melancholy tracks like "Going The Distance"—a true exhibit of New York sentiment.

Make The Road By Walking's soulful vibe and soaring horns, plus Steinweiss's distinctive drumming, were widely sampled in hip-hop, including by 50 Cent, Kendrick Lamar, Ludacris, and Curren$y. But perhaps the most important result of the record was a soul connection with Charles Bradley—the James Brown impersonator and handyman who had been milling around the Daptone family for years, helping with the studio's radiators and singing on a couple of tracks. *No Time For Dreaming*—Charles Bradley's first album, and a monumental accomplishment for the then-sixty-two-year-old singer—would be released in 2011, but it was recorded during the same four-year period where Brenneck was making music out of his Menahan Street apartment.

"Charles came over and I started playing *Make The Road By Walking* for him, and he just responded to it," Brenneck says. A few tracks from that MSB release would become the instrumental basis for Bradley's album, and the singer "wrote away. His response to that instrumental music was immediate and came from a crazy deep place that he had never put into a song before."

CHAPTER NINE HEART OF GOLD: CHARLES BRADLEY REBORN AS THE SCREAMING EAGLE OF SOUL

In July 2011, Charles Bradley stood center stage, his bright red matador jacket with long, sequined lapels dripping with sweat, and let out a guttural howl. At age sixty-two, he had completely done away with pretense (though it's unlikely he ever had much) and laid bare the depths of his soul to a hundred strangers. Bradley shared with the audience at Brooklyn's Fort Greene Park his most painful memories of losing his brother to gun violence, stretching into the distressed cry of a man consistently put down by life and taking a knee through powerful declarations of love. He suggestively wound his hips, dead-dropped onto the stage, and shed true tears of heartache and joy, before running out into the audience to give hugs to dozens of fans, all of whom seemed genuinely moved by his performance.

As the singer and his musicians—Brenneck's Menahan Street Band—came back for an encore of "Golden Rule," the late-July storm that had been looming all evening broke wide open. Cymbals and bongos flew as thunder and lightning crashed; Victor Axelrod grabbed his organ before it was blown away and ran for cover; yet Charles Bradley, dubbed the "Screaming Eagle Of Soul" by his adoring band, remained onstage, drenched and lamenting, "How can we stop the changes going on in America today?" The *New York Times*, long respectful of Daptone and

★ ★ ★ ★ ★ ★

clearly enraptured by Bradley's intensity, noted that, "having shed too many tears for one man, he made the sky cry."[1]

"A lot of artists is out there, but when they get out in the lamp lights they just want to sing and make money," Bradley said from a hotel where he was taking a brief break during a 2016 European tour, his voice raspy but soft. "Yes, I want to sing and make money, but I want to give [audiences] something too, and thank them for the opportunities that I'm given. I want to give up the depths of my soul. I want to let the world know me as a person and an artist. The things that my eyes, my heart, my soul have seen while walking this planet."

By the time Bradley was hugging his audience, pleading from his knees onstage, and wailing in the key of James Brown, he was in the midst of a meteoric rise to fame—which only took most of his life to achieve. His first LP, *No Time For Dreaming*, was released on Dunham/Daptone in January 2011 and almost immediately received critical praise for its orchestration and Bradley's primal take on soul. Perhaps even more than Sharon Jones, Charles Bradley *was* soul music—the love, sorrow, exuberance, and fear written in the wrinkles of his face and his story were a true triumph of spirit which audiences ate up.

Bradley was born in Florida but, like Jones, grew up in Bed-Stuy. Fearing violence from his mother, he left home in 1962 at age fourteen—the same year his sister bought him a ticket to see James Brown's legendary stand at the Apollo—and became homeless, sleeping on the subway. Bradley dropped out of school and spent ten years cooking at a Maine hospital for the mentally ill (a period that would establish his love of cooking for groups—and his inability to make a small meal), then hitchhiked across North America, stopping in Alaska, Canada, and Seattle before landing in California, where he spent most of the 80s and 90s working odd jobs. Once, Bradley sat in a pizza parlor contemplating suicide after a run-in with a state trooper robbed him of his dignity. But when another patron dropped change into the jukebox to play the Eagles' "Take It To The Limit," Bradley was shaken as if "God had blown the spirit into that song."[2] He ran out of the restaurant,

★ ★ ★ ★ ★ ★

encouraged to give life a try once more, and never stopped pushing.

Bradley's big eyes and soft-spoken nature belied his many life challenges, including poverty, illiteracy (Bradley read at a first-grade level through much of his adult life), and near death from a penicillin allergy. After being laid off from his job of seventeen years, he moved back to Brooklyn in 1994 to care for his mother, with whom he had rekindled a relationship. Not too long after, his older brother Joseph—an income-tax broker and Vietnam veteran whom the singer described as the backbone of his family—was robbed and murdered by their nephew. The murder was recounted years later as "Heartaches And Pain" on *No Time For Dreaming*, but in the intervening years Bradley forced himself to take it to the limit while grieving a devastating loss. He worked as a handyman while living on the sixteenth floor of a housing project and occasionally in his mother's basement.

Before his death, Joseph had encouraged his brother to follow his musical passions—first manifest during that 1962 James Brown show, after which a young Charles would do his best impressions of Soul Brother No. 1 by singing into a broom he had attached to a string. With a little liquid courage in the form of gin and 7-Up, and his hair curled to resemble Brown's coif, Bradley made his public debut as a James Brown impersonator during a JobsCorp event at age nineteen.[3] He recalled singing "Can't Stand Myself When You Touch Me" and "Please, Please, Please" in front of five hundred girls; although he felt the rumblings of stage fright, Bradley was hooked.

Forty years after that first James Brown performance, Bradley stood at the apartment doorway of a quizzical Gabe Roth. "I heard you're looking for a singer," Bradley said, handing over his phone number. No one at the then-brand-new Daptone could figure out how Bradley heard about the label or found Roth's address, but the co-founders agreed to see the singer do James Brown impersonations under the moniker Black Velvet with Jimmy Hill & The Allstarz Band.

"It was funny because it was winter, and I didn't have a coat, so I went to a thrift store and grabbed a long leather coat. And I'd like sprained my knee or my ankle or something, so I had a cane," Roth recalls, unaware at

★ ★ ★ ★ ★ ★

the time that his outfit would be on point for the occasion. "So, me and Shugs walk into the Tar-Heel Lounge on Bedford Avenue and it looked like *Sweet Sweetback's Baadasssss Song*. It seemed like it was all fucking pimps, like matching hats and fur coats and shit."

After years of gigging around town at Essence Lounge in Weeksville and the Hiro Ballroom in Manhattan, Black Velvet had evolved into Bradley's safe haven. The singer donned a variety of wigs (which he rarely took off) and wore hand-sewn costumes, shirking off his troubles by embodying his hero.

Daptone musicians were recording *Pure Cane Sugar* around the same time, and had connected with funk and R&B showman The Mighty Hannibal to lend some vocals. But when Hannibal, then in his early sixties, came by the Afro Spot, he was drunk. "At one point, I tried to get him to sing a song 'Take It As It Comes,'" Roth remembers. "He started singing with his nose, which was real weird, and we made a mistake of kind of laughing, which just encouraged him. We couldn't get him to sing anymore. I had Charles's number and was like, *Man, lemme call this weird dude*."

Bradley's guttural grunts and Black Velvet vocals appeared on the funky rocksteady track, and while Daptone would have worked with him again, Bradley was busy hustling outside the studio. Tommy Brenneck, still a teenager, had been petitioning Daptone to work with The Bullets—a new band his Staten Island crew had put together—and Roth shepherded Charles Bradley across New York Harbor for a rehearsal. "I could hardly understand what he said when he spoke at that time," Brenneck says. "He was such a crazy, different person than I'd ever met in my life. And he rocked a James Brown wig all the time, which is an amazing persona."

Wearing a wig and overalls covered in paint, Bradley drove his busted van (which the singer sometimes slept in, next to a busted piano) to work on The Bullets' first 45s for Daptone. "We were thrilled, and our energy level was on fucking way past ten," Brenneck says, though The Bullets struggled to write with the singer. "We weren't really getting anything deep from Charles. He was just serving the purpose that we were championing, which was this funky sound. And it was like, *Charles, don't do James Brown lyrics*."

★ ★ ★ ★ ★ ★

Bradley tried, but he would often toss in James Brown lines—part natural reaction, part fear of digging deep for his own words. Daptone released singles from those sessions years later—"This Love Ain't Big Enough For The Two Of Us" b/w "Twilight Eyes" and "Now That I'm Gone (Look How You're Crying)" b/w "Can't Stop Thinking About You" (which Charles wrote). Although the songs were cool, Brenneck notes, "They weren't Charles's stories." The two lost touch, and while Charles Bradley would remain in the periphery of Daptone's orbit—and help with House Of Soul construction—he didn't record anything for years.

Fast forward to 2006 and what felt like half a lifetime later, Charles Bradley & The Bullets (then just completing their evolution into The Budos Band) were among the stacked lineup for Sharon Jones's fiftieth birthday celebration at Irving Plaza in Manhattan. Brenneck and Bradley rekindled their relationship during rehearsals: "I remember dropping him off after rehearsal at the Bushwick project and just being like, 'Man, Charles, I live like fucking five minutes away from here on Myrtle and Menahan Street. We should hang.'"

Bradley eventually came over, and Brenneck played him some songs from *Make The Road By Walking*; they'd subsequently record Bradley's first real single in the same bedroom studio. After years apart—Bradley working as a handyman and moonlighting as Black Velvet, Tommy touring with SJDK and the Budos, while intermittently recording in his bedroom studio—the two quickly developed a unique personal and professional bond. Brenneck became Bradley's champion, close collaborator, and arguably his best friend; Bradley's unique voice and background were the anchor, and they immediately started writing.

"'The World (Is Going Up In Flames)' is just, like, an insane thing," Brenneck says of the first single from *No Time For Dreaming*. "Probably the best thing we ever did together." On those tapes, he continues, "you hear me, like, counting in his ear. You hear the train going by. That environment is so different from a recording studio. I don't think that record ever would have been made in a recording studio."

ABOVE Lee Fields performs during a Big Crown Records showcase, with trumpeter Todd Simon and Leon Michels supporting. Photo by Farah Sosa.

RIGHT A flyer for a Saun & Starr after party in Los Angeles. Courtesy of Nancy Arte Productions.

ABOVE Sharon Jones performs to an adoring crowd in 2010. Photo by Jacob Blickenstaff.

RIGHT Jones at the keys. The singer never took professional piano or vocal lessons. Photo courtesy of Robbie Busch.

LEFT A poster for Sharon Jones & The Dap-Kings' 2011 West Coast tour. Courtesy of Jessica Lipsky, poster design by Scott Williams/ Swill Design.

BELOW Jones's dance skills were legendary and her energy onstage boundless. Photo by Jacob Blickenstaff.

RIGHT A sick but still strong Sharon Jones readies herself ahead of a show in Noblesville, Indiana, in the summer of 2016. Photo by Jacob Blickenstaff.

BELOW RIGHT A flyer announcing a listening party in Long Beach, California, for SJDK's seventh album, *Soul Of A Woman*, which was released one year after Jones's passing. Courtesy of Nancy Arte Productions.

BELOW Sharon Jones & The Dap-Kings working it out in early 2014. Photo by Jacob Blickenstaff.

ABOVE A rehearsal at Madison Square Garden with Sharon Jones, Fernando "Bugaloo" Velez, Saundra Williams and Starr Duncan-Low, Cochemea Gastelum, Neal Sugarman, and trumpet player Chris Davis. Photo by Jacob Blickenstaff.

LEFT The Budos Band perform at the Teragram Ballroom in Los Angeles in 2019. Photo by Farah Sosa.

ABOVE Tommy Brenneck performs at a Los Angeles Big Crown Records revue in 2019. Photo by Farah Sosa.

ABOVE Antibalas frontman Duke Amayo in the zone during the Daptone Super Soul Revue at the Apollo Theater. Photo by Jacob Blickenstaff.

RIGHT A flyer for an Antibalas show in Los Angeles. Courtesy of Nancy Arte Productions.

LEFT Gabe Roth and the Daptone horns, recording "Soul Fugue"—the label's 100th 45—at the House Of Soul. Photo by Jacob Blickenstaff.

BELOW LEFT Daptone co-founder Gabe Roth works out a tune backstage. Photo by Jacob Blickenstaff.

BELOW The Dap-Kings recording in the live room at 115 Troutman Street. Photo by Jacob Blickenstaff.

BELOW Los Angeles funky breaks band Breakestra, with Mix Master Wolf on the mic and Miles Tackett on bass. Photo by Farah Sosa.

ABOVE Naomi Shelton and Cliff Driver perform with the Gospel Queens in 2014 at the Daptone Super Soul Revue. Photo by Jacob Blickenstaff.

LEFT Gabe Roth, Sharon Jones, Fernando Velez, and Homer Steinweiss in the control room at Daptone's Troutman Street headquarters. Photo by Jacob Blickenstaff.

BELOW LEFT Head engineer/producer Wayne Gordon manning the analogue controls at the House Of Soul. Photo by Jacob Blickenstaff.

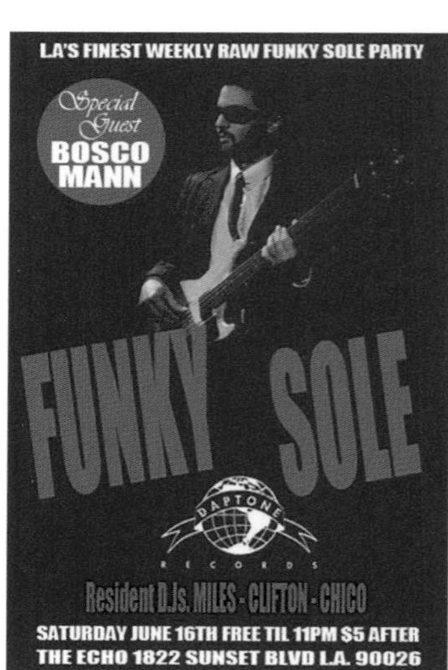

ABOVE A Funky Sole flyer featuring Gabe Roth as a guest DJ. Courtesy of Nancy Arte Productions.

RIGHT A tightly packed crowd enjoys an all-vinyl set at the Funky Sole Weekender, which featured Lee Fields, Los Yesterdays (with Gabe Roth and Tom Brenneck), and Breakestra. Photo by Farah Sosa.

RIGHT Charles Bradley and Extraordinaire Billy Austik get silly backstage. Courtesy of Billy Austik.

BELOW RIGHT A massive, multi-band tribute to Charles Bradley was held in Los Angeles after he passed away. Courtesy of Nancy Arte Productions.

BELOW The Screaming Eagle of Soul was known for his emotive performances. Photo by Jacob Blickenstaff.

ABOVE Charles Bradley unleashes heartaches and pains onstage at the Apollo for the Super Soul Revue in 2014. Photo by Jacob Blickenstaff.

ABOVE The Sugarman Three perform at NoMoore, a longtime Desco Records Haunt, circa 1997. Photo by Dulce Pinzon, courtesy of Adam Scone.

RIGHT Binky Griptite during a SJDK/James Hunter gig at the House of Blues in Boston. Photo by wcmickle/Flickr.

★ ★ ★ ★ ★ ★

Brenneck theorizes that their close relationship was propelled by the physical intimacy required of working in a bedroom studio. "Charles was nervous walking into a stiff, professional environment. But he's at this kid's house, and I was like making him hot toddies and he was telling me about his brother being murdered; it was so fucking crazy. I was just playing the tracks and if he liked it, you'd give him a microphone and it was fucking magic in like three minutes." Brenneck wrote down Bradley's stories and recorded him playing bits of piano, then put down instrumentals with Menahan Street Band and had Bradley sing over them. "It was really, really wild magic. I swear to God, because our friendship was so beautiful, the music that we made was a reflection."

After four years of work, *No Time For Dreaming* was released in January 2011, a searingly unadulterated exploration of Bradley's personal history through midtempo ballads and a continued evolution for MSB, who performed less cinematic and more emotionally resonant 70s-era sounds. The album "is probably one of the best things I've ever done in my life. It's a great record that represents me and Charles," Brenneck says emphatically. "The chemistry of our art was bigger than the two of us and all the musicians involved, which is a small group of musicians that I love very much, but I think the music speaks for itself."

The creation of *No Time* and Charles Bradley's rise from itinerant handyman to his album release show at Southpaw in Brooklyn and onto the world stage is chronicled in *Charles Bradley: Soul Of America*, a 2012 documentary that debuted at South By Southwest. While Brenneck was privately unhappy about some of the film, it was certainly a boost, and it cemented Charles's decades-long struggle for soul. "It's still a little raw to me to see the life that I've been through," Bradley said during a performance on Seattle's KEXP radio. "I think of everybody who believed in me to give me this opportunity to come forward; I say thanks everybody."[4]

Following the album and documentary, Charles Bradley toured widely—the singer's visceral performances were often laced with tears, culminating with hugs and blessings. Charles Bradley was sincerely grateful to be in front of fans, and his earnest, powerful shows elevated him to an almost saintly status. On at least one occasion, a pregnant fan asked Bradley to bless her unborn child; multiple fans named their sons after the singer.

However, Bradley suffered from a powerful stage fright that lasted the majority of his career and was intensified by illiteracy. "Charles was really forgetful with lyrics if I wasn't riding him so hard," Brenneck says. "I fucking paid for him to take reading classes when we were first getting started so he would be a little bit easier to work with in the studio. But the reading classes never really took off, because he was already, like, fifty-nine years old. He just charmed all the teachers; they loved him, but they weren't hard on him."

Bradley would have to memorize lyrics by ear, and he regularly became frustrated. "He'd ask me, 'Why does it matter?' I would have to explain to him that the music is moving around these lyrics and the record's come out and people know the songs. You could change the melody, you could dance around the thing, but you really kind of have to say, 'heartaches and pain.'"

Bradley almost left an early European tour opening for Lee Fields, Brenneck adds, "because he's really not having a good time, because I was giving him such a hard time about remembering the lyrics." Before Bradley was set to take stage, Fields gratefully stepped in and convinced Bradley to stay on the tour, put up with Tommy, and learn the lyrics. "He needed to hear that from somebody else—aside from somebody half of this age and the opposite color," Brenneck states.

Bradley also needed to see his words resonate with the audience. "I was afraid to get on the stage to sing it," the singer recalls, "but then Lee Fields came over and said, 'You better get on the stage and sing it, people came here to see you.' But when I got on the stage to sing it, they just opened their arms and voices and showed me so much love," he adds, the weight of that moment still palpable in his voice through space and Skype.

Experiencing that love—even from an audience that didn't understand the language he was singing in—changed everything for Charles Bradley,

★ ★ ★ ★ ★ ★

who now put great effort into learning the lyrics to his songs. "He would sit in the dressing room and he would iron shirts to relax—for the whole band," Brenneck recalls. "And he would just sit with his reading glasses and study his lyrics." Even for simple songs like the hard-hitting psychedelic "Confusion," which used more of an improvisational vamp than a serious story, "he would be sitting there practicing. Like 'Confusion, confusion, baby confusion. Oooh confusion mama!' I'm like, *Charles, you're fucking crazy.*"

Booking agent Josh Brinkman set Charles up with more than thirty dates, including over twenty festivals, for Bradley's first international tour in support of *No Time*—a schedule that, as with other artists on the label's roster, would require a dedicated band. Brenneck (himself playing with the Budos and SJDK, where guitarist Joe Crispiano would soon become his replacement, in addition to El Michels Affair and MSB) was convinced to assemble The Extraordinaires, a touring band of seven or so mostly younger players who he would lead for two years. Menahan Street Band evolved into studio musicians while offering support during special shows.

Baby-faced trumpet player and Chicago native Billy Austik was set to enter his junior year at NYU's jazz school when he got the call to join The Extraordinaires on tour. The musician had gigged around town with Antibalas—their Afrobeat more in line with the jazz he was neck deep in learning—and he hadn't spent much time listening to soul music, though he was the recipient of a charged hug during Bradley's early Fort Greene show. After previously turning down the opportunity to tour with Charles to focus on school, Austik knew he couldn't let a second chance go to waste. He quit his job at the Apple Store, took a sabbatical from college, and spent the next two weeks learning all of Charles's music.

"Historically, every Daptone band I've ever played with leaves everything to you. We don't have rehearsals, we just play shows," he says, adding that he had to audition with Brenneck and Antibalas trombonist Aaron Johnson. "I had all the music memorized; I was so prepared. But I was also super nervous, and I think they knew. And so they were like, *All right, smoke this*. So we all got stoned, and then it was great."

★ ★ ★ ★ ★ ★

Even if stoned was the de facto state of many Daptone musicians, those who came up through The Dap-Kings had a particularly strict mentality when it came to tightness and showmanship. Austik continues, "Tom was such a great bandleader, producer, and, like, *the* guy. He was just like, *This is what it is. You don't like it, leave. If you don't play right, you're out of the band*. It was pretty intense."

Saxophonist Freddy DeBoe joined The Extraordinaires after subbing in for Cochemea during a SJDK European tour, though he first met the band in Australia while touring with Eli "Paperboy" Reed and regularly played with Austik and Crispiano in Staten Island. Those relationships and experience playing together, even in small gigs, laid an important foundation. "When you're in a horn section, you kind of have to have an understanding," says DeBoe, a Milwaukee native who went to Berklee School of Music but also dropped out to tour. "You have to know where you're going to play, before you play it, so it sounds strong and confident."

Together, the crew that included drummer Caito Sanchez, bassists Ben Trokan and Vince Chiarito, organist Mike Deller, guitarist Alex Chakour, and brothers Will and Paul Schalda became the "patron saints, healers, gurus, and epicureans" for the Screaming Eagle. They first recreated the sound of the records and found songs that could be walk-ons for Bradley, adapting performances to a crowd's energy with the same kind of "showtime" style Sharon Jones & The Dap-Kings were known for.

"As we grew as a band, we started to realize how we should shape it for Charles, because he was such a unique singer and this real emotional guy," Austik reflects. "We were stretching out songs and he was giving himself more time to connect with the audience, rather than just, like, pop out the lyrics." Charles and his Extraordinaires were playing to large and diverse crowds early on, and the singer "broke down any musical wall. It's definitely soul music, but it becomes more than that when he's singing. You can't help but be connected to him or else you're a fucking soulless bastard," the trumpet player says with wistful emphasis.

Clifton Weaver DJed a few Charles Bradley shows when the band

★ ★ ★ ★ ★ ★

did West Coast runs (unlike SJDK, who spent years working up from smaller venues, Bradley's first tour had him at the Hollywood Bowl) and remembers being mind-blown by Bradley's energy. "You always think that if someone has that kind of talent, they're going to be on another level. And you meet them and they're just really humble, down to earth people. Both Charles and Sharon were some of the sweetest people I've met. But then you stand on the side of the stage watching them, and it's just like watching someone possessed, or a supernatural being, perform a miracle onstage. It was an emotional experience."

As he came into his own, Charles brought a lot of sexual energy to the stage, channeling the spirits of Bobby Womack and Luther Vandross to deliver the sort of "grown folks" music that championed slow motion over the raunchy antics of other artists. (Once, however, during a 2015 performance at San Francisco's Hardly Strictly Bluegrass Festival, Bradley's tour manager dared him to take off his pants onstage and suggestively grind his hips through a love song.) "Charles wasn't comfortable with his sexuality anywhere else," Homer Steinweiss says. "So, if you ever asked him, *What's going on onstage?*, he'd just be like, *That's just what's going on onstage. We're not going to talk about it.*" Bradley was rumored to have a male lover for years, but he was extremely private about his relationships; like Sharon Jones, he wasn't known to date anyone at the height of his career. "I think he was really self-conscious, and he became kind of asexual for a long time," the drummer theorizes, picking his words with sensitivity. Bradley told *Vice* that his real love was music, though it took ten years to get over the heartache of one major relationship. "It'll be a strong person who can move that mountain out of my heart again. Because I do have the love inside me to give, but if I stumble this time I don't think I'm gonna get back up, so I'm kind of real afraid of it," he said.[5]

For someone who spent the majority of his life behind a stove and seemed most comfortable donning a persona before getting onstage, performing as himself and tapping a bottomless well of emotion night after night (and also during soundcheck) took its toll. "Charles would put

★ ★ ★ ★ ★ ★

his all into the show, all of his energy, all of like everything he got," DeBoe says. "He would get nervous and had built up anxiety sometimes while getting ready, but we were always there to make him feel comfortable." Brenneck recalled jamming to William Bell's "I Forgot To Be Your Lover" whenever Charles would get weary on the road: "I'd play that opening lick and he would instantly light up and start screaming, *Tommyyyyyy. Tommy you too much. You know me too well*," he wrote on Instagram. The song "would always lift his spirits so he could find the strength to get back on stage and give a 1000 percent of himself as he'd done the night before and the night before that to every audience large or small."

Bradley would often pause during the set, covering his face with his hand or touching his forehead in pain. "When the soul hit me and the spirit hit me, sometimes you'll be watching me onstage, when I just like to be standing in one spot and get quiet," he explains. "I be resouling myself. I'll say, 'Lord this is the gift you give me, teach me how to stand strong with it and give it the way I feel it in my heart.' Sometimes I get very emotional with it."

While the members of his band (who were easily forty years younger than their leader) were down to party and DJ after gigs, Charles didn't indulge in much beyond a good meal. "When the show was over, it was a huge relief for him," DeBoe continues. "He would crash pretty soon after." Bradley didn't sleep in the tour bus bunks, so The Extraordinaires relegated the lounge area at the back of the bus as Charles's chill-out spot. "I think he lived vicariously through us. He saw our youth, and he saw us having a good time, and it kind of made him feel like a kid again. He had a lot of tragic experiences earlier in his life. And he also kind of had his childhood stripped away from him in a way. I think he kind of relived some of that in a positive way by experiencing the world with us."

Charles Bradley's first year of touring culminated with a headlining show at New York's Bowery Ballroom, the first of six performances celebrating Daptone's tenth anniversary. Sharon Jones & The Dap-Kings played four nights to packed crowds in Manhattan and Brooklyn, their latest release, *I Learned The Hard Way*, having debuted at No. 14 on the

★ ★ ★ ★ ★ ★

Billboard charts, reaching No. 2 among independent album releases and No. 6 on the R&B and hip-hop charts—in addition to selling a hundred thousand copies in its first four months.[6]

SJDK's audiences and sales were hard-earned—the result of a decade of rough touring and little pay. While Bradley had come from incredibly difficult circumstances and was earning his stripes by the road mile, Gabe Roth hypothesizes that "Sharon probably had a little bit of resentment for Charles, because she'd worked so hard to open up these doors, and he kind of came straight up into it and was able to play for thousands of people." The singers loved and supported each other, and while the queen of the Daptone universe was never personally petty about things, she often treated Charles in the way a mean big sister might. "I think Sharon did a lot of stuff, publicly and privately, to help Charles and support him. Sharon was always the first one to let everybody know that we're a family and what's good for Charles is good for us," Roth says. "But she would fuck with him a little bit, and it would get to him because he was sensitive."

Earlier that year, Sharon and Charles were guest performers at the inaugural Global Soul Revue, held at the Hollywood Bowl, where Stevie Wonder was also on deck. Bradley was nervous and uncomfortable—he had to learn the lyrics to Otis Redding's "My Lover's Prayer" in a fancy Burbank studio, without Tommy to help him. "In the middle of this rehearsal, Sharon said, 'Hey, Charles, you want a candy?'" Roth recounts. "She had butterscotch or something, and he loved candy. She started laughing at him because, of course, it was weed candy. Charles didn't mess with that shit, so it flipped him out; he was real high for like two days. He was already freaked out and paranoid, it was completely mean." (Sharon maintained that Charles kept bugging her for candy, and she simply gave in.) On his next record, 2013's *Victim Of Love*, Bradley co-wrote a moody, hard rock–influenced song called "Where Do We Go From Here"—which could read as a frustrated love song, but "he's singing, you know, she gave me that candy that made me lose my mind, where do we go from here? It's a song about Sharon," Roth says.

★ ★ ★ ★ ★ ★

As Bradley managed intra-label competition and his own feelings that management viewed him as secondary to Sharon Jones, he was also navigating a plethora of outside influences. "He's a sweetheart inside; a little childlike," Brenneck says. "His success kind of came very quickly with a lot of money and a lot of vultures coming at him. He was not equipped to really make great decisions. 'Confusion' was really about what was just happening to him and his life. Everybody was watching him get successful. His house started getting broken into when we would go on tour. All sorts of people, even his fucking bankers at Chase Bank, everybody was fucking talking to him."

Brenneck and manager Alex Kadvan pleaded with Bradley to move out of his three-hundred-dollar-a-month project. "It's so complicated," Brenneck recounts with residual frustration. "Oh my god, he was so fucking introverted in the projects, afraid to show his sexuality. Just afraid to wear his freak flag that he would eventually wave proudly in his success. We were like, 'Charles, we can rent your apartment, you can buy a car.' He wanted to buy, like, a twelve-passenger van; that was his fucking dream. So he bought a twelve-passenger van. And then we got him to move out and he moved in with his mother. And he spent, like, twenty-five grand hooking up that basement."

Whether that inability to leave his comfort zone was the result of fear or a desire to simply do good for those close to him (or both), Bradley's community spirit was legendary. He hosted annual summer block parties on Monroe Street in Bed-Stuy, where he cooked for the whole neighborhood and invited all his friends from the Essence Lounge to perform James Brown covers. He would host big Christmas parties at his home for family and friends who didn't have a place to be, cooking enough food to feed an army (who would have their choice of turkey, ham, roast beef, an "international" mac and cheese, ribs, and likely a seafood option). The Extraordinaires, who Bradley treated like family, were always invited.

"He took really good care of us and he cared about us. He was a sweetheart," DeBoe recalls. Bradley laid down wisdom with his young

★ ★ ★ ★ ★ ★

band, calling them out but never without love. "They really love me, and I always try to teach them the right way, give them the right motives, the right honesty, as if they were my own sons," says the singer, who never had his own children. DeBoe continues, "Sometimes he'd have his moments, like all of us would, but he was really just a gentle soul. We could tell that he was a special guy. His dreams had come true in a certain way, that he was able to finally be himself and perform music that had come from his heart to all these people. He never imagined that he'd be able to travel the world and find friendship with all these other people."

By the second touring cycle for *Victim Of Love*, however, people from Bradley's community were "whispering all sorts of opinions in his ears," DeBoe says. "There's a ton of people in his life that were trying to take advantage of him, including his family, and were trying to get a piece of his wealth." Charles had gone from handyman to soul superstar and songwriter who made at least $100,000 a year and, for the first time, he had to pay taxes. "Now, all of a sudden, he owes tons of money in taxes, and he has no idea where it's coming from. But somebody else in his business is handling all the money, and it makes him incredibly skeptical." Charles's solution, throughout his career, was to spend time alone, quietly observing and praying.

"I have peoples coming to me, 'Oh, Charles, I like you but you're doing it too hard, you shouldn't be doing that. You should step back and say to hell with the world and do what you wanna do,'" Bradley says. "I'm looking at their faces and see their spirits. I love this world and I love everybody in this world, but I will say not everybody may love and treat me the way I love them. But my mother would say, 'Hold on to the grace of God and keep going, son. Don't change.'" Following the advice of his mother, and with much support from his band and fans, Charles resouled himself again and again.

CHAPTER TEN OUT WITH THE NEW, IN WITH THE TRUE: A CULTURE OF SOUL

Even if they weren't topping the charts, Daptone artists continued to gain fans at record stores, noncommercial radio stations, and on YouTube—enrapturing longtime devotees and new listeners who were floored at the sight of a real, live, big band playing in a tight concert or serving a singer who demanded reverence. Although they never sounded small, the eleven-piece Antibalas could barely be contained while doing promo for their fifth release on the NPR video series *Tiny Desk Concerts*.[1] Launching into the lead single from *Antibalas*, Amayo tapped a cowbell as the white lines painted over his eyes and nose moved expressively (rather than the entirety of his body, per a more expansive dance space). Even if Antibalas looked a little goofy—a large group forced to contain their massive groove behind a cluster of desks, with Victor Axelrod on keys disguised in an alien mask—their sound remained incredibly studied and ecstatic.

Antibalas, the band's first release on the Daptone label (but not their first recorded and produced at the House Of Soul), contains all the elements of the group's Afrobeat tradition: a theatrical performance, with Amayo as lead storyteller, his cries in English and Yoruba answered by an undulating rhythm and a mighty horn section that plows through songs like "Sáré Kon Kon." Yet with the exception of the self-explanatory "Dirty Money," *Antibalas* mostly trades outright fury for more nuanced allegory on tracks like "The Rat Catcher." In a solid, 7.5 review of the record, *Pitchfork* noted that the band "slowly but surely whittled away all the other, subtler Latin, jazz, and funk influences that were threaded through their strain of

★ ★ ★ ★ ★ ★

Afrobeat... they've become both a little less idiosyncratic and a fair amount tighter—predictably reliable, maybe, but not in a context where sudden detours would be worth throwing off listeners (or dancers) anyways."[2]

But as the six-song *Antibalas, No Time For Dreaming, The Budos Band III* (an album of psychedelic, polyrhythmic doom-rock that trumpet player Andrew Greene described as what would happen if you "took Rick James, gave him a fuckin' 8 ball, threw him in studio and locked him in there for two days"[3]), and *I Learned The Hard Way* received positive reviews, a handful of critics were beginning to question whether Daptone was too in thrall with the past, or perhaps even appropriating the sound of another era or race. Others suggested that this label of connoisseurs might be too lost in their own stacks, concerned more with period perfection and exploring the nuances of soul music than with experimentation or more noticeable sonic progression. Although SJDK's fourth record (now with backup singers the Dapettes, aka Saun Williams and Starr Duncan-Lowe) suggested Philadelphia soul and Sam Cooke–style ballads, and even hinted at a Latin influence, *Rolling Stone* questioned whether it was "a record or a museum exhibit."[4]

Even as some levied criticism (though almost always with the caveat that Daptone's roster was sonically solid and impeccably entertaining), however, the label had begun getting recognition as a pioneer in a larger soul revival. "Daptone's creation story is also a reminder that soul never entirely went away," Raj Dayal opined in the *Atlantic* in 2011. "Their continued success has been largely off the mainstream radar, serving as a reminder that the soul revival of the past few years has been taking place at all levels of music, from indie-leaning clubs to the Grammys."[5]

The success of Amy Winehouse's *Back To Black* had created a renewed interest in 1960s-era soul, and a handful of female pop singers subsequently secured ubiquitous radio hits by employing a similar musical (and sometimes visual) aesthetic. In 2008, Welsh singer Duffy topped the UK pop charts and reached platinum status in the US with her jaunty, organ- and bass-heavy single "Mercy," its 60s pop referencing earning her

★ ★ ★ ★ ★ ★

comparisons to Winehouse and Aretha Franklin, as well as a Grammy nomination for "Best Female Pop Vocal Performance." The thunderous pop-soul breakup song "Rolling In The Deep," from British belter Adele, spent twenty-four nonconsecutive weeks at the top of the charts in 2011. (Coincidentally, Adele's breakout hit was mixed by Tom Elmhirst, who had mixed Lee Fields's *My World* for Truth & Soul a few years prior.) The song was so popular and anthemic that even Aretha Franklin did a cover of it. Bands at the intersection of indie-pop and alternative rock were also getting in on the soul game: Fitz & The Tantrums' rollicking 2010 single "Moneygrabber" blasted onto the scene with horns, and, highlighting the collective, broad influence of soul music, indie-rocker Cat Power traveled to Memphis in 2006 to record with the musicians who once backed Al Green. Singer Sean Kingston had an R&B hit in 2007 with "Beautiful Girls," borrowing heavily from The Drifters' "Stand By Me" and using a complementary retro aesthetic for its video. "Coming in with that 'Stand By Me' riff could only have ever happened after us and Amy," Binky Griptite says, reflecting on the mid-2000s musical retromania. "I think that was one of the last times that the pop culture pendulum swung toward an organic sound, even though a lot of people copied it in inorganic ways."

Although Daptone Records and its growing influence was conspicuously absent from an otherwise thoughtful and thorough feature, the *New York Times* declared in 2007 that "more than at any time in recent memory, soul music's pressing syncopation and stirring hollers are churning within the popular mainstream."[6] Contemporary artists such as John Legend, Joss Stone, Raphael Saadiq, and Solange were using studio musicians and classic soul samples to create revivalist-adjacent pop-soul—an alternative to electronica that was palatable for the new millennium's pop charts but indie enough to get people noticing. Legend's Grammy-nominated "Save Room" drew on the lounge-y organ workout of Classic IV's 1968 pop-soul hit "Stormy"; Gnarls Barkley's vocals on "Crazy" drew a direct line to Sly Stone circa '73, both of them fresh pop hits with heavy bass and psychedelic organ; even Christina Aguilera's poppy dance single "Ain't No

★ ★ ★ ★ ★ ★

Other Man" employed late-60s-style horn breaks. Released a few years prior, Beyoncé's now-classic "Crazy In Love" relied on the blaring horns of The Chi-Lites (a Daptone favorite)—though the singer initially thought the sample was too retro.[7]

While inventive for the time, these efforts didn't embody the revolutionary spirit of 60s soul but rather aped convention. Still, thanks to iTunes, file-sharing services, and burgeoning social media, pop acts and their fans could access influential records and build a soul knowledge base once relegated to the "hermetic circle of cognoscenti" collectors, as the *Times* put it. "Blogs like soul-sides.com post MP3s of rare soul and funk recordings that anyone can download. And for just $2.49, cellphone users can download a ring tone of the hook from ... 'Searching For Soul,'" a breakbeat-ready instrumental from the late 60s sampled by Beyoncé.[8] Video sharing platforms like Vimeo and YouTube (launched in 2004 and 2006, respectively) allowed fans to view music easily and provided artists with a platform to share their own work. Such services were buoyed by the release of the iPhone in 2007, which made having a camera and computer in your pocket the new status quo. Streaming services like Pandora and Spotify cracked the algorithmic code of the soul universe shortly after, making through-lines between the mainstream and underground more easily accessible to the average ear.

"If you're a pop music producer, you're no longer looking for the next sound; you're looking how you can rearrange all the old sounds," says Homer Steinweiss, who in the years following *Back To Black* had become a coveted session drummer and a regular collaborator with Mark Ronson. "There's always something new coming along, but everything has this wealth of references now. Now you have the world of music at your fingertips. And it's not just a really cool hip-hop producer that finds an old sample, but everyone is just using found music for everything. There's the revivalists in the scene, and pop music that's always culling from whatever cool scene is going on. It's feeding off each other."

★ ★ ★ ★ ★ ★

While pop was just beginning to sample from the soul buffet in 2007—and the *Times* had yet to give Daptone its propers for cooking up such a sonic feast—hip-hop artists and producers had long been digging in the same crates to create iconic breakbeats. "I might come across a [soul] record and then, shortly thereafter, hear a hip-hop track and be like, *Oh, shit, they just sampled that song that I just learned about*, or the other way around," Victor Axelrod recalls.

By the time Daptone started to press wax, hip-hop was cemented among the milieu of New York City culture, and its hometown acts were requisite knowledge for any curious musician or producer. Yet, from the outside, Daptone's crew and hip-hop were operating in seemingly separate spheres. Unless you were a particularly enterprising fan reading liner notes (or, after 2008, scouring WhoSampled.com) or a musician listening for a specific line in a song, it's unlikely that one would clock Kanye West's use of "Pick It Up, Lay It In The Cut" from *Dap-Dippin'* on Rhymefest's "Brand New" in 2005, or that Menahan Street Band was sampled by 50 Cent and Kid Cudi. Wu-Tang member Ghostface Killah, one of Leon Michel's favorite rappers for a time, sampled *Sounding Out The City* in 2007. The Black Eyed Peas pulled "Ride Or Die" from The Budos Band's second album, and, years later, Eminem would use samples from *Victim Of Love* and MSB's second album, *The Crossing*.

Hip-hop and club DJs like Danny Akalepse—a legendary battle DJ who came up during the golden age of hip-hop and shared stages with Rich Medina, KRS-One, Kenny Dope, and Cypress Hill, in addition to having a twice-weekly residency at APT—would spin whatever records would get a party jumping, regardless of genre. Lepse and others were also fanatical diggers, sharing most of the funk and soul knowledge that informed Desco and Daptone, but not crossing paths. "DJs who are primarily known for hip-hop have the records sure, but would they go to a Desco showcase at, like, Wetlands or something?" Lepse wonders, slouching in a swivel chair at his Brooklyn office. "Probably not. Were Phillip and Gabe going to go see Wu-Tang when they were playing shows? I don't know. I feel like in the

★ ★ ★ ★ ★ ★

early to mid-90s, these soul-scene dudes would have got their ass whooped at hip-hop parties. Because hip-hop was so violent, because New York was so violent, I think people didn't cross pollinate. Everybody was young and dumb; I used to do gigs and worry about people robbing me for records."

While it might seem incongruous for a battle DJ, Lepse had a thing for "slowies"—the late-night anthems and ballads one might use to close down a club at 4am on a weekday. While hunting for Lee Fields's "Honey Dove" (a slow and particularly poorly distributed single) at Truth & Soul's headquarters on North 10th Street in Williamsburg, Lepse met Leon Michels. They shared similar interests, which they came to from different ends: Lepse knew The Meters from hip-hop samples; Michels knew The Meters because they were The Meters, and he'd spent much of his high-school years paying homage to the New Orleans legends in The Mighty Imperials. Lepse became the Truth & Soul's manager almost by happenstance.

Hip-hop was hardwired into the musical minds of members of El Michels Affair and Menahan Street Band, who came of age in the 90s. "New Yorkers have Wu-Tang in our DNA, and we have Nas's beats," says Brenneck, who hails from the same borough as Wu-Tang. "We have all those fucking East Coast hip-hop bands that were super-fucking-heavy and straight, and all sampling soul records. We heard hip-hop beats and we loved them. So it's like, we want to play Booker T. & The MG's, but also we know what a Wu-Tang pocket sounds like. And that's a New York thing." The Budos Band have a direct connection to the rap supergroup, he argues, and *No Time For Dreaming*—with its dusty piano and boom-bap drums—is steeped in hip-hop phrasing. Those records "not only have 60s influence in it, but it clearly has 1993 Wu-Tang influence in it. [Hip-hop] is in the fucking DNA of those bands. We don't have to make hip-hop though, but we couldn't make music absent of that." (Across the country in Los Angeles, The Root Down, Breakestra, and parties like Funky Sole also provided a "really beautiful example of the lineage of jazz and hip hop and soul," Brenneck notes.)

★ ★ ★ ★ ★ ★

Truth & Soul, and by extension Daptone, would close the circle on hip-hop relevance with an unlikely assist from Toyota's Scion brand. In 2005, the car company offered El Michels Affair an opportunity to back up Wu-Tang rapper Raekwon on a promotional tour dubbed the Live Metro series. The setup melded EMA's emotional and cinematic soul with Wu-Tang's traditionally gritty, dark aesthetic, which eventually netted multiple gigs with other members of WTC. EMA flipped original arrangements from Wu-Tang's 1993 masterpiece *Enter The Wu-Tang (36 Chambers)*, then added horn lines and strings to cut two singles: "C.R.E.A.M." and "Bring Da Ruckus," which netted more than ten times the sales of an average Truth & Soul record. "Wu-Tang fans are so nuts about Wu-Tang, and also live hip-hop is—for me at least—such a touchy thing," Michels told the blog *Rollo & Grady*. "I don't really like a lot of hip-hop. We just approached it like it wasn't going to be hip-hop—this was going to be some soul shit."[9]

While RZA told Michels that he liked a few tracks, the band had a falling out with Wu-Tang not too long after. "But we learned all their songs," says Brenneck, "and we were always just like, *Let's just record a fucking instrumental Wu-Tang record.*" Through a contract with Fat Beats Records, El Michels released their soul-inspired take on the Wu-Tang in 2009. *Enter The 37th Chamber*, El Michels Affair's second LP, became the band's most successful record, thanks to its inventive covers of "Shimmy Shimmy Ya" and "Protect Ya Neck," though Michels later told the *Village Voice* that the album was likely successful because WTC's original is so beloved: "It was almost too easy with 'C.R.E.A.M.' My cover was cool, but I didn't think it was special."[10] Ten years later, El Michels Affair would release a more studied follow-up featuring Lee Fields on vocals, *Return To The 37th Chamber*.

El Michels Affair weren't the only band getting the hip-hop hookup. Across the country in Southern California, where cars are arguably more of a way of life, Scion tapped funk ensemble Connie Price & The Keystones (a project led by Daptone friends guitarist Dan Ubick and Todd Simon,

★ ★ ★ ★ ★ ★

who had already released three LPs) to back rapper Big Daddy Kane. CP&K became one of the main backing bands for Scion's series, cementing their hip-hop cred and leading to the release of *Lucas High*—an LP on Fat Beats featuring golden-age MCs and singers including Talib Kweli, Brand Nubian, Pharcyde, and Macy Gray—as well as a handful of other studio projects on Ubiquity and Stones Throw.

Orgone—an instrumental funk/disco group from the San Fernando Valley with records on Ubiquity—supported Bun B and a handful of other artists on Scion tours. "Oftentimes the artist themselves hadn't had a lot of experience playing with a live band," says Orgone guitarist and producer Sergio Rios, "but some of those relationships continued on. It was definitely one of the highlights of our musical career." Work supporting hip-hop legends led to studio sessions with a prominent LA producer named Jack Splash. Over the phone from his home in Santa Cruz, Rios adds, "We're the uncredited band on 'Teenage Love Affair' by Alicia Keys and worked as the rhythm section on CeeLo's 'Fool For You,'" which netted the singer a Grammy. In a further meeting of the minds and connected coasts, Orgone supported Sharon Jones & The Dap-Kings through part of their national tour for *I Learned The Hard Way*.

A little further west from Orgone's HQ, multi-instrumentalist and producer Adrian Younge took inspiration from Wu-Tang and classical composers to create the funk soundtrack for a real Blaxploitation film: 2009's *Black Dynamite*. Unlike Desco's *Revenge Of Mister Mopoji*, the film was a real cult hit.

Back east, Truth & Soul doubled down on its link to hip-hop history, working with Missy Elliot protégé Nicole Wray (an R&B singer who featured on a Timbaland-produced single in 1998 and briefly had a deal with Roc-A-Fella) to write for Lee Fields before producing her own work.

Daptone also got into the hip-hop game, recording and engineering a Mark Ronson–produced track for hometown hero Nas, who did multiple collaborations with Amy Winehouse. Nas's "Fried Chicken" was released in 2008, Steinweiss's syncopated drumming, The Dap-Kings' stabbing horns,

★ ★ ★ ★ ★ ★

and Brenneck's guitar recognizable to a devoted ear. In 2010, the label released a single from the 3 Titans, a group of elementary-aged boys doing 90s-style hip-hop about the importance of education, written by Mighty Imperial guitarist Sean Solomon and backed by Menahan Street Band.

Even as Daptone continued to encounter new opportunities for studio work and collaboration, the growing world of pop-soul and interest from prominent hip-hop artists didn't translate into listenership or sales—at least in Gabe Roth's eyes. "When you talk about producers that are making big records—Jay-Z and Mark Ronson, Questlove—all those people who are kind of at the tip of pop music and shit, are all using our guys and our beats. They are all hip to us, and they all give us daps; they all respect us and stuff, but the people who listen to them don't know what the fuck we are. That's not a connection people make," he adds, noting that an average listener won't think about samples, influences, or a producer's current favorite record. "Questlove would be sitting on the side of the stage watching Homer play drums. People don't know that stuff; that's not part of major pop culture."

Outside of mainstream pop culture, Daptone's touring musicians were noticing vintage soul scenes and bands popping up throughout the world. All-vinyl soul and funk DJ nights (including northern soul–style events like Chicago's Windy City Soul Club) had established themselves in Austin, the San Francisco Bay Area, Philadelphia, and Baltimore, and expanded in the already soul-rich cities of Los Angeles and New York. Where soul nights were the purview of collectors in the early to mid-2000s, appreciation for the genre was growing rapidly. "Amy Winehouse, with the help of Daptone, got people very excited about the label and soul music in general," Jonathan Toubin, a NYC DJ whose Soul Clap dance parties toured the country and local Shakin' All Over nights packed tiny dancefloors, told *Pitchfork*. "I think it would be safe to say that Sharon Jones helped bring an entire generation into soul music."[11]

★ ★ ★ ★ ★ ★

Los Angeles–based promoter Nancy Arteaga booked Daptone's Southern California shows in the mid-to-late 2000s, and first heard SJDK's soulful siren call during a 2005 performance at Sunset Junction—a local festival in Los Angeles's rapidly gentrifying Silverlake neighborhood. Arteaga didn't come up listening to funk, instead preferring punk, metal, and reggae, but Sharon and her band introduced her to the revival scene in her own backyard. "I didn't know about Funky Sole, I didn't know there was a Breakestra," she says. "I learned about all of that through Daptone."

Although Roth didn't see the larger pop lineage, he says, "We were obviously influenced by a lot of people before us, and I think we were big influences on a lot of young bands." The years following *Back To Black*, *100 Days, 100 Nights*, and the exhaustive touring of groups like Antibalas resulted in an international crop of likeminded groups. LA's Mayer Hawthorne did straight covers of soul rarities as well as his own tunes with hip-hop drumming, rising to prominence on Stones Throw Records; DJ Nick Waterhouse took his education at all-vinyl Rooky Ricardo's Records from San Francisco to Southern California, demonstrating his deep affinity for early 60s R&B on a debut LP called *Time's All Gone*. JC Brooks & The Uptown Sound brought a theatrical element to their Chicago funk and soul (including a particularly cool cover of Windy City brethren Wilco's "I Am Trying To Break Your Heart"); blues-rock bands like The Heavy, Vintage Trouble, Black Joe Lewis & The Honeybears, and Alabama Shakes all incorporated elements of funk and soul into their music. Meanwhile, British soul singer Alice Russell and Quantic's *Look Around The Corner* pulled from a variety of soulful sounds; Ben L'Oncle Soul released 60s-style tunes from Paris; Australia's scene cooked up the spacy Afrobeat Shaolin Afronauts, in addition to straight-ahead hard funk from The Transatlantics and The Bamboos. Garage, punk, and rock'n'soul groups like King Khan & The Shrines (an affiliate of Jonathan Toubin), Shannon & The Clams, and labelmates/friends Hunxs & His Punxs also got in on the action, infusing soulful ballads, girl-group harmonies, and snotty 60s pop into their raucous shows and rough records.

★ ★ ★ ★ ★ ★

Daptone Records' influence can be heard in nearly every modern soul group, music journalist David Ma told the *Atlantic*. "To make soul music is one thing, but to sound as brassy, drum-heavy, and project the warmth that can only be achieved with analog equipment, is probably Daptone's biggest influence."[12]

While Sharon Jones & The Dap-Kings' live show shook The Black Keys' Dan Auerbach, Daptone's records "never struck a chord with me because it was too retro overall. It wasn't until Leon did the Lee Fields record *My World* that it really spoke to me," he says, referring to the album released in 2009 on Truth & Soul and cut with players from Menahan Street Band and Antibalas. "That record was so inspiring, so influential to me when I went down to Muscle Shoals to do the *Brothers* record with The Black Keys. Pat [Carney] and I were listening to that record on repeat, driving around in our rental car." Auerbach first experimented with singing in falsetto on *Brothers*, trading his usual harmonies for an intimidating higher register with just a hint of influence from Fields. Fittingly, Lee Fields & The Expressions opened for The Black Keys on their *Brothers* tour in 2010.

Neal Sugarman sees his label's influence as having had a more subliminal effect both within the "retro soul" world and outside of it; Daptone's musicians showed that what had once fallen out of favor could be cool again. "The music had already existed, but somehow playing chanks on the guitar had gone away. And then people heard us doing it and started doing that again," he says, referring to the funk guitar technique developed by J.B.'s guitarist Jimmy Nolen. "It's not like we didn't do anything, because we were wearing our influences on our sleeves and proud of it. I don't want to take any credit for saying that we innovated anything we didn't. The only thing is that we played music we loved, we played it well and executed it well. And hopefully, people are able to realize that you guys can still contribute to that lineage of great soul records that were mostly recorded in the late 60s and early 70s."

Ironically, Daptone never achieved the same level of fame or

★ ★ ★ ★ ★ ★

experienced the rapid ascent of a band like Alabama Shakes—who were often mentioned in the same breath as Sharon Jones for the passionate and compelling performances of lead singer Brittany Howard, as well as the group's soul influences (speaking to British newspaper the *Telegraph* in 2015, Howard said she was frustrated by being "made out to be a retro, cute band").[13] The lead single from Alabama Shakes' first LP was dubbed the best song of 2013 by *Rolling Stone*.

It's possible that Daptone's insistence on grassroots marketing and rejection of distributor pleas to spend big money advertising at major retailers affected the label's ability to "make it" in a traditional sense. Other bands—even those on independent labels—with a less rebellious and consumerism-adverse attitude more easily achieved degrees of stardom. "Bands would open for us and then, the next year, they would have a radio hit and they would be huge," Roth says. "There's a lot of times that happened, which I don't begrudge at all. I'm proud of it."

Sure enough, gospel-soul shouter Eli "Paperboy" Reed opened for Sharon Jones & The Dap-Kings during a 2009 tour of Australia and was signed to Columbia Records soon after. Still, the label heads (and Roth in particular) could be dismissive of pop accolades and recognition, preferring instead the adoration of fans and appreciation of their true-to-period sound by older listeners.

"They sometimes get off on being a little snotty," says Jacob Blickenstaff, one of Daptone's regular photographers, who began shooting Sharon Jones & The Dap-Kings in 2009 and captured some of the label's more iconic images. "It's a little bit of an act. I think it's partly because they want to be judged on their merits. And, with an artist who became as popular as Amy Winehouse, the scale does eclipse what they do. So they don't want that to be the first thing on their resumé because they put decades into all these other artists."

Like many in the fold, Blickenstaff found himself in Daptone's orbit first as a fan and hobby photographer at shows, before eventually making friends with them and shooting the cover of *I Learned The Hard Way*. "I

★ ★ ★ ★ ★ ★

think what is special in the big picture is that Daptone treats soul music as a discipline and an artform unto itself, and not just one note of popular music. And they just live it twenty-four hours a day."

Legacy acts also put out new records in a post–Amy Winehouse world. R&B singer/soul forefather Solomon Burke released three records between 2006 and 2010; Bettye LaVette released more music and sang Sam Cooke's "A Change Is Gonna Come" with Bon Jovi at President Barack Obama's first inauguration. Southern soul singer Candi Staton put out a handful of studio albums, while Isaac Hayes was added back onto the Stax Records roster for an album reissue. Mavis Staples continued to release music, working with Wilco's Jeff Tweedy and performing alongside British troubadour Billy Bragg. (Binky Griptite once had a guitar commissioned in her honor, which Staples christened by signing the head.) New Orleans soul queen Irma Thomas, whose beautiful ballads ripped hearts to shreds but who was most known for her infectious 1964 single "Breakaway," won a Grammy for "Best Blues Album" in 2006. That same year, Darondo, an underground enigma from the Bay Area, was tracked down by Ubiquity Records. The label re-released some of his 60s classics and brought the singer into the studio to finish a few unreleased funky tracks as *Let My People Go*.

Other artists who weren't putting out new music but benefitting from renewed interest in soul and obscurities found space on revue stages and specialized shows. Archival label Numero Group hosted a touring Eccentric Soul Revue in 2009, with JC Brooks & The Uptown Sound backing up Syl Johnson, Renaldo Domino, and The Notations. Around the same time, two New York DJs began bringing lesser-known 60s soul, reggae, and rock'n'roll artists to various Brooklyn stages in a bid of edutainment for its typically young audiences. Dig Deeper provided audiences and inspiration for the likes of Chicago soul singer Darrow Fletcher, an octogenarian Bay Area badass named Sugar Pie DeSanto, and smooth-singing rocksteady artist Ken Parker (whose falsetto is legendary), with backing by local acts including Reed, the Brooklyn Rhythm Band, and, for the Jamaican singers

★ ★ ★ ★ ★ ★

onstage, reggae band Crazy Baldhead. "We're kind of rewriting the history of soul music," Dig Deeper co-founder Richard Lewis told the *New York Times*. "There are all these artists who got really popular and culturally relevant to the overall population ... but there are also all these other artists who didn't make it for some reason, and their music is still relevant."[14]

The musicians behind Daptone Records long recognized that relevance, of course. As a testament to this understanding and torch-bearing status—and after a decade of listening to their records on repeat in tour vans—Sharon Jones & The Dap-Kings opened for The Isley Brothers during a 2007 show at Harlem's United Palace Theater. Recalls Binky Griptite, "We didn't get to meet them or interact with them at all, but it was just nice to be in the same building." Roth engineered *The Road From Memphis*, a 2011 follow-up from Stax legend Booker T. Jones that was produced by Questlove and Rob Schnapfh (of Beck and Elliott Smith fame). The album tapped a dozen notable musicians, including Lauryn Hill, unmistakable Detroit session guitarist Dennis Coffey, Lou Reed, The Roots, and Sharon Jones. Roth brought his trademark engineering techniques from Bushwick to the Midtown session. "I remember being in the studio with Questlove and he's listening to the drum sounds that Gabe was getting using one microphone, maybe two," says Kirk Douglas, a longtime fan of Daptone. "He was getting such explosive, lively drum sounds that just had such a vibe. That was a great opportunity to kind of feel like you're a Dap-King for a day."

Griptite had a chance to work closely with some of his soul heroes a few years later. Recording with harmony legends The Impressions, he and original members Fred Cash and Sam Gooden, as well as Reggie Torrian (who replaced Curtis Mayfield), cut four songs at the House Of Soul with original arranger Johnny Pate. The seven-inch release featured the Mayfield-penned tune "Rhythm" (originally a hit for singer/songwriter Major Lance in the mid-60s) and "Star Bright," a midtempo love song whose melody Griptite wrote as a young boy. To subsidize their trip to record in Brooklyn, Griptite organized a New York soul-scene blowout

★ ★ ★ ★ ★ ★

at Southpaw in Park Slope—he and a few other Dap-Kings, performing as The DeeKays, would support The Impressions, who sang the newest release as well as hits including "People Get Ready," "Mighty Mighty," and Mayfield's "Move on Up." Between sets, DJ Pari (who connected Griptite with The Impressions), Eli Reed, and the DJs from Dig Deeper took turns behind the decks.

As Daptone's profile grew among industry veterans and living legends, show bills would flip in favor of SJDK. By 2010, pianist and songwriter Allen Toussaint—who penned many popular R&B songs throughout his lengthy career, including Lee Dorsey's "Working In The Coal Mine"—was opening for Sharon Jones during two New Year's Eve performances in New York. As he warmed up the revelrous crowd, Toussaint said, "There's no place I'd rather be tonight. I really mean it." Meanwhile, further downtown, Lee Fields & The Expressions were ringing in 2011 at the Bowery Ballroom.[15]

As audiences celebrated the year 2011 with sounds straight from 1965, so-called nostalgia culture was on the rise. Recent years had seen the release of *Dreamgirls*, a musical drama about a 1960s girl group loosely based on The Supremes, and *Cadillac Records*, a musical drama loosely based on Chicago's Chess Records. Both films provided a glossy, silver-screen counterpart to music that was very much alive and strutting on international stages. Among baby boomers, such nostalgia fed into a wistful view of their salad days. Yet their Gen X and millennial kids generally came of age with less economic stability, fewer job prospects, and radically different forms of communication than generations prior. It should be no surprise, then, that the cohort born between 1981 and 1997 would be attuned to soul music meant to be uplifting in times of tumult. After all, one needn't consider the Great Recession while looking back through archival video on YouTube or learning about The Mynah Birds, a Canadian R&B band from the mid-60s featuring both Rick James and Neil Young. Daptone Records, though not intentionally engaging in any "nostalgia marketing," was oddly on-trend.[16]

★ ★ ★ ★ ★ ★

Everyone associated with Daptone would be quick to dismiss any claim that their love of funk and soul music was a marketing ploy. Yet, early in Sharon Jones & The Dap-Kings' run, Boston music critic Siddhartha Mitter wrote that every aspect of the band's performance "was a tad overdone," and that "an odor of exploitation hovered in the room, though its exact source and strength were hard to pin down." Mitter suggested that SJDK were fetishizing soul music—an act that "often carries the false corollary that there is no good new soul and R&B."[17]

As the leader of a crew of musical libertines, Gabe Roth never felt trapped by genre or critical reception, though fear of appropriation (or at least the possibility of others viewing his interests as such) came up early. Playing with Cliff Driver, Lee Fields, and Sharon Jones—all Black musicians who, even without a reductionist view of appropriation, would be the most rightful heirs to a soulful throne—taught Roth that he didn't have to try so hard. "I'm not gonna say it got me over it, because I still don't think I'm over it, but it taught me that I don't have to try to pretend that somebody's history is my history when it isn't. If I'm playing good, everybody's happy," he says. "Right from the beginning, I was very conscious of trying not to imitate shit and not to be a thief. Specifically of licks and stuff like that, but also not to be a cultural, social thief. I'm not gonna say that I was successful or defend myself, really."

The first horn blasts of the soul revival and Daptone's slow but steady ascent into the pop culture pantheon happened concurrently with the 2008 election of Barack Obama—an impossibly hip candidate who employed a soul-heavy playlist on the campaign trail. For many, Obama's presidency marked the first step into a new, progressive dawn, and its soulful soundtrack a resounding recognition of the power of Black music. But as the country experienced a renewed fascination with its pop roots—riding high off the inaccurate notion of a "post-racial America" despite crushing inequality—the audience listening to and buying tickets to see the "throwback" music of Daptone Records was exceedingly white.

"For a lot of reasons, Black people in this country are just interested

★ ★ ★ ★ ★ ★

in new things," theorizes Griptite, who is Black but shies away from discussions on race, preferring not to speak for the band or all Black people. "I would guess a lot of it has to do with a culture that's grown up stigmatized by hand-me-down clothes. So maybe, *I don't want the old, I want the new—and I'm definitely not wanting to listen to the old folks' music.* Black people have appreciation for classic soul music, but that's just not where the party is. You pick your music according to the people you want to see at that party. I hate to admit it, but I've seen it happen time and time again: Black people abandon a band once white people start showing up at the shows and in droves."

Sharon Jones, too, spoke little on race, but she never "made you feel bad for being white," says Austen Holman, who is white and grew up in the less ethnically diverse Seattle area. "Someone even asked, 'What is it like for you to look out in the audience if there are hardly any Black people?' She would always say it's about the music, not the people. She likes to let people be themselves, and that, to me, is what made her so special, because there was zero judgment."

Although the intersectional musical roots of The Budos Band and Antibalas (who regularly confronted the status quo through songs like "Dirty Money" and "Hook And Crook"), the challenging questions about class and inequality posed by Charles Bradley, the message songs of Naomi Shelton, and SJDK tracks such as "What If We All Stopped Paying Taxes" are all political in nature, much of the music of the soul revival seemed to lack overt political themes. "There's a lot of songs that we did that were political, but people didn't even take them that way," Roth says, pointing to "When The Other Foot Drops Uncle" from *100 Days,* a tongue-in-cheek song about holding President George Bush and his cronies accountable for the War on Terrorism. "People hear that song and are like, *Oh, she's telling her lover.* She doesn't say anything about a lover; it's talking about lies and propaganda and war machines."

Tommy Brenneck drew a line between Daptone's contemporary soul and folk singers of the 60s, suggesting that political songs should come

★ ★ ★ ★ ★ ★

from a singular voice. "I don't think that any of us are equipped to write folk songs on the level of Bob Dylan or even Buffalo Springfield. Sharon wasn't a songwriter; Gabe wrote most of those songs. Charles could write a song, but he needed a lot of help, and together we could write songs greater than the sum of its parts."

"Why Is It So Hard (To Make It In America)" was originally a silly song about Daptone's overseas success and inability to "make it" on their home turf. But when Charles Bradley sang it, Brenneck adds, "All of a sudden, he put his story into those lyrics. He pulled the depth out of it; I was just like, *Whoa, man, I'm so glad I showed you that idea.*"

Regardless of the message, soul music is fundamentally political, and the mere presence of Daptone's singers—most of whom were middle-aged, Black, and performing for audiences who might not share their experience—was in itself a progressive statement. "It's inherently political for African Americans to stand up and be proud and loud about anything," Roth declares. "It doesn't matter what Sharon, Charles, or Lee are singing, but the idea that they're up there and putting power and honesty into music, there's something inherently political about that. I don't pretend to think that we are some kind of civil rights leaders, but it's like the old saying: revolution needs a soundtrack. It doesn't have to be Gil Scott Heron; it could be Earth Wind & Fire, it could be anything, man. It can be Fugazi or Rage Against The Machine, or it could be Bob Dylan. The point is, people hear that soundtrack."

CHAPTER ELEVEN YOU PUT THE FLAME ON IT: DAPTONE AND THE SOUL REVOLUTION GROW

Ahead of the release of *I Learned The Hard Way*, Sharon Jones & The Dap-Kings flew from New York to Austin, Texas, for a whirlwind set of performances at South By Southwest. They were set to perform three times in one night, the last of which would see SJDK performing past 1am at Austin Music Hall following the legendary Smokey Robinson. It wasn't the band's first time performing at the legendary festival—a 2006 SXSW appearance netted Jones her role in *The Great Debaters*—but by 2010, the feeling was different. Working the crowd at an NPR showcase held at Stubb's, Binky Griptite announced the arrival of "a much-celebrated sister that's about to get her due"—an evolution of one of his many introductory lines that, at that moment, rang particularly true.

Lounging on a sidewalk earlier in the day while dressed down in jeans and a straw cowboy hat (Sharon would have multiple costume changes in one night, suspending disbelief that she had just sweated through multiple other sets), Jones radiated energy and was seemingly undaunted by the night ahead. Even at fifty-four, and after injuring her toe at the airport, she was excited to break in some new shoes and wow her audience. "I'm proud of my age," she told *Billboard* in a brief interview where she would reflect on her success and gratefulness, in a regular refrain that never tired. "I've been wanting to do this so long, and my inspiration started almost fifteen years ago when I met these guys. … Being turned down when I was in my

★ ★ ★ ★ ★ ★

twenties, I could have taken that another way and went in a shell and never tried to sing again and go get a nine-to-five."[1]

Although she had held a day job in the in between, Sharon Jones's tenacity, vivaciousness, and unequivocal soul were making the rounds. She hit *SNL* with Michael Bublé and tore Stephen Colbert to ribbons with an "I'll slit you where the good lord split you"-level cutting look when he jokingly questioned Daptone's style. And although the majority of Daptone's artists would shirk interest from a major label that might, in Sharon's mind, "try to make me look like Beyoncé and make me expose my behind," SJDK were getting recognition from major pop artists.[2]

From the wings of an Austin stage, Prince watched Sharon Jones & The Dap-Kings work a packed crowd into a righteous, blissed out splendor. Prince had been hip to The Dap-Kings since *Back To Black*, and he'd covered Amy Winehouse's "Love Is A Losing Game" during a long residency in Las Vegas (at the last night of which Winehouse made an appearance, The Dap-Kings having been loosely considered to perform). Blown away by their visceral show and dedication to an era, the Purple One realized that the NYC locals and modern funk pioneers would be a great opening act. The following year at Madison Square Garden, they opened Prince's *Welcome To America* tour; Sharon, the Dap-Kings horns, and Binky (who, in a moment of shocking cool, played Prince's original Telecaster guitar) also came on for an encore of "Love Bizarre."

Jones was shocked and anxious about the invitation, telling manager Alex Kadvan, "I don't want to ask for too much and he'll say, 'Man, y'all must be crazy, I'll get somebody else.'" Instead, Prince met the band's price—and added another five thousand dollars. "Prince taught us a lesson: *Hey, this is what you guys are worth*," Jones continued.[3] SJDK met Prince on the symbol stage, jamming together for a bit between soundchecks; backstage, Prince gushed to Jones about seeing her at SXSW. "That's one of the most funkiest songs I've heard in the last twenty-five years," he said, the singer recalled to *Entertainment Weekly*. In her first "I don't know what to do with myself moment," Prince told Jones, "Girl, you took me to church."[4]

★ ★ ★ ★ ★ ★

The daps continued into the afterparty at the Darby (a nouveau supper club that, in a previous life, was Nell's—an early haunt of DJ Frankie Inglese), where Prince invited SJDK to jam and hobnob with Jay-Z, Leonardo DiCaprio, Mos Def, and Questlove. Sharon—who would always hang, but who by then was hesitant to overextend her vocal cords by yelling and singing in a loud, smoky room—lent her voice to the revelry.

"I got a lot of love from Prince," recalls Binky, who wasn't initially set to do the encore but impressed Prince with his playing and wah-wah pedal skills. "I know a lot of people that have incredibly negative stories about Prince. But he's a great guitar player. I mean, it took me a while to really understand that."

A few months later, SJDK were opening for Prince in Paris; Sharon was in the middle of a nine-minute-long soul-dance montage to "There Was A Time," in which she broke down the boogaloo, the swim, the pony, and a dozen other moves. The roar of the crowd grew louder as Prince, donning an orange velour hoodie, biked to the stage, and jumped on as an impromptu guest star for a few bars. When Prince accidentally dropped his pick, ending the jam, Sharon Jones effortlessly picked up, inviting the audience to hop on her soul train for a ride back to reality and into the bridge of "When I Come Home."

Never a group to mark achievements (though members of the band were getting more songwriting credits and studio sessions), Sharon Jones & The Dap-Kings were finally seeing the seeds from their own soulful revolution grow. "People are still trying to get a handle on these modern music delivery methods, and you can't necessarily gauge your number of fans by record sales or ticket sales," Griptite says. "But the first time we played to ten thousand people was at the Montreal Jazz Festival. It's not like they bought tickets to see us, because it was a free street festival, but we still were holding the attention of ten thousand people." Fans would come up to the band after shows, profusely sweating after trying to keep up with Sharon's fast feet, incredulous about the sheer spectacle they had just witnessed. "How do you make that sound?" they would ask.

★ ★ ★ ★ ★ ★

"It's just like, man, everyone's feeling as one at the same place," says Sugarman. "When, rhythmically, everyone in the group is lined up together, the stage is higher, and everything is elevated to another level. We had a lot of experiences like that, and when it's happening, everyone on the bandstand knows it's happening." That cloud nine height might not always be recognizable to the crowd, but the saxophonist would "get very emotional. Just tears coming out of my eyes. When that was happening, everything was just on fire. Sharon suddenly was free, and everything felt effortless."

By the time SJDK were performing to a ten-thousand-strong Canadian crowd in 2016—and, two years prior, to three sold-out audiences at the Apollo, for the label's Super Soul Revue—there had been multiple fundamental changes in the Daptone universe. A slew of singles and albums had rocketed out of the House Of Soul: Naomi Shelton's funkier gospel *Cold World*; a second LP from Mississippi a cappella gospel singers The Como Mamas; The Budos Band's fourth LP of pandemonium called *Burnt Offering*; and finally a playful single from Dapettes Saun & Starr, "Hot Shot." ("If this 45 ain't your bag, please go lay down on a busy street. There's no hope for you," the label declared.) Players worked on their own side projects, too: saxophonists Cochemea Gastelum and Ian Hendrickson-Smith each released records, while interplanetary missions connected Daptone with Finnish soul label Timmion Records and British R&B crooner James Hunter (whom Roth originally recorded for Concord Records in 2012, in an early use of what would become his West Coast studio).

Antibalas, like Sharon Jones & The Dap-Kings and Charles Bradley, spread their message of "deep, unconditional love" across the planet through a superhuman touring schedule which, though more comfortable, wasn't bringing in much more money. The band's horn section, however, did perform at relatively cushy events, such as a star-studded tribute to Bill Withers—who preferred to eat his own baloney sandwiches rather than catering—at Carnegie Hall.

★ ★ ★ ★ ★ ★

Favoring studio work and local gigs over massive tours, Homer Steinweiss and Tom Brenneck opened Dunham Sound Studios with money from Menahan Street Band's Jay-Z sample. From the comfy couches of the South Williamsburg studio (and likely with a drink from a fully stocked bar in hand), the collective behind MSB and El Michels Affair made records with Alabama Shakes, Dan Auerbach, and even a Quincy Jones/Amy Winehouse cover of "It's My Party"—in addition to producing and recording Lee Fields and Charles Bradley.

Those choices, as well as the multiple bands many musicians performed with, required new members from a growing network of players. "It's rare for people in this particular scene to get mad or selfish," Extraordinaire Freddy DeBoe notes. "We're all friends, understanding and happy for each other. You find out you get a gig and then you go home, or your friends buy drinks and they're happy for you. They're supportive because there's so many gigs that come and go."

But even as the label's impact grew, Sharon Jones remained its anchor, heart, and backbone. Back on the sidewalk in Austin, the singer had quipped, "Major labels don't understand what we were trying to do, you know? So we had to start our own label in order to keep our funk and soul, our idea, what we wanted to do, alive."[5] As UCLA professor Scot Brown told *Ebony*, "It's not that funk artists don't exist anymore, it's just that the record companies don't see Black bands as a sacred unit anymore." While bands existed across geography and genre, Black executives in the business were mostly on the hunt for the next Chris Brown or Beyoncé.[6]

But by being uncompromising in its taste and playing by its own rules—and with SJDK as its headlining act—Daptone far exceeded the impact of other independent labels. With each album, the music got deeper, more complex, and more personal for The Dap-Kings, and for Sharon. Performances became both tighter and looser, the whole band working more as an organism than a collective of players, stretching out tunes, working different parts to Sharon's preferred tempo.

"I don't remember the first time I saw Sharon Jones and it took me

★ ★ ★ ★ ★ ★

a while to warm up to her, actually," WFMU soul DJ Matt Weingarden recalls. "At first, she struck me as a very, very talented, sort of journeywoman singer. It was totally fun to see her, and I liked it. But in later years, she was so at the top of the game. All the hard work and dedication, and the band sounded so good; I was super impressed by their growth. There's always going to be room for Sharon Jones because everybody loves Aretha Franklin so much, and that sort of 60s and early 70s soul diva sound is never going to go away."

★ ★ ★

In the spring of 2013, Daptone announced SJDK's sixth LP, *Give The People What They Want*, an ambitious record with new influences, anchored by a powerful anthem called "Retreat." Austen Holman, a young artist manager fresh from Seattle, had just become Sharon's day-to-day manager, and was responsible for organizing the singer's growing calendar of photoshoots, interviews, and promotion. "She has, like, a ton of vibrant energy coming out in all these promotional pictures. But she was starting to complain about her back hurting—she was tired. She was a very stubborn person and very vocal about whatever she was feeling when she was feeling it," says Holman, who clocked Jones's complaints but initially assumed they were a product of age. "To be honest, no one really took it seriously until her eyes were turning yellow and she was itchy. She'd be like, *Oh, it's my laundry detergent, I'm just getting itchy.* We found out that was a symptom."

In June, just a month after Daptone announced *GTPWTW* and a string of supporting tour dates, Sharon was diagnosed with stage two pancreatic cancer. The singer relocated from South Carolina (where she had been living in the house she bought her mother, later grieving her passing) back to New York ahead of treatment, and crashed at Holman's Williamsburg studio—watching Hulu, scrolling through Facebook, and drinking green health shakes. Holman had been working with Jones, an affable but private woman, for just three months.

"We were in a really unusual situation that forced us to get very

★ ★ ★ ★ ★ ★

close, very fast," Holman says. "And thank goodness it worked. Because sometimes people aren't comfortable around people in that way. What I heard was, *Sharon's great, but she's tough. Don't be afraid, her bark is louder than her bite*. I was so lucky that Sharon accepted me, because if Sharon likes me then, chances were, no one was going to have an issue with letting me into the world."

That June, Jones underwent a whipple procedure—a complex surgery that removed her gallbladder, the top of her pancreas, and eighteen inches of small intestine, leaving a sizeable scar on her chest. "Alex and I would take shifts staying with her in the hospital room," Holman adds. "And at one point, she needed to ask someone to help her in the bathroom. I had no qualms at all. I was, like, rubbing her back and helping her get dressed. And we even laughed about it at the time. Like, *Can you believe this? This is what we're doing*."

Despite moments of levity and a generally positive attitude, Jones thought she was going to die in the early months of her diagnosis. She expected *Give The People What They Want* to be her final testament—one that she'd never be able to perform live. She leaned into her faith, and although she knew she wouldn't go to hell if she died, Jones wanted to right her soul, just in case.

"I did go through the trial and tribulation then," she told *Vice*. "That's a stumbling block in front of me. And I've got to go over this. I'm not going to go around it. And it's another chapter in my life. You know? My sickness ain't forever."[7]

Sharon was characteristically determined, telling herself and her doctor that she had to get out of bed and walk. "I was crazy," she admitted. "But I had also got an infection, so they had to take some of the staples out, and then there was a hole in my stomach that took a couple months to heal… it was really tough."[8]

Once she had recovered from the whipple procedure, the singer made plans to convalesce and undergo six months of chemotherapy in Sharon Springs, New York, at the home of Megan Holken, a friend and

★ ★ ★ ★ ★ ★

nutritionist Jones met in the 90s (and whose wedding she once sang at). Holman traveled with Jones back down to South Carolina, and the two planned to drive Jones's car back up to New York. They spent a handful of days in Sharon's hometown of North Augusta, visiting family and touring Jones's favorite fishing ponds and childhood haunts.

"It was eye-opening," Holman recalls. "She had family members where they were living twelve people to a two-bedroom mobile home with no running water. And it was so clear that she was providing for a lot of these people," she adds, qualifying that as a white woman from the more affluent city of Seattle, she hadn't seen the level of poverty Jones grew up around. "I think everyone gravitated toward Sharon's energy because it was a survival thing. Life was hard for her, but you never really got that sense."

Jones spoke matter-of-factly about the racism she experienced as a kid, both during summers spent in the segregated South and in the mostly Black neighborhood of Bed-Stuy, but she seemed keen to keep those memories in the past in favor of an honorific future. She beamed with delight as she walked Academy Award–winning documentary filmmaker Barbara Kopple—who was following Jones's cancer battle for the film *Miss Sharon Jones!*—past her own display at the Augusta Museum Of History. Sharon Jones's dress, shoes, and albums were set near a larger exhibit of Augusta's original hometown hero, James Brown, further cementing that soulful lineage. But while such positive moments sustained the spirit of Jones's fans, Kopple didn't shy away from showing the fear and taxing nature of Jones's cancer. "The first time I ever met Sharon was when she was having her hair cut and shaved," the documentarian said. "And that was such an intimate and incredible moment, I think it just had a bond between us."[9]

Sharon was hesitant and somewhat dismissive about being filmed, telling Alex Kadvan that she didn't have much of a story. "At first, I didn't want to, but it wasn't about me anymore," she said. "It was about my fans... and my band. I knew that even though I was sick, there was something about me performing, me being on that stage. I felt that my fans can see

★ ★ ★ ★ ★ ★

what I'm going through and feel what I'm going through, and not only my fans, but someone else out there with cancer."[10]

Two months into her chemotherapy, Jones wrote on Facebook, "I wish I could say it's been a breeze, but this is looking to be the most challenging part yet. … I want you all to know that YOU are the reason why I am so motivated and driven to stay healthy and work through my recovery."

Jones powered through months of chemo that burned her skin, caused her eyelashes to fall out, and turned her fingernails black. Her body—once an indefatigable powerhouse of lungs, feet, hips, and potent sass—ached, and she couldn't walk without bending over; showering was an effort, and she didn't want to see many people. Sharon didn't have much energy to sing, which made her unhappy and frustrated, and if Sharon couldn't sing, she didn't want to listen to music or practice the new songs on *Give The People What They Want*—the release of which was put on hold and all tours postponed. Though the stage was her sanctuary and her ability to enrapture any audience the ultimate healing power, Sharon told *New York Magazine* from her kitchen, "I wasn't thinking about no damn stage."[11]

Mostly she relaxed—a state previously relegated to short stints between tours and the occasional special afternoon spent fishing while enjoying a cigar—painting by numbers and indulging in a heavy rotation of talk shows while fantasizing about being a guest on *Ellen*. The Dap-Kings and others from the label called and texted; some made the nearly four-hour drive north to Sharon Springs. But back in Brooklyn, life as The Dap-Kings knew it had come to a screeching halt. Ten musicians who relied on touring for a large chunk of their income (particularly if they didn't have significant royalties or songwriting credits) were functionally out of work; at least thirty-six dates for 2013 were canceled or rescheduled. Money for health insurance, funded by SJDK's touring, became scarce.

"Alex was more like a father figure to Sharon," says Holman. "He was the one to manage the band and had to have a sit down with everyone to talk about what the future was maybe gonna look like. The Dap-Kings weren't anything without Sharon at that time." An entire Australian tour was canceled after a nervous promoter worried Jones wouldn't make it, while news of her illness had other, unintended consequences that resonated beyond the band. Roth, who by that time had moved back to Riverside and was working at an officially unofficial Daptone West, was denied a loan to refinance his home because his bank had heard about Sharon's sickness and thought he was too risky. Binky Griptite essentially lost his job while in the middle of a divorce. Trumpeter Dave Guy, now the father of two young boys, was already tired of touring.

Although one might expect people who would soon be eligible for Social Security to slow down, the forces leading the soul revolution had never stopped. And because no one at Daptone expected their music to really take off, thus making the singers' slightly advanced ages a talking point, there was no thought given to the worst-case scenario. Neal Sugarman bristles at the thought: "Yes, you have Sharon and Charles and Naomi, and all the other artists and myself, and we're all getting older. Things change, and whether it means that there are families involved and less touring, or there's health issues because the artists are getting older… you work a long time to develop as a business, to develop your distribution network and your partners and the branding. You keep going."

The label refocused, developing ways to keep fans engaged without going on the road. In a coincidental return to Sharon Jones's roots, SJDK appeared as a wedding band in the 2013 Martin Scorsese film *The Wolf Of Wall Street* and brought their signature flair to a melodramatic cover of "Goldfinger" for the film's soundtrack. Instead of an album release and supporting tour for *GTPWTW*, Daptone trickled out animated music videos while Sharon recovered upstate. The video for "Retreat" took on new meaning as a smiling Sharon battled hordes of hyena-like goblins while growing to an omnipotent size and commanding, "Boy, you don't know what I'm all about / I'll chew you up and then I'll spit you out / So if you know what's good for you / Retreat!" If the song was ever read as an explosive takedown of a lover, it now became an anthem for kicking cancer's ass.

★ ★ ★ ★ ★ ★

A month before Sharon finished chemo—the final round poetically set for December 31, 2013—she, the Dapettes, and The Dap-Kings boarded a replica of Central Park to float down Fifth Avenue in the Macy's Thanksgiving Day Parade while lip-syncing "Ain't No Chimneys In The Projects." The band were happy to be performing, despite the thirty-degree cool and early call time, and Sharon was too—though the event left her so sore she spent the next three days in bed recovering.

At the time Sharon was processing her diagnosis, Charles Bradley was beginning a thirty-six-date tour that would take him and The Extraordinaires to stages from Nevada to the Netherlands. As press clamored for interviews with Sharon—whose story of perseverance and late-in-life success was made even more compelling by a cancer battle at the height of her fame—Charles's own story of triumph was winning hearts and ears. His intensely emotive performances could still sucker-punch even the deepest fan, bringing an impossible amount of life to howling, confessional lyrics before softening the blow with offhanded, straight-from-the-heart speeches made from center stage.

"I'm moving on to the next level, but I feel like everybody already knows a lot of my hurts and pains," he told the *Village Voice*. "I'm still growing into society and in my own wisdom and knowledge... but I want to do some crazy music, too."[12] Things were going well into the second and third touring cycles of *Victim Of Love*—a period during which Daptone released a handful of singles, including a duet with Bradley's friend LaRose Jackson, a four-song twelve-inch titled *I Hope You Find (The Good Life)*, and a beautifully painful cover of Black Sabbath's "Changes," which would be the title track of his next record. Yet Bradley's new lawyer, playing on lingering feelings of competition and the singer's lack of financial knowhow, convinced him to seek new management.

"Alex Kadvan was also Sharon and Antibalas's and Budos's manager," says DeBoe. "Charles kind of felt like he wasn't given the time of day,

★ ★ ★ ★ ★ ★

like they cared more about Sharon. Which wasn't necessarily the case." Charles's lawyer suggested a management team who worked with Def Jam Records, Wu-Tang Clan, and Mobb Deep. "They hadn't been in the industry for years and weren't experienced with dealing with a band at all. We almost got completely fired; they were trying to convince Charles that he could go on his own without a band. It was a very, very crazy time for a little while but none of us wanted to give up on Charles."

The Extraordinaires were set up with a tour manager everyone hated, but the group of young men rolled with the punches. Meanwhile, Tom Brenneck begged his friend to reconsider leaving Kadvan's Lever And Beam management. "Somebody had gotten in Charles's ear that the money wasn't right, but the money was right, and then it was too late. It really scared Kadvan for his business and his whole livelihood."

Realizing his grave error, Bradley begged Kadvan to take him back as a client, but the manager refused, and then dropped Brenneck and all of his projects as well—The Budos Band, Menahan Street Band, and all of his production work. Kadvan had also been the point person for all of Brenneck, Movshon, and Steinweiss's session work, though he'd continue to manage them in Sharon Jones & The Dap-Kings and Antibalas. Kadvan says he had spent years trying to convince Bradley that the singer was, in fact, his own boss and "not anyone else. My splitting from Tommy was that I was hurt; I was hurt that there were choices made to stick with Charles." Adds Tommy, "Kadvan had managed me since I was, like, nineteen; I was pretty happy to be under his wing. His business was really good for the artist, so the ironic part is that Charles goes and tries to fuck the person that's doing him right."

Now off tour for the most significant period in years, Gabe Roth had more time in the studio and began production on a number of albums. The Dap-Kings laid the foundation for *Look Closer*, Saun & Starr's 2015 debut; released an anthology of The Poets Of Rhythm; helped distribute a salsa album called *Pilon* from locals Los Hacheros (who, like the former Mighty Imperials, were also part of the Friends Seminary class of 2000);

★ ★ ★ ★ ★ ★

and had a horn-section studio session with British singer Paloma Faith.

While the label had always worked on music outside that of its main artists, this period would prove influential for future years' output and set the stage for jumping into soul-adjacent genres. But The Dap-Kings were still anxious to get on the road, make money, and see their queen—the brightest star in the soul galaxy—back in action and propelling across the stage where she belonged. "The band knows if Sharon ain't make it, nobody works," the singer deadpanned.[13]

Sharon welcomed 2014 by completing her final chemotherapy treatment and readied herself to perform on *Late Night With Jimmy Fallon*—first with house band The Roots and then, the next day, with The Dap-Kings—less than two weeks later. She was feeling relatively sturdy and had been diligently studying *Give The People* song by song, though she was still fuzzy on some lyrics, the chemo and months spent not singing having taken a toll on her memory. "If I get there, and I'm not ready, then I'm not ready," she told *Vice*. "But in my heart, and my faith, and my belief, and just the energy what the fans have sent me is enough that I know I'm going to be ready. And I know my fans going to be ready for me. Whatever I bring out to the stage to them, they're going to be ready for it."[14]

"She was amazing; it was just great to have her back," says Kirk Douglas of Jones's *Fallon* performances. "There was an intensity to her performance, and it was just good to have the feeling that we didn't lose her. She'd always been really friendly to us. It was just great to see her smile and just to see her loving performing, and feeling how thankful she was to be back."

With the blessing of her oncologist, Sharon Jones started preparations for a seven-month tour in support of *Give The People What They Want*, which officially dropped on January 14, 2014. Jones knew that there was a long road ahead; she would likely not be able to deliver 110 percent of her explosive energy, and certainly not with the shimmery dresses and flying hair she was used to. The visible changes to Sharon's stage persona were affecting. "When I was on that stage, I was Ms. Sharon Jones. You know? I look in the mirror and sometimes I'm sad at what I see," she continued

★ ★ ★ ★ ★ ★

to *Vice*. "I want that hair back. … I want my happiness. I want what I had before I left the stage. But I know I still got that. And it's just going to be a little different at the beginning."[15]

Equal parts stubborn and self-assured, Sharon never wore a wig but had covered her bald head with ballcaps and fedoras during chemo. Onstage and in the music video for "Stranger To My Happiness," her baldness was emboldening—a powerful visual for all she had overcome, and a defiant statement of both beauty and strength. (Griptite, Sugarman, Guy, and Fernando all donned freshly shaved heads for the video.) With a month still left in her treatment, Sharon appeared on the cover of the *Village Voice*. She gazed at herself on the cover, photographed starkly in black-and-white, her face thinner and eyes looking solemnly at the camera as the definitive, hopeful headline, "Soul Survivor," loomed large across the page. Sharon wept; she wished her mother could see this story. She hoped she wouldn't be seeing her in heaven any time soon.

With a couple of small performances under her belt, Sharon headed uptown to the Beacon Theater on Manhattan's Upper West Side for her big comeback performance. It was early February 2014, and Sharon was officially in remission, though through soundcheck she was worried about being able to remember lyrics or kick herself into high gear—SJDK's last sizeable performance was over nine months prior. The Dap-Kings were anxious too, but they largely played off any concerns they had about Shern coming through.

"Everyone was nervous, like, *Is this gonna go off the rails?*" remembers photographer Jacob Blickenstaff, one of a handful of documentarians restlessly waiting for the singer's grand entrance. Backstage, the vibe was quieter than usual, especially around Jones, who multiple times shirked cameras and forced Blickenstaff and others to leave. "I saw the level of care that was coming from the people around her, and it gave me this deeper perspective on what it means to work with these artists," the photographer says.

To absolutely no one's surprise, the Beacon was sold out with fans

★ ★ ★ ★ ★ ★

desperate to be awash in the soul Sharon Jones & The Dap-Kings pounded into the stage; Jones's oncologist and Megan Holken had traveled from upstate to witness this triumphant return. The Dap-Kings did their traditional warm-up, spending a few minutes getting into tight step as Jones hovered in the wings, waiting for her cue. Blickenstaff tried to make himself invisible, capturing this small but very big moment. "It was the first time I saw the very vulnerable side of Sharon. She's literally shaking—not in fear but just out of this big emotional thing that's kind of going through her. It's like an almost religious doubt and she's looking for some deeper unconscious strength."

"We've taken the longest time off we ever have as a band," Binky Griptite bellowed, ending his soul salutations by welcoming Sharon Jones into a roaring house. The crowd leapt to their feet as the singer bounded onstage, her smile radiant as her designer sparkly dress. "I'm back!" she exclaimed, slightly out of breath. "Woooo! Guess what, I'm feeling good!" The show was strong, with only minor mishaps in lyrics, and Sharon memorably turned *GTPWTW*'s midtempo love song "Get Up And Get Out" into a high-octane, Tina Turner sermon-stomper. Jones didn't think she would be onstage at the Beacon, she told the crowd; just months ago she was laid in a hospital bed with tubes down her throat, her hair had fallen out and her nails turned black. But she was back to give the people what they want, and now she took the nearly three-thousand-seat theater to church in a bluesy ballad turned hyper-shout in praise of her own strength. She kicked off her shoes to do a medley of dances, her legs no longer too weak, and booted cancer right out the door.

"Everyone's rooting for her and she was legitimately scared to get onstage," says Holman, who keeps a framed picture from the performance on her fireplace. "But she did it. We got to have ninety minutes of pure bliss because she did it. We were like, *We made it. It's all good. We got past this.* It was the most magical show I've ever seen in my entire life."

Sharon was stronger than ever. Kicking cancer seemed to have given her a prodigious force that took her already exuberant performance to

★ ★ ★ ★ ★ ★

new heights. Forever grateful for the opportunity to share "the gift that God gave me" with audiences around the world, the singer returned to the stage with more passion and determination—her voice sturdier, her feet stomping harder into the stage, the thrill palpable from the back of the room. "When I walk out [onstage], whatever pain is gone," she told *Rolling Stone*. "You forget about everything. There is no cancer. There is no sickness. You're just floating, looking in their faces and hearing them scream. That's all that is to me."[16]

Audiences who may have worried that the reigning queen of soul was lost wept upon her return. "I remember thinking, *Where does she get this energy?*" DJ Clifton Weaver recalls, on seeing Jones hit a Southern California stage in 2014. "It's supernatural—some otherworldly thing she must be tapping into; something outside of our reality to be able to perform like that after having gone through such an intense health situation. Then, to come back like she hadn't lost a step, like nothing has happened, was truly incredible."

From backstage, LA promoter Nancy Arteaga would "pay attention to the way people would look at her, and it was like they were in a trance." Yet speaking to *Fresh Air*'s Terry Gross, Jones revealed that despite her recovery, she felt different. "I mean, everyone said my energy was great, but I didn't feel it at all. Even now, the days on the stage I'm just not myself, I don't have that energy. The legs don't lift up like I want to with the pain, the neuropathy from certain chemo. It's a hinder, but I do the shows, but it's not the same."[17]

Sharon Jones & The Dap-Kings quickly shirked off any lingering upheaval the cancer had wrought and hit the road with a force. They booked thirty-seven dates in the US before beginning a second round of international performances, including one at the historic L'Olympia theater in Paris. Yet two days before the Beacon show, trumpeter Dave Guy and saxman Ian Hendrickson-Smith (aka Chief) were hired to join The Roots, who were

★ ★ ★ ★ ★ ★

nightly upending the tradition of talk-show house bands from 30 Rock as part of the newly christened *Tonight Show With Jimmy Fallon*.

"It's fascinating to watch them work together because they're like that couple that can finish each other's sentences," Douglas says of Guy and Chief. "They really know how to predict what the other person's going to do and know where to go instinctively. They're just the baddest horn players out there, so it's a real education to watch them play daily." Their addition would prove a boon when The Roots recreated certain songs and hip-hop samples. "There's a real authenticity that we're able to execute them with, because those cats are such students of music from that era, and also participants."

Billy Austik was called in to sub on a three-month SJDK tour, which meant he in turn had to leave a run of dates with Charles Bradley. "It was tough, but I knew and Charles knew and everyone else knew that Sharon's the top of the food chain," Austik says. That first tour was super emotional, and everyone missed Guy. "After they were kind of over the shock of it all, it was just kind of business as usual, and I slid in there. To get ready for the Dap-Kings gig I practiced completely blazed so that I could be ready to play completely blazed. It was kind of an unspoken thing: you had to play stoned or else you, like, were an outsider." Sharon, who was taking daily enzyme pills for her pancreas and had acquired a medical marijuana card to manage her pain, always had weed packed among her toiletries. "Sharon and I would have many a hotel bathroom smoke sesh. After we would land in town, she'd be like, *Everybody come to my room!*"

Daptone capped a nail-biting, turbulent, and exhilarating eighteen months with a three-night stand at the Apollo on December 4, 5, and 6, 2014. The label's entire roster would be on display as the Daptone Super Soul Revue, with Sharon Jones & The Dap-Kings headlining each night in a career pinnacle performance that matched the energy and showmanship of James Brown's historic revues upon the same stage. Label engineers Wayne Gordon and Simon Guzman were brought in to record

★ ★ ★ ★ ★ ★

the concerts, which, depending on which musician you spoke to, were either a dream come true or a really nice working-family reunion.

Daptone proceeded to tear the house down, offering the audience a well-oiled visual representation of the label's linkage and musical philosophy; most musicians played in two or three groups and sat in with others for the first time after touring separately for years. The Sugarman 3 reconvened for one of Gabe Roth's favorite sets, while Antibalas and The Budos Band made their Apollo debuts—the latter messing around in typical fashion and holding little outward reverence for the stage, jokingly slaughtering the space as organist Mike Deller pretended to nearly throw his entire set over only to have saxophonist Jared Tankle fake bash him over the head with his horn. Dressed in a flashy, handmade blue and white outfit with his face painted, Duke Amayo led Antibalas in an exploratory and explosive set that forced the crowd to their feet in solidarity with message songs, calling up extra horn players to bring the total number of musicians onstage to well over a dozen. Sharon Jones and Charles Bradley brought their now-trademark fire to each night of performances, while Saun & Starr, Naomi Shelton, and others rose to the occasion, taking their searing soul and brassy, percussive gospel to Harlem heights.

"Every one of these bands can go to a club and play for two hours and tear it down," Roth told me during an interview for *Vice*. "When you're doing a revue you're only playing for like 40–45 minutes; you kind of trim the fat and everybody puts a fire under each other's asses. It made the whole thing fun. The wings of the show were packed, everyone was watching each other's set and if they weren't, they were downstairs laughing and jamming. It was a lot of beautiful connections between people."[18]

On December 5, prior to the start of the night's uninterrupted three or so hours of music, the family found out *Give The People What They Want* had been nominated for a "Best R&B Album" Grammy. Backstage, Sharon Jones gathered the sprawl of musicians for a toast: "There should not be one hand that don't," she hollered, pausing to tell someone to quit standing on the table. Raising a glass of champagne, she recognized "Daptone, The

★ ★ ★ ★ ★ ★

Dap-Kings, Antibalas, the Menahan and the Budos, and the Como Mamas and everyone . . . we been *nooooominated!* To the sound, to management, everything we've done, we've worked hard. No one gave us this!"[19]

Onstage that night, Sharon coolly announced the nomination, the Apollo acting as a fitting stage to share some long-overdue industry acknowledgment. "Sharon never was egotistical about it, but it was very validating for her to have those opportunities and to get recognition," Blickenstaff says. "Some people were very joyous and felt very validated. There were others that were like *Fuck this shit. It's all bullshit.*"

As expected, Gabe Roth was less than moved by the Grammy nom—*GTPWTW* went up against The Robert Glasper Experiment and Aloe Blacc (who'd worked with Truth & Soul on a 2010 record), and they all lost to Toni Braxton and Babyface's *Love, Marriage & Divorce*. "I'm not saying we didn't do anything, man. I'm very, very proud of it. But to me, it's like, we go play a show and somebody'll come and tell me, 'I brought my boyfriend and I've never seen him dance before and he danced all night'; 'My mother died and I was in tears a whole week and could barely get out of bed and it's the first time I've smiled since that happened.' Or somebody will write me a note about how a record we did or a show we did really touched them. And that, to me, is like unbelievably rewarding," Roth says.

Where would Daptone even put the award at the House Of Soul? Perhaps in the overfull kitchen-storeroom, or on one of the crowded desks in the main office, or somewhere unassuming in the control room? Amy Winehouse's platinum record was already taking prized space above the second-floor toilet. "I'm way more proud of it than I ever would be of this other shit—pop studio sessions, Grammys, radio. Because that's not something based on making good music and connecting with people. Look who's getting a Grammy—that's where you want to be? There's an award for *that*? Then look at all the records that you love; do any of them have Grammys? No."

CHAPTER TWELVE SOUL TIME! REVIVAL SOUNDS GAIN STEAM

Publicly, Sharon Jones was never bitter about losing out on a Grammy—a win would have been nice, but validation from fans and the pride of beating cancer was no consolation prize. The award ceremony itself "sucked," she told the *Oxford American*. "I left an hour and a half before they ended."[1] Instead, she focused on the music and set to work promoting the genre that had given her life.

"What they call R&B and funk today is really pop," Jones said backstage at *The Queen Latifah Show*. "This music industry needs to know about soul; know that we are out here and not going anywhere."[2] In an interview with *Vice*, she pointed to Taylor Swift and Justin Timberlake, who in 2013, won multiple awards in R&B for his *The 20/20 Experience*. "I'm not saying R&B and soul is Black. It ain't got nothing to do with that. It's the pop singers. . . . And then you've got people like me and Charles Bradley. Just because we're independent we're not even recognized up there. And my next goal is for people to recognize that soul music is now. Soul music did not die in '69 and '70."[3]

By championing a specific pocket of funk and soul, Daptone Records was, somewhat unintentionally, continuing a folk tradition. "What we do is keep random musical traditions alive that we love," says Homer Steinweiss. "Like very specific era James Brown, from '65 to '69—how did they all play together? We'll learn that language exactly, which is almost frozen in time because it was so perfect."

Grammy notwithstanding, Daptone's influence had greater resonance

★ ★ ★ ★ ★ ★

beyond the here-today-gone-tomorrow nature of pop music. Over time, the label had centered itself at the forefront of a soul revolution, its dedication to genre, showmanship, and analogue recording the catalyst for a soul train that made stops in the global underground. Jones, for her part, had thoughts on the term "underground," telling Queen Latifah, "There's nothing underground about us—everything we're doing is clean, and it shouldn't be under, it should be over!"

In the 2010s, a second generation of independent labels and artists had cropped up, cementing a soul revival that was in full swing. The majority of these artists pulled inspiration from the same well of soul that Daptone and family had been tapping for years, in addition to the label itself.

Terry Cole was first bowled over by *Dap Dippin' With The Dap-Kings* while digging at RamaLama Records in Toledo, Ohio, in the early 2000s. He was no stranger to collector culture—he had paid for two degrees with money made from dealing 78s to fellow Midwesterners with his dad—and harbored an obsession with Blue Note and Atlantic records, as well as everything from James Brown (who launched his career through Cincinnati label Federal Records).

"At that time, there was so much bullshit being produced, and so little that was new that was really engaging to me," Cole reflects. "There wasn't a soul space. So, to hear *Dap-Dippin'* was literally a cosmic shift, and it just blew my mind. That was sort of the kick I needed to be like, *Oh my god, if they can do this, I want to do this. I want to figure out how to make records that make me feel the way I feel right now.*"

In 2007, when he wasn't teaching high school, Cole began slinging instrumental funk 45s (including his own singles and LPs as The Jive Turkeys) from up-and-coming bands across the country. Headquartered in the Cinci suburb of Loveland, and later from the top floor of a building housing his brick-and-mortar Plaid Room Records, Colemine Records continued a long tradition of Midwestern soul. "Cincinnati, Ohio, has been and will always be the epicenter of funk," drummer Questlove said during a DJ set streamed on social media in 2020. "There was industry, and Black people could move and buy houses. And then they buy their kids instruments. They form bands and the next thing you know [funk is] spreading."

Over the years, Colemine Records has put out hard funk from The Grease Traps in Oakland, cinematic soul from San Diego's Sure Fire Soul Ensemble, boogie from Orgone, and a popular 45 called "Comencemos" from Los Angeles ten-piece Latin funk outfit Jungle Fire. G.E.D Soul Records in Tennessee, Detroit's Funk Night Records, and Culture Of Soul in Boston would join the tribe of independent funk and soul labels circa 2010, adding a particular regional taste to a rapidly growing community that was also seeing soulful releases from Stones Throw, Now Again Records, Timmion, Record Kicks, and others.

"Daptone and Truth & Soul were sort of closed doors back in the mid-2000s, to, like, 2009 or 2010," Cole says. "I'm not criticizing them for that, but they did their own thing. If you were in, you were in, but if you weren't, you weren't. And I think, honestly, I capitalized on that," he adds, his Midwestern nice attitude creeping into conversation to cool any hint of competitive judgment. "There wasn't really a West Coast analogy to Daptone; there certainly wasn't a Midwest thing. These groups are making this cool shit and we're all inspired by Daptone, but we're trying to put our own spin on it."

Members of the Daptone family did collaborate with their friends at these newer labels as producers, session musicians, and connectors. Proving they were still dedicated to obscurity as much as fame (and with a connect from longtime supporter Kenny Dope), The Dap-Kings backed an older singer from Florida named Rickey Calloway on a couple of superbad early-70s-style funk tunes for Funk Night. Members of Antibalas, MSB, and The Budos Band recorded an instrumental soundtrack for the film *Postales* as Los Sospechos in 2010, which was released by a Colemine subsidiary. Brooklyn instrumental soul group Ikebe Shakedown fit Daptone's vibe, but with enough instrumental bands already on the roster, their debut LP was released on Colemine instead. Yet *Hard Steppin'* was produced at Dunham Studios by Tom Brenneck, who, like Gabe, had developed a notoriously picky (or

★ ★ ★ ★ ★ ★

nuanced, depending) taste. "The only thing I like is Los Sospechos. I like Terry Cole. Terry's so sweet; I'll drink tequila with Terry in a bar anytime and buy drinks all night," Brenneck says. "I think what he's doing is cool, but it . . . just makes it harder for people to find a Daptone record."

Unlike Daptone, next-gen labels like Colemine are not restricted by recording location, house band, or genre; they favored licensing and distribution contracts over production credits. "That Jungle Fire 45 that we put out was a breakout DJ thing," Cole says. "Cut Chemist was ordering them by the dozen because he knew he was gonna burn it out. That was great for the label, and it would have been a silly business move to be like, *No, I didn't produce it, so I'm not gonna put it out.*"

From the large front porch of his Riverside home, Gabe Roth reflects on the humor, or perhaps irony, of being looked up to. "People always come to us, especially young bands and funk and soul singers. And they would look at me to, like, open doors for them—as if I had some big opportunity to present them. You realize, like, we're straight punk rock. Like there's three of us in a fucked-up building, like, packing the records. What do you expect me to do? You want me to sign you and write you a check? From the inside, I think it's smaller than it looks like from the outside. We're kind of as big as you could possibly be and still be underground."

Yet as elder statesmen in the soul scene, it's undeniable that Daptone Records had done serious wayfinding. The label's grind on tour, relationships with distributors and popularity among independent retailers was a boon to new musicians and smaller imprints, who had a popular reference point for their own sales. "It wasn't like they had paved the road, but they had at least gone through the forest a few times," says Cole. "And, like, trampled some of that shit down and got some of the debris out of the way so that we can get in here and try to start building our own thing." He adds that by 2013–14, Colemine was experiencing a rapid growth in popularity as Daptone's own star rose.

★ ★ ★

★ ★ ★ ★ ★ ★

Although Daptone's—and specifically Sharon Jones & The Dap-Kings'—brand of funk and soul was gaining steam and a number of copycat groups, a handful of bands on the West Coast were aspiring to a different sound. Organist and singer Kelly Finnigan arrived in the Bay Area from Los Angeles in 2008, joining instrumental funk band Monophonics square in the middle of the larger cultural fascination with soul. And if British bands and East Coast groups were following a Daptone-derived formula, the West Coast was on its own trip.

"Nobody out here was doing the fucking step, in the fucking suit like a soul band, straight trying to be James Brown or do The Dap-Kings' classic soul thing," Finnigan says from his Marin County studio, Transistor Sound. "We were very much like, *We don't want to be in suits, we don't want to step*. There were so many bands doing that already." Nor were Monophonics foolish enough to send a demo to the ultra-cool and exclusive Daptone. "We just knew based off the vibe of their records and their pictures, Daptone ain't signing no other young soul bands." Monophonics did, however, perform with the Daptone Super Soul Revue during a 2014 gig in France.

With an instrumental album under their belt, Monophonics dug into the music of Isaac Hayes and Curtis Mayfield, early Funkadelic, and Norman Whitfield–produced Temptations records, as well as hometown hero Sly Stone. The six-piece were most interested in psychedelic soul, a subgenre that emerged in the late 60s, "when Black musicians started to figure out that there's a white audience out there and they're tapped into psychedelic culture, free speech and the antiwar movement, and peace and love and drugs and also the darkness that comes with that. That's where we want to be."

While Charles Bradley dabbled in psychedelia on singles like "Confusion" and on a few *No Time For Dreaming* tunes, Monophonics' sound was unique for the era. Their 2012 sophomore album *In Your Brain* (Ubiquity) was a mind-melting journey that layers Finnigan's searing Stax-style vocals over heavy organ, fuzzed-out guitar, and sharp horns. Their sound caught the ear of Bud Light, McDonald's, HBO, and even the San Francisco Giants, whose 2013 slogan was "All Together"—the same name of a heavy singalong on *In Your Brain*. While the song was played at every home game and on TV, the band were busy connecting with Colemine to distribute 45s; Finnigan and Terry Cole developed a deep friendship that would lead to a variety of co-produced efforts. Monophonics also established a large fanbase in Greece, recorded with Ben L'Oncle Soul, and made friends with local funk and soul outfits like Gene Washington & The Ironsides, organ quartet The M-Tet, and Los Angeles's Orgone. Together, the Northern and Southern California soul scenes created a new West Coast vibe.

Further north, in Seattle, the nine-piece Grace Love & The True Loves were making their own Puget sound with Betty Wright meets Mahalia Jackson vocals and serious Hammond B3 action. Guitarist Jimmy James—a shredding virtuoso from South Seattle whose great uncle played in a band with Jimi Hendrix in the 1950s—said his group was absolutely inspired by Sharon Jones & The Dap-Kings, who became his friends.[4] "Sharon—words can't even explain. I had a crush on her, yes I did. I had a huge crush and I would consider her the hardest-working woman in showbusiness," he told KEXP host John Richards, adding that he sat in with the band at Seattle's Moore Theater. "I can't even put into words just how great they were. They really helped, for a person like myself not be so shy about the music that I love to play ... every show that we do, it's always a dedication."[5]

Even as the coastal sound of the soul underground became more distinct, the majority of labels were propelled by trends set by Daptone—the most successful among the indies specifically dedicated to funk and soul. The genres had developed a much broader appeal by 2014, which allowed artists room to stretch their legs and their style, furthering the evolution from hard funk into 60s soul. Hypothesizing about the revival's auditory

★ ★ ★ ★ ★ ★

trajectory, Cole surmises that, early on, Daptone (and, by extension, Colemine) were appealing to DJs and collectors. "As that shifted to the LP format, it became more about growing an artist than just, like, a banging-ass 45. That was part of the shift from funk to soul; I think once it got past the DJ thing, it could just be a cool song," he says. "They didn't have to be uptempo burners, they didn't have to be super funky for the dance floor. They could just be the songs that anybody can enjoy. It's also a sign of the passive listening nature of Spotify and shit too."

Daptone, and all the musicians who looked up to (or just dug) them, had created a diasporic soul sound, which touched different subcultural pockets while also making its mark on major label aesthetics. In 2015, Warner Bros and Columbia planted their own flags in the soul revolution, each releasing Grammy-nominated debut albums by young Black singers.

San Diego native Andra Day first made waves by performing R&B takes of Eminem and Muse online before letting loose the heartbreak of an eight-year relationship on *Cheers To The Fall*; the album's leading single, "Rise Up," would even be a rally theme for Hillary Clinton's presidential campaign. Her raspy voice oozed over a bed of moody R&B which, when combined with a tendency toward 60s dress, netted Day multiple comparisons to Amy Winehouse, with *Billboard* noting, "At times, she so closely resembles Winehouse that it's hard to tell where *Back To Black* ends and *Cheers To The Fall* begins."[6] Connections to the late British singer went beyond vocal stylings: like Winehouse, Day's "Only Love" relied on Daptone session players including baritone saxophonist Cochemea Gastelum, Victor Axelrod, Dave Guy, Homer Steinweiss, and Leon Michels (who are listed in the album credits alongside Questlove and Raphael Saadiq).

"Andra Day was cool as shit, but her producer, Adrian Gurvitz, was a prick," Roth recalls of the Day session, which paired melodramatic organ and castanets with Day's personal lyrics. "We did one song with her, and she said, 'I love you guys, do the whole record; I would love to work with you some more.' And I said, 'I'm sorry but we're not going to work with your producer, he's out of here and never coming back.'" Missing the opportunity

★ ★ ★ ★ ★ ★

to work with a major-label rising star and the cadre of big-name producers was no loss for Roth. "I think it would be pretty fucking hypocritical at this point to put any pride in being acknowledged or respected by some fucking industry that just seems like garbage," he deadpans.

While Day released an EP and a handful of singles, *Cheers To The Fall* ended up being her only album. Her contemporary, Leon Bridges, had a bit more staying power. Two months before *Cheers*, the twenty-six-year-old singer from Fort Worth, Texas, released *Coming Home*, a critically acclaimed album of Sam Cooke– and Arthur Alexander–inspired blues and early-1960s-style soul. There was a bidding war for Bridges's contract among big-name record companies (an almost unheard-of event circa 2014), and the singer checked all the boxes for pop-soul success: he was young, handsome but not unattainably so, with pensive eyes, a sharp dresser, and a good dancer who could croon but didn't shy away from pop inflection.

Bridges's debut charted at No. 6 on the *Billboard* 200 and twice netted the singer an invitation to perform for the Obamas—a feat that shouldn't be looked upon as simply good marketing by Columbia Records—where he'd share the stage with Stevie Wonder and other legends. At the president's birthday celebration in 2016, Bridges recalled Obama pulling him aside to whisper, "This morning I was getting ready, and I was listening to [the song] 'Smooth Sailing.' I love your sound. Keep it raw."[7]

While Bridges bagged accolades and invites, he was also drawing significant criticism from journalists who questioned whether the world—which, one year prior to the release of *Coming Home*, was rocked by the fatal police-involved shooting of a young Black man named Michael Brown and subsequent weeks of uprising in Ferguson, Missouri—needed Bridges's brand of pre-civil-rights-era soul. At a pivotal moment in history, *Coming Home* was less of a rallying cry for the young, gifted, and Black and more a digestible throwback. Bridges's clean-cut, respectable image (regardless of whether such a look was designed by Columbia) and earnest love songs nailed the sort of colorless soul music Motown was known for in its early years. His ethics and place in America's larger racial reckoning

★ ★ ★ ★ ★ ★

were further called into question by the presence of a white lover in the otherwise sparsely populated music video for "Coming Home."

As with many artists in the soul revival, Bridges's audience was mostly white—"When I sing 'Brown-Skinned Girls,' I always say, 'Where my brown-skinned girls at,' and there'll be like maybe seven or eight of them girls in the crowd," Bridges told *Vogue* in 2015. "But I think a lot of Black people aren't as aware of my music yet."[8]

"Leon Bridges is a little bit bullshit to me, but I wouldn't put the weight of civil rights on him," says Roth, comparing Bridges's vocals to Daptone's own early-60s crooner James Hunter, a white singer from the UK whose *Hold On!* was released on the label in February 2016. "The songwriting and the singing is so much deeper; James Hunter and Leon Bridges live in different worlds, and that's why I'm just kind of like, *Man, fuck your world.* Also, he's real pretty; I have a hard time with people who are real pretty, even if they're talented."

Terry Cole loves Leon Bridges but acknowledged that the smoothness of his vocals makes his records less aurally engaging than other bands in the soul revival. "It blows my mind how many people come into my store and buy Leon Bridges that have no interest, or historical purchases, of anything in that world. Leon Bridges checks their soul box. It's a really strange bit of irony when you're seeing white folks consume soul music that might be about Black pride and Black power and getting over," he continues, with the caveat that his brick-and-mortar customer base is a majority white, suburban group. "They're not hearing any of that on *Coming Home*. They just like how it makes them feel. I think Leon Bridges definitely touched that nerve with people." Whenever a customer purchases a Bridges record from Cole's Plaid Room Records, he'll write a list of five other soul revival acts to check out—Sharon Jones and Lee Fields always top the list.

However, Bridges was more a product of Columbia's attempt to tap into revival sounds than a genuine fan. Sam Cooke wasn't on heavy rotation in Bridges's childhood home—but Usher and Genuwine were. "Writing [for *Coming Home*] was very restrictive," he told me for a *Newsweek* article in

★ ★ ★ ★ ★ ★

2018, ahead of the release of his sophomore album. *Good Thing* pulled from a wider R&B tradition, with nods to Michael Jackson and Bruno Mars, effectively plucking Bridges from the world of revival soul. "I think [*Coming Home*] was a great opportunity to be able to educate people on the foundation of what Black music is ... but what I'm speaking about in my songs is something that anyone can relate to, and I wanted to gain a wider range in my audience as far as ethnicity."[9]

Regardless of their talent and relative authenticity, Bridges's *Coming Home*, Andra Day, and SJDK were featured on multiple playlists of favorite songs curated by President Obama and his First Lady—arguably the most taste-making and culturally relevant First Family since the Kennedys.[10] These playlists, made widely available on social media and Spotify, also included Frank Ocean, Common, Aloe Blacc, D'Angelo, Alabama Shakes, and U2. The First Family's varied musical tastes reflected the complex emotions of the American people, and sent the message that Kendrick Lamar's politically influenced hip-hop was as relevant as Leon Bridges's hopefully saccharine soul.

If Andra Day and Leon Bridges's ventures into 60s-style soul were marked but fairly short lived, Mark Ronson's contributions to funk were indelible. His "Uptown Funk" featuring Bruno Mars—a hook-heavy, explosively danceable single with roots in 1980s electro-funk and a Michael Jackson–esque pop sensibility—was released in November 2014 and immediately rocketed up the charts. "Uptown Funk" spent fourteen weeks atop the *Billboard* 100, hitting No. 1 in 18 countries and being certified platinum by the RIAA eleven times over.

"Funk has had such a dodgy connotation for so long, because it's been hijacked by terrible jam bands and whatever," Ronson told *Spin* magazine. "But I remember saying to Bruno, 'Can we really put "Funk" in a thing in 2014?' He was like, 'Yo, we've got to own it.'"[11]

Although they didn't *entirely* own it—Ronson was sued multiple times by artists and entertainment groups for copyright infringement, and in 2015 quietly amended the songwriting credits to include five members

★ ★ ★ ★ ★ ★

of The Gap Band—the single was ubiquitous, appearing on late-night television, commercials, clubs, and streaming sites. The song incited mass euphoric dancing, and as one *PopMatters* critic gushed two months after its release, it might be the "only song on planet Earth right now."[12] By 2021, its official music video was the sixth most streamed video on YouTube, having garnered more than four billion views.

Ronson had admittedly become lazy following *Back To Black* and a handful of other smash hits, but he leaned into the creation of "Uptown Funk" so hard that he would often become nauseous, and his hair (still full and unreceded, unlike other musicians on the record) began to fall out. The multihyphenate spent seven months recording "Uptown Funk," setting up shop in London, Los Angeles, Memphis, Toronto, and at Electric Lady Studios in Greenwich Village—whenever and wherever he could get a hold of Mars—and working the tune into the ground over fifty takes. Ronson's determination to turn the bass line he and Bruno had developed during a jam into something that could meet the approval of both Bootsy Collins and Prince required a large creative team—one that would be bolstered by a horn section that could emulate badass blare in the vein of Chaka Khan and Morris Day without sounding like they were trying too hard. Naturally, Ronson reached out to The Dap-Kings and Antibalas horns, bringing in Neal Sugarman, Ian Hendrickson-Smith, Dave Guy, and trombonist Ray Mason, as well as Truth & Soul house trumpeter Michael Leonhart to supplement Bruno Mars's own horns. "Production-wise, this is the most progressive record I've ever done" Ronson told *Billboard*. "I wanted that shit to sound tough, crisp—and fucking massive."[13]

Other musicians in the Daptone universe played on *Uptown Special*, released two months after "Uptown Funk" exploded. After doing sessions for Mars's Ronson-produced *Unorthodox Jukebox*, Steinweiss and Nick Movshon (then playing bass on Truth & Soul records while doing session work for TV On The Radio and Dr. John) each played on three tracks on the album. Tommy Brenneck played guitar on two as a somewhat conciliatory gig.

★ ★ ★ ★ ★ ★

"I refused to play on *Unorthodox Jukebox* because Bruno Mars wrote a song for CeeLo called 'Fuck You,'" Brenneck says. "I was rocking with CeeLo before he made that song and was trying to push him in a different direction that wasn't so fucking teenage bippity boppity. They made that song and it was a hit, and then CeeLo went right into the fucking shadows. I never got to work with CeeLo, and I held it against Bruno Mars. Then Mark produced [*Unorthodox*] and called me up and was like, *Dude, are you mad at me?* I was like *No, I don't wanna play fucking supermarket music.*"

Instead, the El Michels Affair crew shared writing credits on *Uptown Special*'s "Feel Right," a horn-forward, singalong banger featuring rapper Mystikal. "When you're in the fucking game, man, you get mad at people. It's like, I hold what I do close, so if I don't respect the person's art, I don't really like to fucking lend my talent to it. But I've come to really respect Bruno Mars as an artist now. I love the record he made after 'Uptown Funk' by himself. I thought it was fucking great."

Beyond production credits and royalties, "Uptown Funk" continued to be a boon for Daptone's musicians. Ronson took *Uptown Special* on tour in 2015, tapping Extraordinaires horns Freddy DeBoe and Billy Austik—players he'd watched from the wings of Daptone's Super Soul Revue in Europe, then vetted through Antibalas's Ray Mason and the band's former drummer Chris Vatallaro, both of whom recorded on *Uptown Special.* "It definitely felt different," Austik says. "A lot more pressure. But it still felt like a homie vibe, because Mark knew all of our friends; he trusted us kind of just from reputation."

The crew held daily rehearsals in London ahead of a handful of shows in the UK—including the Glastonbury festival—as well as a few private events and an Australian tour. "Everybody was in their area with their instruments and we'd just work on one song a day, kind of break it down piece by piece and try to recreate the song live," DeBoe recalls, noting that he was impressed by Ronson's mental capacity. "Mark would take moments to himself just to think; he was always seeing the big picture of things." Although Bruno Mars (who was still the biggest name on

★ ★ ★ ★ ★ ★

"Uptown Funk") wasn't on the tour, Ronson brought out all the stops for Glastonbury, a massive festival and his first full-length set in three years. Ronson trotted out Boy George, Tame Impala's Kevin Parker, and a handful of others throughout the show, closing the performance with a star-studded version of "Uptown Funk" featuring Grandmaster Flash, George Clinton, and Mary J. Blige. "The shows were crazy," DeBoe says. "This shit was Hollywood. It was just one of those gigs that don't happen very often. They're very temporary, and if you enjoy them while it lasts it can be kind of surreal."

While some of the Daptone family toured with Ronson, Dapettes Saun Williams and Starr Duncan-Lowe were celebrating the release of *Look Closer* with a small US tour and a few UK dates. Their debut album featured ten lushly orchestrated originals that ran the gamut from silly summertime pop ("Big Wheel," "Blah Blah Blah Blah Blah Blah Blah") to devastating and dramatic ballads ("In The Night," "Another Love Like Mine"), all anchored by the singers' deep rapport and natural chemistry. Ronson gave the record his seal of approval, tweeting, "Just bought the new album from Saun & Starr (who sung on Amy's 'Will You Still Love Me Tomorrow'). So so good."

Williams and Duncan-Lowe met at a Harlem open mic in 1986 and reconnected while working in the Good 'N' Plenty wedding band, fronted by Sharon Jones. Although they were initially offered three weeks of work supporting *I Learned The Hard Way*, the singers spent five years backing Sharon on the road and in studio before readying their album debut. The chance to move centerstage was a perk of coming up on Daptone. In a home video, Williams recounted how "Sharon would always say to us, 'I'm telling you girls, sooner or later you all are gonna get asked to do your own thing.' We were like, *Get out of here, we're fine in the back, doing our shoo-bop-bop-shoo-wops*. And when it actually came to pass ... it was surreal."[14]

In an interview for Daptone's fifteenth anniversary, Duncan-Lowe told the UK's *Independent* newspaper, "Growing up, you had Motown, Stax ...

★ ★ ★ ★ ★ ★

their input was very strong and positive for us, but over the years, [the business] started getting different. But when I first came here, by the third day it was like click, you're family."[15]

That summer, the Daptone family was growing further with the addition of a reggae and rocksteady four-piece from Jamaica, Queens, called The Frightnrs, helmed by singer Dan "Brukky" Klein. Produced and engineered by Victor Axelrod—who had been busy as a studio player on a handful of pop sessions while doing his own reggae and dub work—The Frightnrs represented Daptone's first major foray into an entirely new genre. Rocksteady in the vein of Jamaican crooner Alton Ellis (rather than in the hard-hitting style of Aretha Franklin circa 1971) melded soul and R&B with Jamaican riddims, usually in the form of a love song. It first seeped through Jamaican sound systems during the blistering summer of 1967, when it was too hot to dance to music that required anything more up-tempo than a steady rocking motion, before spreading around the world through reggae collectors and revivalist bands like Los Angeles's Hepcat and New York locals The Slackers. "Each style has its own vocabulary and structures, but underneath it all is African rhythm," Axelrod notes. "It's totally conceivable to me that somebody who's good at playing 60s-style rocksteady would play American soul really well, or vice versa."

Axelrod first encountered The Frightnrs in 2011, at East Village tiki bar Otto's Shrunken Head; he was immediately struck by their unique instrumentation and Klein's vibrato tenor. However, the singer—a thin, tattooed white man in his late twenties who was rarely spotted without a scally cap and a beer in whatever hand wasn't holding a microphone—looked incredibly uncomfortable, his eyes closed to the audience. Axelrod later told NPR, "There were subtleties in their playing and the way they sang together that really resonated with me. Dan's energy was simultaneously subdued and manic... but there was a sound that came from him that had everyone in the room mesmerized for the whole show."[16]

With three EPs under their belt and a dedicated following, The Frightnrs were at the forefront of new bands in New York's thriving reggae scene, yet

★ ★ ★ ★ ★ ★

they actively shirked its ska-punk and rasta trends by going for a distinctly late-60s, early-70s vibe with rub-a-dub overtones. Axelrod had used The Frightnrs' rhythm section for a handful of his Inversions reggae records over the years, and produced two of the band's singles: "Admiration," released on DJ/producer Diplo's Mad Decent label, and a tearjerker cover of "I'd Rather Go Blind," which he handed over to Gabe Roth.

The label head had been looking for a rocksteady band for years (rocksteady being the sweetest form of Jamaican soul), and he'd even recorded a never-released rocksteady version of James Hunter's *Whatever It Takes* featuring the harmonic Greg Lee and Alex Désert of Hepcat. Yet nothing ever felt quite right until that Frightnrs demo. The band quickly got to work recording *Nothing More To Say*—their first studio record and the first full-length produced by Ticklah for Daptone after two decades of association—which created a fair amount of pressure for everyone involved. Axelrod spent two days setting up the House Of Soul studio to his meticulous standards before the four Frightnrs (brothers Preet and Chuck Patel, Richard Terrana, and Klein) arrived, and each day he spent hours adjusting for the session.

"[Victor] would say one or two things and all of us would have lightbulbs above our heads," organist Chuck Patel told the *Observer*. "He instantly got us and helped us do what we wanted to do ... he's our producer, but we kind of treat him as the [fifth] member of our band." Drummer Terrana continued, "In the morning we would come in ready to play it really fresh, but by the time Victor was ready to record and had all the sounds ready, we were exhausted to play the same song over and over again. It ended up in us getting this laid-back, very relaxed sound."[17]

Klein wrote nearly two dozen songs ahead of recording, but the twelve on *Nothing More To Say*—a majority of originals, and mostly painful love songs that draw a parallel between modern day New York and late 1960s Kingston, Jamaica—embody Daptone's particular lo-fi sparseness. Yet the record is sumptuous and awash in dub, and guaranteed to make a home stereo feel swollen with sound. It's a favorite of Gabe Roth's (one of perhaps

★ ★ ★ ★ ★ ★

five Daptone LPs he says he'll actually listen to for enjoyment), but the otherwise smooth record is laced with an audible schism—an enigmatic vocal tone that belies a deep sadness.

In the middle of The Frightnrs' weeklong recording session, Klein's voice began to keen; he seemed out of it, and he was walking slowly with a hunch. "To be honest, Dan can be a real complainer, so we all chucked it up to him pulling his [expletive] at the worst possible time," Axelrod later told the *New York Times*. None of us had any idea what was really going on."[18] By the end of the summer, Klein had quit his job and was falling down regularly—a phenomenon he chalked up to a chiropractic issue—and by the autumn, his mobility had deteriorated so that the now incredibly thin thirty-three-year-old was using a walker. In November 2015, Klein learned he had ALS—a degenerative and fast-moving disease that weakens muscles and other bodily functions.

Although his bandmates and friends would describe him as loving but negative, the period around the *Nothing More To Say* recording and his ALS diagnosis forced positivity out of Brukky. "I literally don't have time to not enjoy my life," he told the *Times*, recalling that he drew strength from his band. He once told them, "I'm high right now because you guys are here."[19]

As Brukky made peace with the disease that would eventually kill him by getting tattoos and spending time with his friends, Axelrod and Roth rushed to ready the album for release before Klein died, using demos and early takes to round out lead vocals he was no longer capable of singing.

"It was a horrible feeling to work with," Axelrod told NPR. "It felt ugly and surreal for all of us in the final months of completing the record. It felt like we all had fifty-pound weights strapped to our chests while we did it."[20] That heart-heavy feeling wasn't exclusive to Klein's illness, though the label and much of New York's reggae scene were despairing.

While the House Of Soul was busy recording the tough sounds of The Frightnrs, Sharon Jones & The Dap-Kings had spent the summer dipping in and out of the festival circuit with blues-rockers Tedeschi

★ ★ ★ ★ ★ ★

Trucks Band on their Wheels Of Soul tour. That September, Sharon Jones was backstage at the Toronto International Film Festival, where she was set to debut the Barbara Kopple–directed documentary *Miss Sharon Jones!* The day prior, Jones had learned that the cancer—which Kopple lovingly depicted as being crushed to a pulp beneath the singer's low-heeled stage shoe—had returned. She would start a new round of chemotherapy the following week.

"Sharon's whole thing was like, *I'm not gonna lie to anyone, I'm not gonna lie to my fans. I'm not gonna get up there and say I'm okay when I'm not,*" Austen Holman recalls. Standing next to oncologist Dr. James Leonardo, Sharon announced her prognosis onstage and promised that she would continue to give the people what they wanted—her song and spirit. "I'm gonna keep fighting. We got a long way to go." True to her word, Sharon Jones & The Dap-Kings performed in Ontario that same night. Her voice ever strong, Jones's eyes were heavy, and she felt pins and needles through her hands and feet.

CHAPTER THIRTEEN I'M STILL HERE: DAPTONE'S STARS FIGHT FOR THEIR LIVES

By 2015, Daptone had well established its belief that age ain't nothing but a number when dealing in the intergenerational power of soul music. Yet the label was reckoning with some of the more serious aspects of aging—for a second time. As *Miss Sharon Jones!* gained critical acclaim alongside documentaries about established divas Mavis Staples and Nina Simone released the same year, the label was busy course-correcting its marketing and promo plans for SJDK. The push for *It's A Holiday Soul Party!*—a Christmas record that carried the lighted string in the great the tradition of soulful holiday albums—would give Sharon some time to recover from surgery and another bout of chemotherapy. The album's bubble-gummy "8 Days Of Hanukkah" (a tribute to the Jewish heritage of a handful of band members) was animated to 70s pop perfection, working toward holiday classic status. The record also featured cheeky yuletide flair like "Big Bulbs" and a radio-friendly cover of "White Christmas"—which SJDK performed during an NPR *Tiny Desk* holiday special.

Much as the label did during Jones's first cancer battle, Daptone wisely looked for licensing opportunities, which included putting out an animated video for *Holiday Soul*'s "Ain't No Chimneys" and featuring in Netflix's adaptation of the Marvel comic *Luke Cage*, which brought Sharon & co to the stage of a swanky fictional Harlem nightclub alongside Charles Bradley, The Delfonics, Raphael Saadiq, and Faith Evans.

★ ★ ★ ★ ★ ★

Meanwhile, Daptone's second-biggest star was working on a third record, *Changes*, and utilizing additional writers. Although Charles Bradley had recently broken with Alex Kadvan's management, thus making a mess for the other groups his songwriting partner Tom Brenneck was involved in, Tommy stuck with him: "I went ahead and produced Charles's record because no matter how mad I was at him, I could not *not* make music with him. His voice lives inside of my head," says Brenneck, whose manager was furious. "It was a super-turbulent time; he was touring with the group that I wasn't in. I actually didn't get to produce the whole album: [Charles's management] kind of took it away from me and added some songs. On the first two records I really had, like, full control which makes it easier for me to be proud of. *Changes* is a bit of a mess for me; it was super rushed."

Released in April 2016, *Changes* was a typical (though not exhaustive) blend of funk and sorrowful soul born from Bradley's guts, as well as James Brown–inspired groovers like "Ain't It A Sin," which pit nasty, honking horns against the singer's potent, stage-induced sexuality. And at a time when the country was on the precipice of almost inconceivable tumult—Donald Trump would announce his presidential campaign just two months later—the album opens with a hopeful, gospel-tinged take on "God Bless America." The singer introduces himself as "an old brother from the hard licks of life / That knows that America is my home," one which had been "real honest, hurt and sweet to me." But Charles wouldn't trade his life story, quietly proclaiming that the most painful parts of his life had given him strength as well as the faith that America "represents love for all humanity and the world."

Charles Bradley had, to say the least, been put through the wringer before landing onstage in his mid-sixties, and he was dealt another blow in 2014 when his mother passed away. Inez Bradley, whom Charles had grown extremely close to in recent years after being estranged from her for most of his life, died on the same night he was set to headline a sold-out show at the Bowery Ballroom. Just getting to the Manhattan venue took all of Bradley's emotional will. "His mom was older aged and she

★ ★ ★ ★ ★ ★

died in the house," Sharon Jones recounted. "I heard her body was still there—he had to leave his mother's body to go do the show. I was proud of him. I told him, 'Be strong, do what you gotta do.'"[1] A year later, Charles anchored his third album with an impossibly heart-wrenching cover of Black Sabbath's 1972 ballad "Changes"—an emotional tribute to his late mother.

"When we first started playing 'Changes,' none of us liked it," says Extraordinaires trumpeter Billy Austik. "It was too slow, and The Budos Band backed him on it in studio, so it always seemed a little different. We never quite figured out how to play it. Then he turned the lyrics to make it about his mom and was able to find his meaning in it. And once he found his meaning in that song, we found our meaning. We would end every show with that song, and I think it was one of the best because he was able to really just break it down to the core and connect with everyone. Black Sabbath even tweeted at him."

After the management shakeup, Brenneck only saw Charles Bradley perform live once, when he and The Budos Band shared a bill. "Most of the set I was just talking shit about the band, how shitty they sounded, and that they couldn't play songs right. And then they played 'Changes' and we all started crying. And it was just like, okay, we can sit here and talk shit about the band as much as we want but Charles fucking got it with tears."

Charles and his Extraordinaires hit the road hard touring *Changes*, racking up famous fans such as Bill Murray, Margo Price, and Helen Mirren along the way; actor Craig Ferguson from the TV show *The Office* randomly announced Bradley's encore during a show in Santa Cruz, California. Yet the singer was still battling demons. Even having achieved international fame and a sincere adoration for his visceral, soul-shaking performances, he was never without a sense of ache. "My life is just truly bittersweet," he told me for a 2016 *Vice* article. "I'm still going through my emotional changes deep inside of me. I'm hoping this album can help me with my life. I hope I can just keep going. Sometimes I want to just run and hide and fade away from the world, but ... I think the world wants

★ ★ ★ ★ ★ ★

me, so I'll just find a way to open my heart and keep going forward." Charles Bradley had officially arrived, a pure but complicated man leading a soul revolution that needed "to come back. Because today's music ain't got the same soul," he continued. "What I've been hearing from peoples is, 'Charles, we needed you a long time ago.' You come out with truth and your hope and your heart, and that's what the world needs today."[2]

Where Bradley carried a sizeable emotional weight—one that could be gutting but still left fans wanting more—it wasn't all heavy in the Daptone universe. The label was cooking up new records and doing sessions, while announcing new releases and another imprint. In addition to *Daptone Gold Vol. 2*—a compilation with a couple of new tunes thrown in for good measure—the label released *Panola County Spirit*, the third in a series of traditional gospel field recordings from Mississippi that provided further connection between spirituals and contemporary soul. Back up north, the House Of Soul studio was buzzing with fuzzed-out guitar and soulful screams and awash in the influence of 70s art-punk from local garage-rock bands The Mystery Lights and The Jay-Vons (a rock and soul quartet featuring Daptone Production Manager Mikey Post on drums), as well as The Ar-Kaics from Richmond, Virginia. Those groups would provide the first four releases on Wick Records, a long-in-the-works rock imprint spearheaded by Post and songwriter/head engineer Wayne Gordon—a Daptonian take on the rough and raw, often raucous, sometimes understated underground rock scene.

Gordon and Post started as Daptone interns around the same time, each working on a different floor of the crammed building on Troutman, and soon became friends. "He wanted to get into recording," Post says, "and my band, The Reigning Sound, wanted to record. Gabe would let Wayne record us after hours for free so he would get practice using the equipment and we'd get free recording time. And while we were doing that, we would talk about how we'd love to do a rock label at Daptone. I

★ ★ ★ ★ ★ ★

love soul music, it's my life, but I come from a rock'n'roll background, and most of the bands I play with are rock bands."

When the five-piece Mystery Lights—whose garage teen-beat single "Too Many Girls" backed by the swampy psychedelia of "Too Tough To Bear" was Wick's first release—first came by the House Of Soul, they were treated to a deep hang soundtracked by 60s rockers The Remains and The Standelles. "We had always been huge fans of Daptone and loved the fact that you could go into a record store and into the Daptone section and pick out anything and know that it's going to be a good soul record," Mystery Lights frontman Mike Brandon told the *Guardian*, adding that they felt an instantly familial vibe.[3] Neal Sugarman, too, grew up on rock and punk. "Wick is just something diverse," he says. "If there was a rock band we liked, it could've been on Daptone, but it didn't make sense. This is fun—we love record labels and we love record labels with a brand that have a certain sound. It's no different than Stax and Volt, or Gordy and Motown; a lot of labels did it."

In a parallel universe with a bigger stage, Daptone players and extended family had formed The Arcs, a psychedelic-rock-meets-cinematic soul band that sounded like a more spiritual Black Keys—likely because it was fronted by The Black Keys' own Dan Auerbach. Having called on Leon Michels, Nick Movshon, and Homer Steinweiss for a variety of projects over the years (including Lana Del Ray's *Honeymoon* and Dr. John's 2012 album *Locked Down*, which also featured Poets Of Rhythm drummer Max Weissenfeldt), Auerbach's utility players had long since become friends. And while some friends work on cars together or play games and drink beer, this crew spent their free time making records—while also drinking.

"We'd been recording for years and compiling these demos," Auerbach says from his antique and ephemera-laden Easy Eye Studios. "We would get together sporadically, just for fun, just to record. I would go to New York and the guys would come to Nashville—and we didn't really have any rhyme or reason for it. And then we just decided to put an album together because that's what we liked to do. I've just known those guys in some

★ ★ ★ ★ ★ ★

sort of capacity for so many years and I love what each of them brings. Everybody in the room made my favorite records and getting to create with all those people is just, like, pure joy."

Yours, Dreamily was produced by Auerbach and released in 2015, featuring two drummers (the second being Richard Swift, a multi-instrumentalist who toured with The Shins and The Black Keys) and members of all-female mariachi band Flor De Toloache. The album received much positive press, and the collective did small tours in addition to releasing a handful of singles. But while Auerbach insisted that The Arcs were a full-fledged band and not a Black Keys side project, its members were soon pulled into other production and performance obligations.

Studio work continued to keep Daptone's large family of musicians busy. Steinweiss lent his unique drum sound to rock duo The Kills and played on the Bruno Mars song "Perm," a lesser-known track from *24K Magic*; Gabe arranged for British rock'n'soul group The Heavy, while the Dap-King horns played on Sturgill Simpson's *A Sailor's Guide To Earth*. Tom Brenneck, Victor Axelrod, Roth, Ian Hendrickson-Smith, and Antibalas guitarist Luke O'Malley all worked on the soundtrack to the aesthetically pleasing (but ultimately canceled) 1970s-set HBO show *Vinyl*.

When the Wu-Tang's Ghostface Killah teamed up with Canadian instrumental hip-hop group BadBadNotGood to record *Sour Soul*—an album heavily inspired by 70s funk and jazz—producer Frank Dukes called on Daptone to bring the soul sounds, not samples, to life. Brenneck, Extraordinaires DeBoe and Austik, as well as Wayne Gordon and Budos saxophonist Jared Tankel all worked on the record, enlivening *Sour Soul*'s immersive arrangements. "Frank Dukes came to our studio to basically learn how old records are made," Steinweiss recalls, noting that the Grammy-nominated Dukes also produced for Drake, Post Malone, Cardi B, and Frank Ocean. "He was like, *I sample records and now I want to make new records*. He really liked Menahan Street Band, so he finds us, who are making records that sound old."

Visiting the House Of Soul studio "opened my eyes to a different way of recording," Dukes told the *Toronto Star*. Soon after, he began recording live music and making original samples. "A new period of collaboration opened up a lot of doors for me. It evolved the way I look at the whole process: putting all the pieces together in a way that is greater than the sum of all its parts."[4]

Singles kept coming, too. Daptone distributed a fast-selling northern soul 45 called "Light Of My Life" from local act Benjamin & The Right Direction on Palmetto Records, while Dunham issued a seven-inch from family band The Sha La Das—a soulful take on California coastal sounds and very reminiscent of the Beach Boys.

In spring 2016, Sugarman, Antibalas's Aaron Johnson and Michael Leonhart (now Steely Dan's musical director), Lee Fields drummer Evan Paznner, and the Michels-Movshon-Steinweiss-Guy collective assembled to create a "temple of sound" as The Olympians. Originally dreamed up by keys/vibraphone player Toby Pazner during a 2008 tour in Greece, the resulting self-titled album was wistful and astral, a lush orchestration with hints of strings and the bombastic horns Daptone fans would expect from an instrumental band.

Meanwhile, Sharon Jones was eager to get back to music after a brief period off the road. "Not too long after her surgery she was back, and everyone was like, *Let's go, Sharon wants to go*. All she wanted to do was be onstage; she wanted to perform," manager Austen Holman remembers. True to form, Jones spent precious little time recuperating, and by the fall of 2015 was doing a West Coast tour, proving the message in the newly released, bluesy defiant "I'm Still Here"—an autobiographical single in the vein of "Longer And Stronger" that was released alongside *Miss Sharon Jones!*

Although Jones continued to perform with her trademark verve, hitting several New York stages in December, the illness was beginning to wear on her. Monophonics' Kelly Finnigan recalls seeing her on the street in Brooklyn that December. "We had played the Apollo the night before,

★ ★ ★ ★ ★ ★

and I was super-excited to tell her that, 'cause I knew she knew the feeling quite well. But you could tell she was going through it."

Following a similar crowd to that of Tedeschi Trucks Band, Sharon Jones & The Dap-Kings joined Hall & Oates on a nationwide spring tour that would have the band sandwiched between the blue-eyed soul duo and Trombone Shorty & Orleans Avenue at venues from Madison Square Garden to the less storied Florida State Fairgrounds in Tampa. Jones was playful and generally energetic during those early shows opening for Hall & Oates—her smile wide, her hair grown out into a small but tight natural, her vigor seemingly undiminished.

"It was only really in that last year that suddenly I was just like, *I'm really lucky to see this every night*," Binky Griptite reflects quietly. "And not just with Sharon. I remember this one time, Starr leaned back to hit this one note. I was just like, *I have a really good seat for this point*."

While SJDK's commitment to showmanship knew no bounds—their fury unleashed on every stage, regardless of audience or inevitable technical issue—the band achieved new heights on a warm June night in 2016 as the opening act of the Celebrate Brooklyn! festival. Performing to a packed hometown crowd at the intimate Prospect Park bandshell was particularly special, and called for a full family lineup. SJDK set up for two drummers—Steinweiss and longtime touring player Brian Wolfe—and were joined by Axelrod on organ, as well as nearly two dozen horns and drums, to play the massive, symphonic, and vaguely militaristic "Soul Fugue." Saun & Starr sang cuts from *Look Closer* before Griptite big-upped Sharon, who leapt onstage and into "Stranger To My Happiness" from *Give The People What They Want*.

"Sharon had just turned up to another level because, at that point, she had nothing to lose," remembers Jacob Blickenstaff, who was unsure whether he'd be shooting the show until he caught a contact high from Sharon's energy. "And she was gonna turn up the brightness of what she was doing to whatever her limit was. The band would be synced up and Sharon was the turbo boost on the car. She force-fed this energy that got

★ ★ ★ ★ ★ ★

them all going and made them perform at their best. And that allowed her to perform at *her* best. I think she just realized that the time we have is precious—so everyone was more attuned, more empathetic to what she's feeling and going through."

If the audience wasn't already bowled over by Sharon Jones's energy and the excitement of The Dap-Kings, Griptite was quick to remind the sold-out crowd, "You just got your ass kicked by a sixty-year-old cancer patient."

The Celebrate Brooklyn! performance was also a special one for Dan Klein, who attended despite concerns regarding his deteriorated health. He watched the show from a wheelchair, beaming with excitement, and sent congratulatory after-show texts to both Gabe Roth and Ticklah. By the following morning, Klein had died in his sleep at age thirty-four. *Nothing More To Say* was released three months later, a deeply bittersweet success that fulfilled Brukky's wishes to *go out with a bang*, even if he wouldn't live to enjoy it.[5]

Blickenstaff—similarly invigorated by Sharon's indomitable spirit—followed SJDK through the rest of the summer as they toured with Hall & Oates. The band hit a string of outdoor venues during what they jokingly referred to as the "No Limits" tour for the seemingly infinite amount of weed floating around. Guitarist John Oates became particularly friendly with the band, which was working up a cover of a northern soul single he cut in 1966 as The Masters called "I Need Your Love." Oates played the rare tune during one of SJDK's opening sets, sending The Dap-Kings into fits of record-collecting nerdom.

Although she remained ever committed to the show, the now-bald Sharon was showing signs of fatigue. She could no longer wear heels, and she needed to strut atop a carpet rather than the bare stage. She didn't have energy for certain songs or the hour-plus sets she once thrived in, and each performance required her to muster more strength by homing in on both good and bad feelings. Backstage, personal assistant/merch manager Abbey Simmons and day manager Megan Frestedt rubbed Sharon's taut

★ ★ ★ ★ ★ ★

legs and numb feet, and sometimes administered medicine—two of the many people behind the scenes sharing the burden of the singer's feelings and pain.

The last time Blickenstaff found himself alone with Jones was in Nobelsville, Indiana. His stark and intimate images show Sharon in an unglamorous, summer steam–filled dressing room, her face gaunt and body thin, prepping for a performance that would be both triumphant and exhausting. "In the dressing room she was saying, *I want to keep going as long as I can to give all the people around me stuff to work with and keep going after*. She had a very acute sense of her mortality and this very generous desire to leave things behind that people could keep," he says, with the caveat that the singer wasn't hopeless. "There was positivity in both of those acts. She was affirming that she wanted to keep doing everything she could, as long as she could, for herself and for others. That's what the performance was. She needed those performances; it took away her pain and made the suffering and discomfort on a daily basis worth it."

Yet SJDK traveled on two busses—the guys' bus acting as the hang, with records, weed, the occasional haircut from Starr to keep everyone looking sharp, and food (guitarist Joe Crispiano got really into making pancakes during that tour). Sharon, Saun, and Starr traveled on a quiet bus with Abbey, making Sharon's care somewhat separate from the rest of the band. "The guys all loved her in their own way, but just like a kid, they can shut down a little bit from their own feelings," the photographer speculates. "It's hard to talk about; you just want to be there with them and kind of have everything feel normal. Sharon wasn't, like, stoically hiding anything, but everyone had a desire to have a certain kind of normal routine." After all, the singer told Terry Gross, "I don't wanna be home, just taking medicine and waiting to die... I just want to be onstage and moving."[6]

Part of that routine entailed making time to record new music. The band would fit in sessions whenever they could, though finding studio time was always difficult as the eleven-piece toured heavily and Sharon considered her priorities. Recording the songs that would fill *Soul Of A Woman*, SJDK's seventh studio album, came with a sharp sense of timeliness. However, Sharon needed to convalesce after the intense performance schedule (often four shows in a row), which was particularly difficult on her body as she underwent chemo and radiation for an increasing amount of tumors. Where concerts were Sharon's true opportunity to lose herself and touch her audience, recording could feel tedious, and the singer's occasionally stubborn, diva-like tendencies became more frequent.

"There's always an urgency to that process, just because whatever you're working on is fresh and new, and everyone's anxious to bring it to people," says Roth. "Obviously, when Sharon got real sick, we were anxious to get it finished and out. She wanted to sing those on the road." Sharon did bring some of *Soul Of A Woman*'s songs to audiences, including the particularly moving ballad "These Tears," a symphonic and devastating song of loss that Roth and company were considering developing into a larger album concept. Although she always preferred up-tempo numbers, an album of ballads and strings might have been a fitting theme for the distressing possibilities lurking in the periphery.

"It's been a while since I've been outside and seen the sun," Sharon said casually, under a blanket of rare Northwest sunshine, to a particularly excited audience outside Seattle's KEXP radio that May, before Saun & Starr began harmonizing the opening bars of "These Tears."[7] Yet as *Miss Sharon Jones!* director Barbara Kopple told *Rolling Stone*, "There wasn't a minute where she thought she wasn't going to get better. She was striving because she wanted to be on the stage even when sometimes the news wasn't that good."[8]

As Sharon Jones & The Dap-Kings wrapped up their time with Hall & Oates—returning to New York to rest and reconvene in the already busy studio after canceling a summer European tour—the label was dealt another blow. The year 2016 had taken Charles Bradley & The Extraordinaires from Alaska to Ecuador, then to New York and out to Europe; they spent

★ ★ ★ ★ ★ ★

nine months touring *Changes*, with little time between shows to rest. The band were nearly done with the summer leg of the tour in Europe, where they had played a string of outdoor festivals, and were up early waiting in their hotel lobby to move onto the next gig when they saw Charles being pulled out of the building on a stretcher.

"I had no idea what had happened—I was stunned," DeBoe remembers. "He had a really high fever and had struggled through the night to sleep. They took him to the hospital, and he had to stay there for a few days." The band canceled performances in Dublin and London, though they still traveled to England for a radio interview. "We visited him in the hospital, and then there were a couple days in London where he wasn't able to see anybody. Eventually, he was cleared to fly, and they flew him back to New York. And it was unclear to us for about a week what had happened to him, how he was doing or what was going to happen next."

Bradley visited multiple hospitals in New York before being diagnosed with stomach cancer. On September 28, 2016, The Extraordinaires were prepping to open for Miike Snow at Radio City Music Hall—one of the largest venues they had played to date—when Charles shared his diagnosis. "We all kind of knew it was something bad, because he was having some issues, but we didn't know it was gonna be that bad," Austik says. "That was kind of in the background: *I hope it's not cancer*. That show was super emotional for everyone. We couldn't cry so performing was like the outlet for us."

Like his soul sister, the Screaming Eagle underwent chemotherapy and surgery to remove most of the cancer. During the months Bradley spent recovering, Austik opened a local PO box for fans to send goodwill letters. "It was nuts," he recalls. "Every week I would go down there and then walk to his house and bring him the letters. People sent some really cool stuff: little gifts, really thoughtful letters, music, food, everything."

That cancer had put the kibosh on six months of planned tours – including runs in Europe, Australia, and India—caused Charles great anger, and depression. "He wanted to go to India; he wanted to do all the

★ ★ ★ ★ ★ ★

shows. He felt like he was letting all these people down," DeBoe remembers. "That was just his personality. Like, he was given this opportunity and he wanted to make the most of it and didn't want to stop. He wanted to die onstage, kind of. Sharon was a similar way."

After six months of convalescing, Bradley's booking agent asked whether he wanted to take the rest of 2017 off or get back on the road. Charles chose the stage, expressing his gratitude and excitement in a Facebook post that May: "I am so grateful to my beautiful fans and touched by all the love and support they showed me through my crisis and time of sickness. They truly lifted me up and kept me going. I am honored and glad to be back and am going to give you all of my love."

The band's first show back, according to Austik, "was crazy, just because we had gone so long without playing. Having Charles back out there was a special show, for sure. Just to get back to that level."

After some pitstops, the soul train was again chugging along. Yet away from the road, the natural habitat for many of Daptone's musicians, some of the label's most painful moments existed in the awkward balancing of business and personal needs. Whatever tepid complacency had developed was regularly shaken by conflict calls, staff meetings, social media posts, and release dates—all of which had to be negotiated with care. Daptone's in-house and contracted teams had to determine when it would be appropriate to announce a new record when someone else was publicly handling hardship. How do you keep fans informed about changes with their favorite artists without ruining your label's distribution deals?

"You want to be successful and do the business right; it's very hard to work on that stuff when your friends are sick and dying," Roth says matter-of-factly. By September 2016, Austen Holman wasn't taking those crisis calls. She had moved to Los Angeles and was no longer managing Sharon Jones (though she did continue to work with Antibalas and The Budos Band, marrying one of its members). She and husband Jared Tankel had snagged great seats to see SJDK open for Hall & Oates at the Hollywood Bowl, but the singer "was really not well. She had to go off stage and

★ ★ ★ ★ ★ ★

take oxygen. I remember going backstage to see her afterward, and Sharon was just *white*. And I remember thinking, *This doesn't feel good*," Holman recalls tearfully. "To see her at a time where she was really not doing well but still trying to perform was hard to watch."

Los Angeles promoter/booker Nancy Arteaga would drop everything to see SJDK live, and she had been faithfully championing Daptone for years. But the memories that stand out most from 2016 are of watching Sharon from side stage, taking oxygen during instrumental breaks. "That's the part when I knew my superhero was running out of batteries—like, *Oh my god, she's still sick*," Arteaga reminisces. "I didn't think it was gonna end. It was like water—you didn't ever think there was not going to be enough for everyone."

A few days later, SJDK were performing in Las Vegas, at the MGM Grand Garden Arena—a venue on the Strip about three-quarters the size of Madison Square Garden—and Sharon was still struggling to maintain her next-level energy. Griptite remembers watching her stop to talk to a few fans as the band crossed the casino floor to get to their hotel rooms. "Those were the last fans that she talked to at a gig," he says. "I wonder if they know that."

CHAPTER FOURTEEN KEEP PUTTING SOUL UP: SOUL'S BIGGEST LABEL LOSES ITS STARS

Back in 2012, Sharon Jones & The Dap-Kings traveled to the Kennedy Center in Washington, DC, to revive Marvin Gaye's storied 1971 performance of *What's Going On*. After an opening set, Sharon Jones joined headliner John Legend—already a nine-time Grammy winner whose silken vocals laid over piano lent to the notion that he was Gaye's modern equivalent, not to mention equally pop friendly—for a set of Marvin and Tammi duets. Backed by the National Symphony Orchestra, Jones and Legend conjured their forebears for covers of "Ain't Nothing Like the Real Thing," "Ain't No Mountain High Enough," and "If I Could Build My Whole World Around You," their voices a complementary blend of lounge smooth and showcase bombastic.

The Legend duet was one of Sharon's favorite big gigs, and one she would revisit in 2014 with the LA Philharmonic, but perhaps the bigger get was a chance to meet First Lady Michelle Obama. Sharon "definitely told Michelle, 'Get us in the White House,'" Roth said at the time. "As far as [President Obama] ... everyone has seen him online singing Al Green songs, so I assume we aren't too far outside of his tastes."[1] As a testament to the import of that gig, a framed thank-you letter from the First Lady lived among other souvenirs and career highlights in Sharon's yellow family house in North Augusta, down the street from her childhood Baptist church.

★ ★ ★ ★ ★ ★

At the end of his second term, President Obama announced that he would host the first festival at the White House: South By South Lawn, a mix of "ideas, art, and action" organized by the makers of South By Southwest. The October 3 event would feature bands such as Gallant and The Lumineers, a spoken-word performance by Common, an NPR *Tiny Desk* recording of Robert Glasper inside the White House, as well as appearances by the cast of Netflix show *Stranger Things* and Leonardo DiCaprio.

After years of begging (or, rather, playfully pestering) Kadvan to get Sharon Jones & The Dap-Kings to perform for the Obamas, Roth remembers, "We finally got the call. They wanted her to come, but said they didn't have room for the whole band—just her and, like, four or five guys." Jones was obstinate, refusing to perform at SXSL unless the whole band could come. "She was like, *This is my family, if my family's not good enough for the White House, I'm not going*," the label head continues, his voice still recalling a mix of astonishment and awe that Sharon would be so bold as to turn down the president. "And everybody was like, *Yo, Sharon, you better go to the White House. We don't give a fuck, man*. Any of us were all down to bow out; it was so important for us that she go to the White House. Like, *don't give them a hard time, just get in there and we'll go with you next time*. And she was fucking adamant, you know, which drove Alex crazy. He had to go back to the fucking White House to tell them, but eventually they said, *Okay, bring the whole band*."

Despite her insistence on attending the White House event as a family, the powerhouse singer was conspicuously absent from the festivities. Instead of joining the band for a performance on the South Lawn, or shaking hands with President Obama, Jones spent the October afternoon recovering from pneumonia at home in Augusta, Georgia. Most of the band didn't want to go without the singer's 110 pounds of soul dynamite, but Jones insisted that they represent. "She told us she would never forgive us," says a resigned Roth. "She said she wouldn't go back onstage with us again if we didn't go play it without her—so we had to go play without her."

★ ★ ★ ★ ★ ★

Even as the band snuggled tight next to the president for a photo op in the Blue Room, with Saun & Starr beaming on either side of Obama, Jones's absence was palpable. What was supposed to be a triumphant event for Sharon was reduced to a group phone call made on speakerphone from the White House lawn. President Obama wrote Sharon Jones a get-well note the same day, sharing his hope for a speedy recovery and that "we have a chance to see you perform in the future." The whole event was really difficult, Roth says quietly. "It was really a bittersweet thing. It was amazing but also really sad not to have her there. That was kind of the beginning of the end."

Sharon Jones's health had taken a turn for the worse by November, and Holman had purchased a flight back east to see her friend. "I was going to go to her house and thought I'd get to hang with her, spend some time together. When I landed in New York I was calling to find out what time I could come over, and was told that I had to go to the hospital." Jones had suffered a stroke on November 8—election night—and joked that the election of Donald Trump was the root cause; another stroke on November 9 left the singer unable to talk or move much. "She was totally out of it, and as time went on she was losing more and more of herself," says Holman, who recalls holding Sharon's hand at her bedside in Cooperstown's Bassett Medical Center. "We loved singing 'Midnight Train To Georgia' on those road trips that we took, and so I started singing." Jones, who was mostly unconscious, started to stir. "And I was like, *Oh my god, did she just hum?*"

Holman and Roth left Jones's bedside to attend a nearby screening and Q&A of *Miss Sharon Jones!*, doing their best to pretend the film's star wasn't dying minutes away; when they returned to Bassett Medical, the entire band had arrived. Binky quietly strummed his guitar, playing Sharon's favorite gospel songs—"His Eye Is On The Sparrow," "Go Tell It On the Mountain," and "This Little Light of Mine"—and whenever the music would stop, she'd pick up a few lines of "Amazing Grace." Finally exhausted but still stubborn, Sharon was determined to commit the ultimate hyperbole: she would die singing.

★ ★ ★ ★ ★ ★

"She was humming, but in the most soulful way," Holman says through tears. "It was her spirit, like, pushing through whatever was going on with her body. And it was the most amazing, beautiful thing. It was such a testament to who she was as a person—this was a woman with a spirit that you could not hold down."

After a valiant battle, Sharon Jones succumbed to cancer at age sixty on November 18, 2016, surrounded by her sister Willa and niece Gene, friend Megan Holken, as well as Alex Kadvan, Megan Frestedt, and Abbey Simmons. News of her passing spread quickly—any DJ with a soulful bone in their body and a gig on the 18th played nothing but Sharon Jones tunes; tributes and remembrances were published in nearly every music blog and paper of record, including *Rolling Stone*, the *New York Times*, *Pitchfork*, and the *Los Angeles Times*. Throughout, Jones was heralded as a powerhouse singer, a transformative "comeback queen," and the "twenty-first-century godmother of soul." The loss of Sharon's dynamic energy created a collective feeling of mourning.

"I was devastated for those guys," says DJ Matt Weingarden. "I was worried that it was going to be the end. I mean, I knew that they had built up a business that wasn't completely reliant upon Sharon, but I was still worried about the future of Daptone. And just personally devastated for their loss." Yet the label received an avalanche of support after Sharon passed: words of encouragement flowed; flowers poured into the studio; donations were made to charities in the singer's name; and an enormous amount of orders came into the House Of Soul. "We've actually had to cancel recording sessions because our little house in Bushwick has been so overly jammed with outgoing packages full of records and merchandise that you can't walk into the studio," Roth wrote in a Daptone Records Instagram post. The whole of the label pitched in to pack boxes. Roth was in "awe of the amount of love, respect, and support that I am seeing... this is what's getting us through. Not just getting us through, but inspiring us to continue to do more."

A private burial was held, followed by public memorial services "to celebrate the singer's life and endless spirit" in Brooklyn and Augusta. New York's soul community (the entire Daptone family as well as Fine Wine, The Roots' Captain Kirk, DJ Jonathan Toubin, longtime supporter and WFUV radio host Rita Houston, and dozens of fans) packed Brown Memorial Baptist Church in the Clinton Hill neighborhood of Brooklyn to listen to tearful readings, performances of "His Eye Is On The Sparrow" from Jones's church choir, and happy memories from decades spent onstage. The service was led by Reverend Miller and Pastor Fields from Sharon's Universal Church Of God, and fittingly MC'd by Binky Griptite.

"It was amazing," Brenneck recalls. "I didn't know how he did it. I was crying the entire time, and Gabe did too." Speaking to the crowd of musical family and fans, Roth reflected on the constant refrain of, *We should have done this; we should have done more*. Working with Sharon for the better part of two decades was a blessing, he surmised, and as a whole, the group did so much.

"The thing that makes Daptone so special is they do not compromise," says Holman, who between tears read a poem called "Gone Fishin'" at the memorial. "They have had so many opportunities to do things for people and it just didn't feel right to them. It didn't feel authentic; it didn't feel like it was true to the way that they are as artists. You can imagine with seven different people, it gets hard to get everyone to agree on things, but everyone agreed on Sharon. And that's where the magic was." A year later, Holman would fulfill a promise and name her firstborn son after the singer—Jones.

Soon after Jones's memorial, Gabe Roth flew back to the West Coast, where he began mixing *Soul Of A Woman*—Sharon Jones & The Dap-Kings' final studio album. The album would be a fitting capstone for the band, its eleven songs showcasing their live, raw energy as well as their penchant for moodier, orchestrated string-driven ballads like the skin-tingling, hopeful yet melancholic "When I Saw Your Face." Prior to

★ ★ ★ ★ ★ ★

Sharon falling ill again, Daptone envisioned a record of slower songs that could possibly incorporate a string section or orchestra. Yet as it became clearer that the singer wouldn't survive, they pivoted to focus on up-tempo soul tunes like the leading single "Sail On!" and message songs like the Binky Griptite–penned "Matter Of Time." *Soul Of A Woman* also features tunes with Latin influence alongside the cheeky, *Schoolhouse Rock*–esque love song "Rumors." The album's closer, an impassioned but unvarnished gospel tune titled "Call On God," which Jones penned as a teenager, features several singers from her church choir. "I think she would have been really happy to know she had those women's voices on there," Roth told the *Irish Times*. "It was amazing for them too because they got to go into the studio and one last time put on the headphones and hear Sharon's voice and sing behind her."[2]

Soul Of A Woman also saw more of the band writing songs, each working at the height of their musicianship. "The band was really cresting onstage in the months before Sharon passed," Roth told me in an interview for *SF Weekly* ahead of the album's release. "As a show band, I don't think any band out there could have competed with us at that level. We hit the studio hot off the road and you could feel it in there."[3] But the heat was off in Roth's Riverside studio, where he mixed *Soul* alone, and in mourning, over several months. Although the end product was big, beautiful, and cathartic, each step of the process—from sifting through old photos for cover art, to doing interviews and sourcing press materials—held its own well of pain.

But, Roth was quick to note, no one can sit on their laurels. Business has to be taken care of. Roth recounts Sharon, near death but ever forceful, encouraging him to "'exploit the shit out of it. Whatever you can do to sell records.' And I was like, 'Dude, Sharon, I don't wanna hear that shit.' But there is no shame in selling those records. We worked really hard on them and want to share them. It's paying musicians and paying the people at Daptone," he says. "On the one side, you don't wanna deal with any of that. People I love are sick or passed away, and I wanna honor them and

★ ★ ★ ★ ★ ★

that's a private thing. On the other hand, you have a business and label and everyone's depending on that, and the fans want the music. It's a good thing to put those out there."

Soul Of A Woman was released nearly a year to the day of Sharon's death on November 17, 2017, its cover a throwback to Jones serenely basking in the warm glow of stage lights circa 2010. The release brought up a myriad of feelings for its players and those who handled publicity. "It's hard to think that we're not gonna play this music," said Sugarman, who had just finished a small tour with the Sugarman 3, on the eve of the album's release. "It's hard to know what's gonna happen with the band. Sometimes it's really just hard to take a step back when you're coming in here every day and grinding it out. But, looking back, especially with this last Sharon record, it's like, *Wow, we killed it.* It's a weird business because you have a lot of emotional connections to the music."[4]

If creating the record was emotionally and physically taxing, the alternative would have been even more gut-wrenching. "We did it for her and for ourselves," said Roth. "It's kind of delivering on a promise to Sharon to get her voice out, and delivering on a promise to her fans."[5]

Sharon Jones was the third Daptone musician to die in 2016. Pianist Cliff Driver passed away in March, at age eighty-five. Although he didn't have the same name recognition, Driver was an integral part of the Daptone family: he was Naomi Shelton & The Gospel Queens' musical director and bandleader for forty years, as well as an early mentor to Gabe Roth. Driver had a rich musical history prior to his work with Daptone and Desco—his band, The Ramrods, had a hit with the original *Soul Train* theme, and the blind piano player gigged with everybody from Ruth Brown to The Coasters to Tito Puente. "He was really a legend," Roth says. "I've known him longer than Sharon, and he was a real musical force and inspiration; he taught me a lot about music and gospel."

Driver's funeral was also a testament to his legacy of music and community, as Brenneck recalls. "The officiant at the service said, 'Will all the gospel queens stand up,' and all of a sudden, like, seventeen women

★ ★ ★ ★ ★ ★

scattered throughout the church stood up; it was incredible. Then you notice that there were like fucking twenty microphones set up across the front, and they all went up and sang a song. I was in the second row and bawling. I've never experienced anything like that; it was just so moving and just so impossible not to cry your ass off."

As the Daptone family mourned, Charles Bradley & The Extraordinaires continued to tour, until the Screaming Eagle got sick again. "We did it as long as we could, then it all happened really fast after that," Austik remembers. "The way it all went down was a little weird; I'm still not really sure about it. Charles was looking for treatment and, like, something happened with that and he went down the wrong path treatment-wise and it didn't work out."

A West Coast run would end up being the band's final tour, taking an ailing Bradley into the smoky mountains of Canada and the Pacific Northwest. "There were wildfires happening up in British Columbia, and the air of the whole northwest corner was really thick—not only were people blazing crazy amounts of joints, but it was hard to breathe," DeBoe recalls of a performance at the Pickathon festival on a wooded stage outside of Portland, Oregon. Standing behind Bradley as he wailed, bawled real tears, and dropped to his knees, the saxophonist says, "I was just amazed, thinking about everything that was happening and how he still sounded super strong. There was never any weakness shown." The final show of tour took Bradley and company into the ski town of Whistler, British Columbia where the high altitude and heavy smoke made for a difficult performance for everyone.

A couple of weeks after returning from the West Coast, Charles decided to go on an isolated retreat in Mexico, against the advice of his doctors. They had encouraged him to instead endure another round of chemotherapy that would prolong his life but wouldn't completely rid his body of cancer. "He didn't want to go through it all again, so he decided to go to this retreat, which was entirely holistic, all natural, and it was just very, very damaging," DeBoe says. "He wasn't on any medications, and

★ ★ ★ ★ ★ ★

he was away from everybody, scared. He was doing all these things that seemed very strange and foreign, and he was gone for two or three weeks. Nobody knew where he was—it was freaky, and a lot of us were really concerned about him. I know a lot of us were told not to say anything."

At some point, Charles reached out to an old neighbor, who picked the singer up outside of Juarez and drove him across the border. Bradley went into hospice care in a hospital in Fort Greene, Brooklyn, soon after. "We were just relieved that he was able to come back, because there were a lot of people who were really concerned about him," DeBoe says, remembering gathering at the hospice with members of his musical community as well as Bradley's family, friends, and neighbors. "The hospital was right next to Fort Greene Park," says Austik, "which is where I saw Charles for the first time in 2011, which was very full circle. And I told him that."

Musicians would sing and play songs for Bradley, DeBoe remembers. "One of my last memories is playing a Junior Walker tune that got his eyes open, got him moving a little bit. It's really hard to see somebody in that condition. I was able to see him like the night before he passed away."

On September 23, 2017, the Screaming Eagle Of Soul moved onto another plane. He was sixty-eight years old.

"It's so fucking crazy," Brenneck says. "I thought that me and Charles would write songs—I thought he would live to be, like, a hundred. I did not expect a friend to pass so soon. At all, at all. I think none of us thought that, because we were all really trying to just make the music that we loved, to fucking imitate the music that we were so obsessed with you know?"

Roth was a little more wary of Bradley's condition. "We weren't expecting it that particular month, but we knew he was sick. Especially coming off what we went through with Sharon, we were on some level prepared that he was fighting a similar battle. It's a lot of sadness dealing with the loss of everybody. These are people who were in with us, day to day."[6]

A memorial for Charles Bradley was held at Sugarhill supper club in Bed-Stuy. "It was really crazy emotional and fun, and we all got real wasted," Austik recalls. "All his family and friends were there, and they

★ ★ ★ ★ ★ ★

had the Essence band play from his James Brown days. Then we all sat down and played, and after went to [Fort Greene bar] Great Georgiana and spun records."

Although all the Extraordinaires had unique, close relationships with Charles, the singer and Tommy Brenneck shared a specific, inscrutable, and intense bond that went beyond music. Bradley was the godfather of Brenneck's first child and a fixture in his life beyond work. "I was paralyzed at Charles's funeral," he recalls, slowly drinking a strong beer. "I couldn't say anything else. I was completely broken and furious at the same time. I was so fucking angry, so upset. I couldn't say a word. I miss him. His birthday just passed, and I've been really in a rut. I find it more sad than his day of passing. My birthday is November 6, right after his birthday, November 5. And my one-year-old daughter's birthday is November 4. So it's a crazy wave of, like, I'm really happy for my daughter, then I'm really sad for Charles and very sad for myself."

Bradley remained a very real presence in Brenneck's life. "When he first passed, I'd be on these long drives and just talked to myself as if he was there. It's just kind of like, Charles is my fucking spirit guide now or something. If some lights flicker, even my son says, *It's ghost Uncle Charles.* Anything funky in the house, he blames Charles. He also predicted that me and my wife would have a daughter, which I thought was crazy. And lo and behold..."

Just as with *Soul Of A Woman*, Daptone prepped the release of a posthumous Charles Bradley record—fittingly titled *Black Velvet.* "That was really fucking awful to make," Brenneck says. "There's always a lot of emotion tied up in making music with Charles, and I don't think the music on *Black Velvet* is anything that glorious—it could have come out later. But Daptone kind of asked for it right away. I think they were going through it and just lost Sharon, and they were like, *Just collect all the old tracks and do it now*. And I was so fucking sad, with my head down for like two years, and I was just like, *Okay*, you know?"

Brenneck pored over old reels and demos, searching for unreleased

★ ★ ★ ★ ★ ★

songs and reliving the sometimes painful, sometimes magnificent memories of recording. "We make music in a frenzy sometimes—you mix it and never listen to it ever again. So, when I go back to the tapes, it's like a time machine. I remember everything about it, every note. I'm really attached to, like, everything on those records. In a way, I'm kind of glad I did *Black Velvet*, because lord knows I'm not gonna fucking revisit any of that shit." Brenneck continues, "When I'm done with a record, I mix the records, I attend the mastering session, then I listen to the test pressing of the vinyl and I never listen to it again."

Black Velvet was released in 2018; its ten tracks span the breadth of Bradley's Daptone career, though only three were previously unreleased. The final song on the album was an eponymous instrumental recorded when the former James Brown impersonator was too weak to sing. While most critics lavished praise on the record—particularly for its inventive twist on Nirvana's "Stay Away" and unique rendition of Neil Young's "Heart Of Gold"—some said the album-as-elegy didn't have the same tightness or cohesion of previous efforts, or capture the intensity of Bradley's stage presence.

Charles's creative partner never basked in the glory of their music, always assuming they could do better and that time would allow them to do so. Where Brenneck might be shy about this songwriting process with another singer, he and Charles were so comfortable that the music flowed. "He was my favorite singer to collaborate with because I could sing him a simple idea. Sharon was really hard to write for—she wanted an empowered female perspective and I like to usually write from a more sad perspective, which Charles just chewed up. So, pitching it to Charles and hearing him sing it back was like really one of the most thrilling things ever as a musician. There are very few singers that I'd be able to do that with."

Brenneck has an additional album's worth of unfinished music, which, like *Black Velvet*, was recorded while Charles was going through chemotherapy. "I would go visit him and kind of get an idea, then record it, but he was never healthy enough to sing on any of the stuff that I

★ ★ ★ ★ ★ ★

was recording," he says. "At that time, if I got time with him, I didn't particularly want to be fucking coaching him through vocal takes, especially when his voice sounded tired. So we would just hang out, talk and enjoy time together. We would mostly just cook and eat together—orange peel chicken was a Charles Bradley special. His favorite food's shrimp but I'm allergic, so he'd make a wicked fried chicken or macaroni and cheese."

Charles's death came as a shock to many fans who were keen to forget a string of canceled concerts due to illness in favor of the singer's larger-than-life, sometimes emotionally devastating performances. Seeing Charles Bradley perform was so spiritually ascendant, one could easily assume that he was divine, impervious to any more of life's adversities. But for members of the Daptone family, most of whom were still mourning the loss of Sharon, Charles's death was another step in the circle of life. Resigned and cautiously choosing his words, Roth takes a more macabre view. "Everybody kind of prepares for it differently. You try to be very positive and will your way through these things, but at the end of it... we're all dying on one level or another. None of this is forever."

Where some of the Dap-Kings had pop studio work, side projects, and, in the case of Binky Griptite, a paid DJ gig on Fordham University radio station WFUV, The Extraordinaires mostly relied on touring to make a living. Without Charles, the youngest generation of Daptone musicians also had to reevaluate. "You have all these guys who've basically sacrificed all their time and their lives to make it happen," DeBoe reflects. "It reaches a peak, and then something like this happens and it comes crashing down. The whole thing is kind of traumatic depending on how you handle it. It's a livelihood, for sure, but when you have a close relationship with that person, and they're gone, you look at your friendship more than you think about like, *Oh, man, I don't have a job anymore*."

Although being unemployed was scary, Austik contends, "Most of all, it was just being thankful for that time with him. Every person in the band felt lucky to have this gig. I think we all tried to see the bright side of it." Austik had opened Hive Mind Recording with bassist/engineer Vince

★ ★ ★ ★ ★ ★

Chiarito and saxophonist Mike Buckley—whose collective credits included work with Antibalas, Lee Fields, Austin-based psychedelic soul group Black Pumas, and Ikebe Shakedown—and before he died, Bradley came to the studio's opening party. The singer gifted Austik a bottle of wine, a stick of Palo Santo to clear any lingering negative energy in the space, and a fan-made portrait with a hundred-dollar bill in the frame of the picture.

Hive Mind had Charles Bradley's blessing, and when he died, Austik continues, "at that point we were home and interested in recording, mostly because of what we had been experiencing. We were so inspired and the idea for a studio had been brewing for a while off the road"—much as Steinweiss, Brenneck, and Leon Michels had done with Dunham Sound and Diamond Mine Studios.

DeBoe spent six months working locally before joining Lee Fields's touring band, then gigging with R&B crooner James Hunter Six—whose second Daptone LP, *Whatever It Takes*, was released in 2018. "Your life goes on," he says. "It was a pretty drastic thing for me for sure, but I was really lucky that I had a lot of close friends, guys that I played with, and a family. I really pushed my own project with [Dap-King] Joey Crispiano and other guys in the scene, and played for close friends." DeBoe and Crispiano performed instrumental R&B in the style of Junior Walker at local bars such as Freddy's in South Slope and Our Wicked Lady, a Bushwick bar-venue co-owned by Daptone tape-op Wayne Gordon.

Perhaps it's Daptone's punk ethos and its players' eternal surprise that their modern take on soul actually panned out that allows for a Vonnegutian, so-it-goes attitude. As deep grief and gratitude permeated the family—as well as among fans, who, despite a flowering soul scene, continued to mourn the loss of Charles Bradley and Sharon Jones—the next years required hustle. Survival would be sink or swim, with some musicians digging deeper into the world of revivalist sounds while others expanded their palates.

The Dap-Kings, once the gravitational center of the Daptone universe, were rethinking things without their brightest star. "Nothing goes on

★ ★ ★ ★ ★ ★

forever," Sugarman notes. "I think we had a longer run than most people do, but there was always the *what are we gonna do now?* People were coming out of the woodwork after Sharon passed," he adds, though no singer felt like the right person to support following the massive loss of a true showwoman. "There were a lot of expectations from people. I think our manager was hoping that we would have continued, and maybe we will."

Speaking between songs during a live performance on their local KEXP in 2017, True Loves drummer David McGraw said he was impressed by Daptone's strength through struggle. "No matter how difficult it is for them . . . every single one of those guys I've ever met . . . have such good attitudes. They're good people with great attitudes and keep it positive and forward thinking. They're very inspirational."[7]

Daptone also had to contend with the perception that, along with its biggest stars, the label itself was dying. But morale remained strong among its small staff; Mikey Post was quick to dismiss anyone who thought Daptone Records would fade into a saccharine sunset, telling *Consequence Of Sound*, "[People say,] 'Oh so Daptone's over?' And it's like, no, we still love this stuff. Those records are still around, it's a tragedy, and we're all heartbroken that we lost our friends, but we're still gonna make records and do what we can."[8]

That attitude of *keep on pushin'* would be a persuasive and heartening tale if more of the second-generation soul bands were fronted by older artists. Instead, those older artists and first crop of bands showed what could be created as a family and collective, setting the stage for the next phase of the revolution. The lesson is truly in perseverance and sticking to one's guns.

"We have to keep going for the folks who passed away," says Post. "Just because they're gone doesn't mean their history and legacy is gone; it's our responsibility to keep that going." Adds DeBoe, "that's the beauty about that music, it's kind of never-ending. The records will always be there and like a time capsule, but the live shows are a whole other thing. That can't happen again, and people can only really hang on to the memories."

★ ★ ★ ★ ★ ★

There is some self-preservation involved. After all, much of the original Daptone crew and extended family of musicians are in their forties and fifties, over the hill and certainly nearer the grave than when they started at Desco. When many of these musicians began working together, as teens or young adults, there was no air of destiny guiding their musical journey. Instead, the energy that carried musicians from Desco to Daptone and beyond launched its headliners into stardom at the same rapid clip that it took them away.

Rather than feel shortchanged by these losses, Roth insists on putting Charles and Sharon in context. Young pop singers explode on the scene and then disappear years later, but "what you'll notice when you maybe step back, is those are different names everyone's excited about and they all come and they go," Roth says. "They're always comparing it to some neo soul so-and-so who's on the radio at the moment, but those people fade in and out. Maybe it's Adele or Macy Gray or The Alabama Shakes. Or Amy Winehouse." While some of those big names might have five to ten years of staying power, "Sharon stuck around a lot longer than all that stuff."

CHAPTER FIFTEEN WHATEVER IT TAKES: DAPTONE IN THE MODERN ERA

After a professionally prolific and personally miserable two years, Daptone found itself in the unique position of having achieved success while gazing out at a new frontier. The family love was still there (and always would be), but several key OG members had fractured. Gabe Roth, who had long since moved back to Riverside to be near his family as his three kids grew, was exploring new sounds on the West Coast. Neal Sugarman was trying out life in Europe where he could ride his bike through the Swiss countryside and attend business meetings remotely. Dapette Starr Duncan-Lowe moved to Atlanta, making touring as Saun & Starr financially impossible, while Saundra Williams supported Low Cut Connie and Mavis Staples. Absent work with Charles Bradley, guitarist Tom Brenneck headed west to his wife's native Southern California where he had more time to produce bands through his Dunham Records subsidiary and run Mark Ronson's Hollywood studio. Binky Griptite had started his own jump-blues orchestra and announced his departure from The Dap-Kings in a July 2018 Facebook post—though, at the time, there wasn't much to depart from.

While Sugarman and Roth had a business to run, they also had caché and the creative freedom that came with fame. For years, genre heads and fans had sent demos and emails, messaged on social media, and came through headquarters hoping to record. But Daptone also had taste—that amorphous and often ineffable thing that set the label apart from others and provided the exceedingly cool basis for its entire being. What the label

★ ★ ★ ★ ★ ★

did next could determine its future and legacy in a post-Sharon, post-Charles world.

Nearly two years after Jones died, The Dap-Kings returned to the stage behind Jon Batiste, a thirty-ish New Orleanian pianist and singer who came to late-night fame as the bandleader for *The Late Show With Stephen Colbert*. Batiste was a talented songwriter and arranger with mainstream appeal but also serious music-industry cred as a child prodigy and, later, director roles at the National Jazz Museum in Harlem and the *Atlantic*; he'd also shared stages with Stevie Wonder, Prince, and Willie Nelson. The Dap-Kings and Batiste had first performed together in March 2018 during a Newport Folk Festival Foundation fundraiser, and vibed over a shared love of roots music. A tour with Batiste provided the perfect opportunity for a Dap-Kings "comeback": Batiste could hang, his show mixed ballads and up-tempo numbers that a band used to keeping up with Sharon Jones could easily pull, and the money was right for a group of middle-aged musicians skeptical about getting on the road for just anyone. Further, much of their collaboration would consist of covers of New Orleans classics along with a few Batiste originals, easing the group back into the groove with tunes they were passionate about.

"We share a deep love and respect for New Orleans musical roots," Roth said ahead of their tour, which would take the musicians from jazz festival to jazz festival throughout the spring and summer of 2018. "[Batiste] is a distinctly talented dude with a rare feel for that music and we can't wait to tear up these tunes together."[1] Sharon's spirit was with the band, noted Batiste, who refrained from imitating the act of a musical matriarch who shook the world: "Her presence is going to be unavoidable with anyone who joins that band, because that's still going to be her band. I didn't try to fight it or try to live up to that."[2]

With Batiste, The Dap-Kings performed a hometown show at the newly opened Pier 17 rooftop, a beautiful stage in lower Manhattan that gazed out on the East River and Brooklyn skyline, the Statue Of Liberty shining in the distance. Batiste did his best version of Stevie Wonder circa

★ ★ ★ ★ ★ ★

'73, alternating between singing behind the piano and dancing for the audience in a palpably uplifting performance. At Roth's request, the band closed the set with "Beating Like A Tom Tom," a lesser-known tune from singer Ernie K. Doe. The 1962 song is simple in its original incarnation, with stripped down bass and piano, and doo-wop harmonies; it's the kind of song Sharon Jones could easily sing (and she did dig into a similar sound with "Mama Don't Like My Man" on *I Learned The Hard Way*), except it would likely be too slow for her taste. Roth intermittently closed his eyes, tapping on his chest while he sang the refrain.

Despite positive reviews and good cash, the Batiste tour was relatively short, and the soul engine had to keep chugging along. Fortunately, the label had developed an extensive catalogue of albums and singles as well as steady revenue (however small and piecemeal) from streaming services like Spotify—all of which could help float the label and some of its players. Daptone's obsession with and dedication to vinyl was also coincidentally prescient. By 2018, vinyl record sales had been steadily rising for thirteen years to a whopping 16.8 million—a record high since Neilsen began tracking sales in 1991—even as purchases of physical albums dropped overall. While rock albums (and particularly well-packaged reissues of classics like *Abbey Road*) dominated purchases, *Back To Black* was the fifth best-selling record on vinyl in 2017, eleven years after its release.[3] After a decade-plus of putting up soul, Daptone had built a solid foundation and was now playing the long game.

"We don't need to have the new hot stuff," Sugarman told me. "We just need to bang out like one great fucking classic record a year, and with what we have in the can, that helps to keep breath blowing through this house. Some of the records we'll go deep on, others we'll just sell a limited amount. It's a tough business; it's not like slinging hamburgers. We're just this tiny music company trying to figure out .0001 cent per play so we can make it work and make records."[4]

★ ★ ★ ★ ★ ★

From the outside, anyhow, it seemed as if Daptone had it figured out; 2018 was the label's busiest year for output. Antibalas's sixth album, *Where The Gods Are In Peace*, continued an Afrobeat evolution with epic compositions that meditated on ancestral courage while offering messages of a peaceful collective future.[5] The James Hunter Six dug into the poetry of love (likely due to the eponymous singer's recent marriage to a younger fan) for *Whatever It Takes*, simultaneously evoking Ben E. King, Sam Cooke, and Bobby Bland on songs like "I Don't Wanna Be Without You," while showing an incredible vocal range on devotional pop numbers like "I Got Eyes." The Budos Band put the finishing touches on *Budos V*, which would be their fifth album in fifteen years. "We're super active," saxophonist Jared Tankel, now one of two Budos living on the West Coast, later told Seattle's KEXP radio. "The two coasts and the growing families ... actually made us more focused on what we're doing and why this is important to us."[6] Sharon Jones even came through with new music from beyond. Her first gospel funk recordings as E.L. Fields's Gospel Wonders, "Heaven Bound" b/w "Key To The Kingdom," were released on Daptone's Ever-Soul imprint in a custom picture-frame jacket showing Jones's high-school portrait. The Frightnrs' *Nothing More To Say* was so well-received that Ticklah inverted the album to create *More To Say Versions*—a dub record with a psychedelic 3-D cover and Dan Klein's vocals echoing through the ether.

Wick Records hadn't stopped either, offering a healthy sampling of Daptone's rock sensibilities with nuanced but still raw garage and rock'n'soul platters. The imprint released more from Virginian teen-beat aficionados The Ar-Kaics, a sophomore effort titled *In This Time* that was recorded in a properly punk three days and produced by Wayne Gordon. Montreal-based singer/songwriter/producer Michael Rault came into the Daptone-Wick fold after catching Gordon's ear during opening gigs for Charles Bradley and Australian rockers King Gizzard & The Lizard Wizard. With an assist from the Wick engineer, Rault's *It's A New Day Tonight* broadened Daptone's offerings into 70s-style folk-inflected rock à la Badfinger with the breeziness of early Wilco or "Hey Jude"–era Beatles.

★ ★ ★ ★ ★ ★

The Mystery Lights' *Too Much Tension!*, another sophomore LP, rounded out the Wick catalogue.

At the dawn of a new decade, Daptone released its 100th 45, a family record featuring a soul version of The Frightnrs' "Hey Brother" highlighted by the ghostly voices of both Sharon and Charles, backed by the funky psych tune "Soul Fugue"—which corralled all of the label's horn players past and present into the studio on Leap Day 2016 as The 100 Knights Orchestra.

While previous years' releases centered on Daptone's house bands or a smallish group of musicians taking turns as music director and producer, then releasing records under various names to differentiate projects with similar lineups, the label's later releases reflected a wider reach. Daptone's house bands took a back seat to new projects from existing family members and those just coming into the fold. "I look at a guy like Freddy DeBoe, who has a great new band doing Junior Walker songs—he's doing what I was doing when I was his age with the Sugarman 3, basically," Sugarman says, adding that he no longer has energy for the grind of working all day and gigging every night, especially with two young kids. "There's a weird feeling, like I gotta get working and back to doing more records. But then it's like, *No, it's cool.* There's the next guard, and hopefully we can stay involved with them and offer them a platform to put records out."

Expanding its scope of funk influence beyond the mid-70s, the label dipped into the post-disco sound known as boogie. Multiple singles from Chicago's Doug Shorts, the result of a session with Frank Dukes and Steinweiss, promised to make listeners "feel as though you're on the way to the beach in your folks' 1982 Buick Riveria convertible," while bouncing along to a production Rick James would approve of. On "Lover Like Me," Victor Axelrod turned back the clock to Jamaica circa '64 by flipping a tune from the Sugarman 3's *Sugar's Boogaloo* to create heavy traditional ska with singer Leon Dinero (an alias, in grand Daptonian tradition, of NYC scene stalwart Screechy Dan). The two would later rock steady in the style of singer Hopeton Lewis, while the producer explored reggae

★ ★ ★ ★ ★ ★

with Screechy on "Bandits," a condemnation of gentrification told rub-a-dub style.

In early 2018, Dap-Kings saxophonist Cochemea "Cheme" Gastelum released *All My Relations*, a spiritual jazz record that mined Brooklyn's impressive community of percussionists for an improvisational recording session and meditation on Indigenous rhythms. "The session was a beautiful gathering of people, and everyone just walked away with such a good feeling. Everyone was so giving and kind," recounts Gastelum, an easygoing California native whose playing is both cosmically derived and studied. "Once people started setting up and playing, it just felt right." *All My Relations* was a return to roots for both Cheme, who had been plumbing the depths of his Yaqui and Mescalero-Apache heritage, and fans who might have been missing transcendent and soul-affirming Daptone performances.

The album release party was held on a rainy July night inside an impeccably lit, intimate club on the Lower East Side. The show began with an ancestral incantation, rollicking percussively through the record's ten tracks, which, collectively, tell a tale of unity. "That was the first time since seeing a Sharon show that I felt that incredible locked in, collective brain kind of music," says Jacob Blickenstaff, who also shot cover art for the record at Cheme's Woodstock home, delicately engaging with a variety of sacred objects. "And that was like getting a drink of water after a long time in the desert."

At the same time, Daptone was also sewing a web of soul, connecting the fibers of "world music" and doo-wop to its original sounds. Among Daptone's ambitious forays was an album from Orquesta Akokan, a Cuban group playing mambo in the style of Perez Prado and conceived of by New York–based Jewish bandleaders/arrangers Jacob Plasse and Michael Ekroth. As reggaeton and salsa dominated the pop charts, the tune "Despacito" providing an earworm crossover hit to a trend already in the works, Daptone's first Spanish-language record was predictably punk in sensibility—channeling the sounds of yesteryear rather than kowtowing to popular taste. Continuing a generations-long trend of Jewish support

★ ★ ★ ★ ★ ★

of big-band Latin music, Plasse and Ekroth traveled to Cuba to produce the record in November 2016, just ahead of Donald Trump's increasingly isolationist policies.

Orquesta's self-titled debut featured all original songs recorded at Havana's historic state-run Estudios Areito with Cuba's finest players, young and old. "Mambo was a sound that became an ambassador for Cuban culture, opening the doors for writers, musicians and arrangers to a public beyond the island," said singer José "Pepito" Gómez. "We wanted the music to have the beauty and power of those original mambo recordings, while being true to our [current] lives and experiences."[7] The interest from Daptone was more than Plasse—who had gone to high school with The Mighty Imperials—had ever expected.

Akokan's horn section had impressed Neal Sugarman, who didn't consider himself an aficionado but had a handful of Latin records at home. "I always wanted to put out a Latin record, but it just took a while for the right record to come into our world," he says, remarking that Daptone is a team of curators as well as a record label. "It's super-well played, organic grooving music. The same people who bought a Sharon Jones record could really connect with [Akokan]. It will appeal to people who don't necessarily have a whole shelf of Latin records but are open minded to music that grooves."

After a series of gigs at swanky New York venues where Akokan dressed sharply in suits and performed with a seriousness absent from some other projects, the band began recording a second album. Blickenstaff flew to Cuba to shoot the session, held at the slightly more modern A-Room studio. "It's a different configuration of music, a little more broken and intricate with more styles and bigger arrangements. It's more complicated, and a little bit conceptual. I think Neal's original reaction was that it's too fussy, but I really dug it. It's very cinematic." A couple of years later, Daptone released music from Virginia's Miramar; the Spanish-language single was produced by Victor Axelrod and founding Antibalas member Giancarlo Luiggi as a desperate-sounding and spookily scorching bolero-soul 45.

★ ★ ★ ★ ★ ★

Daptone put out soul from yet another corner of the world, working with longtime friends from Finland's Timmion Records as North American distributors of singles, a compilation of the label's funk and sweet soul called *Bad Education Vol. 1*, and an LP from Carlton Jumel Smith, a former Harlemite now living abroad. "They have been a big help and it's always good to have a chat about your ideas and releases with them," say Timmion owners Jukka Sarapää and Sami Kantelinen. "Daptone has had a huge impact on the scene. They've also proven that you can still create this type of music and it's a beautiful example of what you can do independently without major labels when you put your heart and a lot of work into it."

Daptone's musicians continued to lend their heart and ear to a variety of pop acts, doing session work for Adele's *2015*, R&B singer Kali Uchi's studio debut *Isolation*, and The Jonas Brothers, as well as co-writing tracks for the Mark Ronson–produced Miley Cyrus album *Nothing Breaks Like A Heart*. Brenneck, Michels, Steinweiss, Movshon, Axelrod, Cheme, Hendrickson-Smith and Guy are all credited on Lady Gaga's 2016 album *Joanne*, a massive A-list undertaking that had soul's biggest musicians playing everything from wild country romps to pop-funk. Although Brenneck rarely thinks about how he's contributed to the larger pop music landscape, or if his crew's soulful roots have affected Top 40 sounds, he concedes that he enjoys these sessions, adding, "Good musicianship can always pop its head up in pop music.

"I think that we've been in a bubble for our whole career and those of us that can sustain it stay in that bubble. I make records for Daptone as passion projects; anything I do outside of that I couldn't do every day. I wouldn't, it's not why I play music," he continues, gazing toward a wall adorned with award-winning records at Sound Factory—the studio he shares with Ronson, and which has also hosted greats such as The Jackson Five, The Bangles, and Marvin Gaye (who mixed *What's Going On* at the legendary space).[8] "If I get a phone call to write a song with Mark and it ends up being a Miley Cyrus song and that leads me to play some bass

★ ★ ★ ★ ★ ★

guitar on Miley Cyrus's record, of course I'll fucking go do it," he adds. "It's fun, and I don't take it that seriously. If Lady Gaga wants to use the whole band, that sounds like a wild experience and of course we're gonna do it. Sometimes it's just nice to get out of the fucking bubble." In typically cool fashion, Brenneck is quick to note that he will say no to 90 percent of sessions he's offered.

The producers for pop singer Kesha coveted the upbeat swing of Daptone's horns too, and in 2017 they recorded the power anthem "Woman" with extra vocals from Saundra Williams. Gastelum was enthusiastic about the session, telling *Billboard* that the singer was engaged and lent a cool, familial vibe to the recording, which took place shortly after the Women's March On Washington.[9] The empowering message of the song felt timely and relevant to Cheme, but for Gabe Roth—a self-described contrarian who wasn't at the session, "I don't think that shows anything." Speaking for himself rather than the label, and properly hopped up on the midnight indignation that followed a challenge of his punk ethos, Roth says such session work isn't a feather in his cap. "If Kesha hears our music and she gets joy out of it and is inspired to make music and wants to work with us, that I'm into. But I don't give a fuck what some fucking pop so-and-so thinks. Whether Amy Winehouse or Jay-Z or Mark Ronson wants to take our sound or put us up, I don't give a fuck." Just as Groucho Marx wouldn't want to be a member of any club that would have him, the label head says, "Any respect or acceptance from that scene is not something I'm proud of. It's something that makes me stop and think, *Fuck, I better watch what I'm doing.*"

The real pride comes from older fans—the kind Roth might have played for with Cliff Driver at storefront churches in his early twenties—acknowledging the band's skills, watching audiences dance, and meeting fans who obsessively follow Daptone's catalogue. "What a hypocrite I would be if I tell you that those people aren't doing shit, and then I started drooling when they come here. I'm not saying we didn't do anything. I'm very proud of what we did. I'm just using a different measuring stick," Roth

★ ★ ★ ★ ★ ★

says. "At the first really big Women's March, people were playing Sharon's 'This Land Is Your Land' real fucking loud on boom boxes and marching with banners. I'm unbelievably proud of that. Pete Buttigieg used a Sharon Jones song for his [2020 presidential] campaign. I was pretty excited about that—somebody who's actually trying to do something political or social in the country."

Jay-Z came back into the Daptone orbit in 2017 after songwriter/production duo Cool & Dre brought a sample developed by Brenneck, Michels, and Steinweiss to Hova and Beyoncé (then performing as The Carters). Steinweiss's drumming sticks out in the demo, an undercurrent to Brenneck's slightly trippy guitar work, which would form a large musical bed for Beyoncé's voice on the track "Summer" from 2018's *Everything Is Love*. Brenneck recalls running into producer/songwriter DJ Dahi at a party, and learning that the Kendrick Lamar and Dr. Dre collaborator (who was also credited with writing and producing 21 Savage and J. Cole's 2018 hit "A Lot," its musical bed based on the 60s soul song "I Love You For All Seasons") was a fan. "He was just like, 'Oh, man, I fucking study your shit.' And I was like, *Wow, that's incredible*. I had no idea he even listened," Brenneck says, somehow still sounding generally surprised. "Our shit getting sampled so much is really dope and a really good gauge of success—more than how many people listen to records or go to shows," he continues, in stark contrast to Roth's view of sampling. "I always find that to be the greatest compliment. If producers are sampling your shit, that's as close as we can come to assurance that we're making records that our heroes made."

But the Carters sample, or any of the other interest from producers, wasn't a flash in the pan. Hip-hop was experiencing a soulful resurgence that went beyond soundbites—the likes of Travis Scott sampling Lee Fields or Eminem twice using Dunham beats. R&B had made a comeback by the mid-2010s, spurred early by Frank Ocean's acutely emotional *Channel Orange* then iterated on by The Weeknd, Solange (who early sampled Sharon Jones), Anderson .Paak (a Stones Throw collaborator) and his group The Free Nationals, The Internet, and others, each using a traditional singer/songwriter's introspection with electronic beats and live instrumentation, often with a seriously 70s bent. This indie/alternative—or, at worst, hipster—R&B culminated in 2018, with Childish Gambino's *Awaken, My Love!*, an album of deep influence and vocal range that worshiped at the freaky footstool of Funkadelic, Prince, and Sly Stone. The Internet's guitarist Steve Lacy was experimenting with soul and boogie as a solo artist the following year. In 2020, Missy Elliott was using 60s soul phrasing and groovy styling on her single "Why I Still Love You," a trip through time that showed the rapper performing as "Missy & The Demeanors" while evoking The Supremes and Tina Turner.

The continued relevance of funk and soul—as fodder for samples or self-contained boogie machines—is evidence that the genre never left the public consciousness. "That style came in in the late 60s and then kind of stayed in pop music in various iterations. "Bowie used funk in the 70s; in the 80s a lot of pop music like Rick James was just funk music. And then in the 90s hip-hop was sampling funk records," Steinweiss hypothesizes. "That has continued on to now. Even big pop records like Maroon 5 have that funky back beat."

In the decade following the breakout success of Amy Winehouse and Sharon Jones's long road to stardom, the aesthetic and production style of revival funk and soul had become a foundational part of mainstream sound across genre. Analogue and live-to-tape production, the pleasing warmth of vinyl, and the pride of wearing influences on your sleeve had permeated pop music, rock, country, and hip-hop. But just as Leon Bridges felt boxed in by the "retro soul" label years before (as well as the pressure of being one of few young Black men in the scene), the pervasive association with revivalist bands was still frustrating artists in 2018. Singer Kam Franklin—whose Houston-based Gulf Coast Soul collective The Suffers blends disco, gospel, cumbia, and soul—said comparisons to Sharon Jones were so constant that she felt compelled at one point to sign with Daptone, even though The Suffers' sound didn't fit the label's aesthetic. "It's been almost

★ ★ ★ ★ ★ ★

soul-crushing for me sometimes: at what point do I get to be myself and not just another Black girl singing soul music to you people?" Franklin told the *Guardian*, adding that such categorization is "something that affects every woman of color in this industry."[10] (The band didn't sign with Daptone.)

Soul isn't defining for singer/songwriter Curtis Harding (who used to write for and back up CeeLo Green, and worked with Billy Austik on a record) or for psychedelic soul Grammy nominees The Black Pumas. Instead, the genre is an integral part of their musical histories and a convenient descriptor. "We didn't really set out to be a soul revival band or anything like that. I wanted the soul to be that it came from our souls, not so much a carbon copy of any particular era or artists," Pumas producer/guitarist Adrian Quesada explained to *Rolling Stone*.[11]

Even within the wider Daptone family, people were stretching their legs and making work that explored the far reaches of soul. After Truth & Soul petered out, Leon Michels and Danny Akalepese founded Big Crown Records in 2016 with a diverse catalogue. The label's offerings included ballads from Lee Fields, steel drum covers from Bacao Rhythm & Steel Band, disco-soul from 79.5 (who backed up LA indie-rockers Chicano Batman, another band Michels helped produce), Bowie-esque pop from The Shacks, hybrid reggae-rap-soul from British singer Liam Bailey, Brainstory's Inland Empire psych-rock, and power-soul from Lady Wray, as well as a handful of reissues from the likes of Chicano soul vets Sunny and The Sunliners.

For Lepse, Big Crown was a welcome opportunity to work outside a soul scene he was never particularly passionate about. "Soul singing is not really my thing," he says from Big Crown's tidy Greenpoint, Brooklyn office. "It's one kind of records I like, a lot, and always did, but when somebody makes a dope new record, I'm into it. I don't like the masquerade bit, when people go retro on purpose. That's why Truth & Soul to me was like a one trick pony. That revival thing kind of painted itself into a corner. So, when we dumped that shit finally and did Big Crown, we purposely wanted to be

★ ★ ★ ★ ★ ★

able to put out a wide amount of things. To be honest, it doesn't seem that wide to the average person because there's a tone and aesthetic to it all. But you wouldn't find these records in the same section at the record store."

Steinweiss joined Big Crown as the drummer for indie-folk three-piece Holy Hive, noting, "I love old music. I want to keep a tradition alive, but I don't like the idea of, like, being stuck in the past as a musician. So how do you take some things and not completely cop something that was from a different time?"

Seated below an oil painting of Lee Fields, Akalepse coolly insists that "what we're doing is unique. We're doing our own thing, we're not doing what no one else did, in particular at least. I'm not looking at no other record labels for cues."

This isn't to slight Daptone's dedication to era-specific sounds; some bands really pulled from that tradition. Canadian eleven-piece The Soul Motivators carried the deep funk torch in North America; Oakland organ quartet The M-Tet and Seattle's Delvon Lamarr Organ Trio followed in the tradition of the Sugarman 3 and The Scone Cash Players; Boulevards drank from the same well of Southern funk and soul that inspired Daptone; Prince protégé Judith Hill blended rock with Bettye LaVette reminiscent vocals; eight-piece Alabama group St. Paul & The Broken Bones took gospel soul to the masses, though their performances often felt like a mimicry of Otis Redding/the Muscle Shoals sound.

Durand Jones & The Indications, a five-piece that got their start during weekly jam sessions after jazz courses at Indiana University, evolved into a heavy-hitting funk and soul group with two singers and a taste for harmonies. Aaron Frazer—the slight, soft-spoken, and thoughtful drummer-songwriter-vocalist for DJI—grew up in Maryland with many of the same influences as Daptone artists but also had the label's catalogue to grow with. In high school, Frazer heard the groovy doom of the *Budos II*'s "Chicago Falcon"; the song's melding of funk, soul, and hip-hop was blindsiding. "It sounded like biker meth, a country-like soundtrack. It's cinematic soul in its highest form. As a hip-hop head, I was like, *Man,*

★ ★ ★ ★ ★ ★

you can't tell me this is contemporary, but it was." A few years later, "The World (Is Going Up In Flames)" reached Frazer's ears. "It was just like hearing this dispatch from another planet. It sounded so classic, but it also sounded so hip-hop. I was blown away that you could make a record that sounded like that. That and Sharon Jones's *100 Days, 100 Nights* was kind of the basis for us."

On their self-titled Colemine release, DJI put out gritty but fairly straightforward funk and soul, culling influences from around the country and throughout the soul renaissance. If Frazer were to put a finer point on the band's sound, however, it's "post-hip-hop soul"—the kind of sound Tommy Brenneck couldn't help but create with Charles Bradley, the Budos, or Menahan Street Band. "Imagine if, instead of Nas growing up listening to The Delfonics, what if The Delfonics grew up listening to Nas, what music would they make?"

Although Durand Jones & The Indications never intended to tour their debut album, the band hit the road with a vigor in 2017 after a video of their gentle, falsetto-anchored ballad "Is It Any Wonder?" began gathering millions of views on YouTube. DJI filled a void left by Sharon and Charles's passing, Roth says. "They've been on that road paying those dues, which is not about playing where the oldies scene is, but playing Denver, Pittsburgh, and places where it's about getting your friends out and hearing a new band."

The nod from Roth—who later asked DJI to record backing vocals for James Hunter, though that session and another for the band itself never came to fruition—was genuinely flattering and humbling for the young Indications. "It was a really beautiful, gratifying thing to get those calls," Frazer says from his home in Brooklyn. "When I was in college I would have been buggin' out. Back then, we thought why would Daptone even bother with what we're doing? In the end, the tree grows fruit, then the fruit falls to the ground and another tree grows. It's this kind of beautiful cycle."

CHAPTER SIXTEEN CAN I CALL YOU ROSE? DAPTONE HEADS WEST FOR THE SWEETEST SOUL

As Durand Jones & The Indications carried the torch of soul singers not-too-past, their cinematic declarations of love sung at a slow tempo had found another audience—one whose soulful waters ran deep but had received little representation in the revivalist scene. The band had tapped a nerve among fans of sweet soul—a smooth but not slick pocket of mid-60s to early 70s output with a heavy concentration on ballads often sung by amateur teens. Also known as rolas, slowies, and souldies, sweet soul offered a contrast to the high production of Motown, the grit of Stax, or the blues from Chess Records (though these labels certainly have their sweet soul hits, for example Mary Wells's "The One Who Really Loves You," Smokey Robinson's "The Agony And The Ecstasy," and Brenton Wood's "I Like The Way You Love Me"). On the West Coast, these songs are often called lowrider oldies—a regional classification for the tunes dedicated on Art Laboe's long-running KRLA request radio show; songs made for cruising in a lowered vintage car along East LA's Whittier Boulevard with an arm slung around your lover.

Those classics, often released on small labels, were predated slightly by a wellspring of rock and soul from Boyle Heights, Montebello, and other areas of Los Angeles County east of the 5 Freeway. While Chicano bands like Cannibal & The Headhunters and Thee Midniters made hits by mixing rock'n'roll with soulful influences, dozens of other groups—from The

★ ★ ★ ★ ★ ★

Blendells to The Romancers, The Perez Brothers to The Royal Jesters and others—made teen hearts swoon at CYO dances, high schools, and county events with catchy love songs. Their "Eastside Sound" became known as Chicano soul, which defined much of Southern California ahead of (and even through) the British Invasion. Chicano soul influenced mainstream soul singers as well; according to DJ and historian Ruben Molina, Wilson Pickett heard Cannibal's version of "Land Of 1000 Dances" and vowed to make it his own. Chicano soul from Texas received less national spotlight but was equally prolific if not more soulful, dominated by Little Joe & The Latinaires, Sunny & The Sunliners, and "El Gato Negro" Ruben Ramos.

While the East Coast has long loved ballads and slowies were heard on the West Coast for generations, the sound didn't hit among contemporary audiences until the singers who so possessed a James Brownian energy had gone to another plane. Some of Daptone's catalogue could fit into the back seat of a lowrider: the hypnotic harmonies on "Making Up And Breaking Up (And Making Up Over Again)" from *Give The People What They Want* would qualify; the ephemeral surf-soul of The Sha La Das (Dunham Records) is cruise-ready; a handful of Saun & Starr tracks and James Hunter tunes like "Mm-Hmm" from *Whatever It Takes* could be categorized as sweet; Expressions/Jay Vons bassist Benny Trokan released a stellar and haunting lowrider single, "Turn Back You Fool," on Wick. Yet, perhaps for the first time in the label's history, Daptone Records were not leading the charge into the next frontier of soul.

On their 2019 release *American Love Call* (Dead Oceans), Durand Jones & The Indications added a four-piece string section and horns. The band were so inspired by fan support of their sophomore release and for "Is It Any Wonder" that they penned a lowrider tribute called "Cruising In The Park." Meanwhile, Colemine Records released slow singles from Ben Piriani & Thee Sinseers, a Los Angeles harmony group led by singer/producer Joe Quiñones who had spent a handful of years in the soul-adjacent rocksteady group The Steady 45s. The label also distributed a handful of sweet soul 45s from Monophonics' Kelly Finnigan as The

★ ★ ★ ★ ★ ★

Sentiments, then released the singer's debut solo LP—the falsetto-heavy *I Don't Wanna Wait*, which he recorded with studio support from Billy Austik, Terry Cole, Sergio Rios, and Dan Hastie from Orgone, as well as Seattle guitarist Jimmy James and Connie Price's Dan Ubick.

"It takes time to mature into that sound and be like, *I can handle string arrangements, I can hit backgrounds*," Finnigan says between sessions on a warm summer night, leaning against the doorway of his Marin County studio, Transistor Sound. "Fifteen years ago, I just don't think anybody thought they could get away with this and not sound corny. Those Impressions records, The Miracles, and, like, all the big names—those are good musicians being recorded by professional people, arrangers, background singers." Finnigan's debut received rave reviews, including from The Black Keys' Dan Auerbach, who says, "That's my fucking jam. That album took him a lot of work; it's not easy to do. The first time I heard it, I just put it on repeat. I texted Terry Cole immediately." Two years after its release, rapper Curren$y used The Sentiments' "She Won't Be Gone Long" as the musical bed for a song about the Coronavirus and police violence.

Timmion Records had been releasing ballads with help from Daptone's distribution network since 2009. Early tracks like Willie West's "The Devil Gives Me Everything" evolved into "Lost Lost Lost" by Pratt & Moody, and then a handful of sweet tracks by Bobby Oroza. The Finnish-Belizian singer knew his audience, and he killed two birds with one crooning stone by covering Chicano soul classics by Sunny & The Sunliners and looking remarkably like Morrissey. "Ballads are what we've been loving for years, as you could find these on B-sides of those gritty funk 45s," Timmion's co-owners say. "It seems like more and more people are doing ballads nowadays."

With just a hint of competitive edge—and despite efforts to eschew categorization—Big Crown Records was also becoming one of the bigger names in sweet soul music. Once a funky powerhouse, Lee Fields now had set upon set of mid- to slow-tempo love songs, and in 2017 he released

★ ★ ★ ★ ★ ★

an album of grown folks' music called *Special Night*. The label received much love for its one-off souldie single with Los Angeles's Thee Lakesiders, who brought a particular pachuco sensibility to the scene. They'd also hit big with Bobby Oroza, whose *This Love* drew throngs of screaming fans, young and old, white and Brown, to an outdoor Los Angeles stage where he offered up a solid take on Sunny & The Sunliners' classic "Should I Take You Home?" Says Lepse, "I really dig how much people love souldies out there. The Cali contingent, the Southwest contingent, the Chicanos, fucking ride hard for us. The strong support is fucking dope." The Big Crown head isn't into the term "lowrider soul," however, opining that it's an umbrella for singing in falsetto. "That's ballads. Meanwhile, doo-wop is the same music but happened totally different in New York. People don't drive here!"

Outside of dedicated (or at least adjacent) soul labels, Nacional Records released the Adrian Quesada–produced compilation *Look At My Soul: The Latin Shade Of Texas Soul*, highlighting Tejano sweet soul music. Even actor/entrepreneur Danny Trejo dipped his toe into the scene, launching a record label with Sinseers' Joe Quiñones as a producer for artists such as Malik Malo and Tarah New. Rapper Snoop Dogg would later produce and promote a sweet soul revue in Southern California.

Meanwhile, the House Of Soul was humming with projects that would grace turntables on the other side of the decade. In 2019, The Budos Band released their fifth album and finished recording a sixth; the James Hunter Six announced plans for their third Daptone LP, *Nick Of Time*; and Adam Scone distributed his *As The Screw Turns* through Daptone (with cameos by Naomi Shelton and the Dap-King horns). Antibalas were putting the finishing touches on *Fu Chronicles*—a mesmerizing orchestration of kung fu meets Afrobeat that Amayo had been working on since the Afro Spot days—which packed seventeen players into the House Of Soul live room. Tom Brenneck finished mixing a new record from Menahan Street Band and made a rare live appearance with El Michels Affair, backing Lee Fields during a mini sweet-soul tour in Southern California. Billy Austik was readying the release of a northern soul, four-on-the-floor-style single called "Runnin' (To Get To Your Love)" from Bobby Harden—a friend of Sharon Jones's from her Good 'N' Plenty band days whom Austik met at a screening of *Living On Soul*—on his own Dala Records with studio band The Soulful Saints. Yet with what was, by Roth's measure, the pinnacle of the soul scene three thousand miles west of Daptone's Bushwick HQ, 2020 would require ingenuity for the label to get back on top of the game—not that they ever really cared about status to begin with.

Riverside is the so-called jewel of the Inland Empire—a former citrus grove in an increasingly arid valley approximately one to three hours east of Los Angeles, depending on the area's inevitable and pervasive traffic. Nestled in the foothills of Mount Rubidoux on a tree-lined street is Gabe Roth's large but not stately family home. It's old, with a distinct lived-in feel, a sizeable pool that was once the backdrop for Saun & Starr's video "Big Wheel," and a spare bedroom for visiting musicians and journalists. The house is right down the street from Roth's parents and partially purchased with settlement money from the accident that damaged his eyes decades prior, affording the musician and his young family an enviable amount of space most New Yorkers would salivate at. Roth moved home around 2010, flying back and forth to New York for sessions and gigs, typically mixing and mastering records from a studio inside downtown Riverside's historic Life Arts Building. The former YMCA and Scientology center is a convenient five-minute drive away in the producer's nondescript manual-transmission sedan.

The country seat has also been a longtime home for misfit LA bands who would schlep along the 10 Freeway through hilly farmland and characterless suburbs to play local venues. This scene was familiar to Roth who, by his forties, had one foot in the underground, the other in the occasionally glamorous echelons of the music industry, and was considering where next to take his popular label. Ever a digger, the Daptone co-founder began checking out the local music scene—a potent pocket of mostly Chicano collectors and musicians who performed soul music at car shows, festivals, barbecues, and small parties—and spinning his massive collection of 45s at local bars.

The aloof record head found himself drawn to the tearjerker ballads and sweet harmonies played by groups of mostly twenty- and thirtysomething Latinos. Musicians in Thee Sinseers, The Altons, and Los Yesterdays—the latter a duo in their forties who Roth and Brenneck met at a barbecue they hosted—drew from a generations-long dedication to sweet soul. Many of the groups "play at the edge of their ability or sing at the edge of their range," lending a struggle and passion to their performance which similarly informed Daptone's perfectly imperfect early sound. Local DJs and collectors also pressed demos into Roth's hands, connected him with likeminded artists, or, in the case of San Diego three-piece Thee Sacred Souls, piqued Roth's interest with clips from Instagram.

Thee Sacred Souls hadn't released a single song when the trio were invited to Riverside to record the pining "Can I Call You Rose?" for a new Daptone subsidiary: Penrose Records. Named for his daughters Penelope and Rosalie, Roth envisioned Penrose not as a West Coast recreation of Daptone's magic but an opportunity to invest in an existing community and new generation of musicians.

"It's important for me on a personal level to contribute something musically," Roth said during an Instagram live broadcast that required him using a neighbor's account, the producer having never cared much for social media. "With the passings, it was kind of the close of a chapter for us. We still have a lot of great Daptone artists, but Penrose to me is a different chapter. Now more than ever, there's young bands and singers getting into it. And I'm in a position right now to amplify a scene that's already there. All these bands would be doing this whether or not there was a Penrose."

The California sweet soul scene has a foundation in the same Impressions records the Desco/Daptone crew had been listening to for decades, as well as a similar collective mentality. "I'm really happy for

★ ★ ★ ★ ★ ★

Gabe; we're all in a different stage in our lives and it took a bunch of years to kind of get our flow," says Neal Sugarman, who took a lengthy flight from Switzerland to Daptone West to play on a few records and check out the bands on his partner's new project. "Now he's able to create something out there similar to what was happening in Brooklyn when we started in the early 2000s. Those bands have an amazing opportunity to hang out with a master, you know? I don't know if that would be happening in Brooklyn now."

Over the course of a year or so, Penrose became a gathering place for those local musicians—many of whom, like the original Daptone crew, played in each other's projects and produced. Quiñones, who plays with The Altons and Thee Sinseers, was among the Penrose players who helped Roth build out the control room and live studio: a sun-drenched facility with high ceilings, echo, and a slightly bohemian vibe that provides a properly California contrast to the tight quarters of Daptone HQ.

"It's been very welcoming," Quiñones says from his home studio in nearby Rialto. "There's an understanding of, *Let's just help each other make good records*. It's a cool environment to be surrounded by so many good musicians and engineers, and basically a bunch of nerds who can shred." The singer/producer/guitarist might have cut his teeth in Southern California's reggae scene, but he truly came up among lowriders. Quiñones met Brenton Wood at his father's car club as a child, then later played in his band; the ballads he heard at those events and family parties directly influenced JQ's affinity for a higher, harmonic register.

Sacred Souls vocalist Josh Lane is not Chicano, though he grew up listening to the classic soul and R&B that was more popular in Black communities. In his teens and early twenties, Lane fell in love with the music of Sharon Jones and Charles Bradley. "Having some of the contemporary greats pass on left a void in the young people, who would see a show and be like, *Oh, yeah, soul's still kicking*. There's plenty of good artists doing soul today, but I think people are ready for way more selection," the singer reflects, while barreling down the freeway with his bandmates, en route to

★ ★ ★ ★ ★ ★

Riverside for a session. "To be in a lane where all this is happening is both stressful and really, really exciting. Passion on this scale is kind of surreal."

Daptone debuted Penrose in March 2020, launching with five singles from five bands native to Southern California: The Altons, Thee Sinseers, Thee Sacred Souls, Los Yesterdays (which had Roth and Brenneck playing together for the first time in years), and Miami-based singer Jason Joshua, who toured with OG Desco player/Sugarman 3 co-founder Adam Scone, himself a Florida resident. "In California, there is so much fucking talent; everyone can play instruments and everyone is a hustler," says Joshua, who considers Gabe Roth a mentor and keeps him on speed dial; his own Mango Hill Records label uses Daptone's blueprint as a guide. "Gabe is finding the raw, real, right talent, taking these demos and making these younger cats stars." The singer released an LP of ballads, *Alegria y Tristeza*, on Fat Beats Records shortly after the Penrose launch; the album cover features a shot of Joshua atop the isolation booth at Penrose—a pose equal parts awkward and excited.

Penrose Records is a return to the sounds preceding the funk and soul that made Daptone so popular, and it follows Gabe's natural inclinations as a listener and musician. "When I first got into making records, I was all about ... everything just being fast and funky and stuff people could dance to," he told *Billboard* ahead of the subsidiary launch. "Over the years I got older and tireder and got more into ballads and slow stuff."[1] Roth's strength as a producer partially lies in knowing when to step back and when to give a creative push—insight that was put to the test with the more experienced players in Los Yesterdays and the green Sacred Souls.

"Gabe Roth knows how to bring out the sound out of anybody," says Joshua, whose "Language Of Love" b/w "La Vida Es Fria" brought a taste of East Coast Latin soul to Penrose's initial releases. "These younger cats are easy for him to push on—he got The Altons to do soul, and they're a rock'n'roll band!" The Altons, having smoothed their rock edge, recorded "When You Go (That's When You'll Know)" and "Over And Over"—the latter's mesmerizing harmonies and delicate falsetto from Bryan Ponce

★ ★ ★ ★ ★ ★

quickly becoming a favorite of both Joshua and Roth. As with Desco and Daptone's early releases, Roth wasn't looking for technical proficiency. "It's about pushing somebody into someplace that maybe they're not as comfortable in, or playing in a way they're not as used to."

"There's only so much you can do with song forms and still have the funk," considers Binky Griptite, himself a big fan of harmony groups. "So as a songwriter, I'm sure Gabe is just more interested in branching out and being able to utilize different textures." The Penrose subsidiary was launched just weeks before the world plunged into the Coronavirus pandemic, which forced shelter-in-place orders in most cities, as well as international uprising following the police murder of George Floyd, a Black man from Minnesota. The MC continues, "It's a really politically stressful time, so we're in the mood for soothing sounds."

A general sense of vulnerability may lend to the increased popularity of sweet soul, Freddy DeBoe theorizes. "There's a lot of crisis happening and there's a lot of uncertainty, which is pretty scary. It's not really the time to go out there and be crazy and have a party. We need to get together with the ones that we love, and embrace the time that we're together. I feel like a lot of that music is there for people. Everybody's got a heart."

Yet sweet soul music is couched in a specific cultural and political history, which is outside of Roth's personal experience. Some of the genre's greatest songs were originals and covers of soul and R&B classics, performed by lesser-known Latino musicians in the Southwest. These Chicano soul songs were passed down through families and survived generational changes in taste, were chronicled in numerous articles, documentaries, and at painstaking length by Ruben Molina in *Chicano Soul*. It's been revived and prized through the *East Side Story* LP compilation and honored with contemporary parties in Los Angeles including Hello Stranger and East Side Luv. Chicano soul and lowrider oldies may have been made by people of all colors, but their heartbeat is strongest among Brown people, making the genre's long-lasting power and cultural nuance inherently political. Yet sweet soul knows no ethnic line.

★ ★ ★ ★ ★ ★

When Tom Brenneck moved west in 2017, he "learned about Chicano culture and their affinity for soul music and how deep it is and how dope it is," he says. "We'd play these local little parties, and the DJ would always have fucking incredible records. I feel like soul music is at its best if it's small. Those people are carrying the torch through the generations; that exists in LA and it does not exist in New York." To Molina, a sixty-something Chicano DJ and historian from East LA who's opened for Big Crown acts, the color of a sweet soul band's members is irrelevant so long as the culture is respected. "These new soul labels will give it a little sunshine because they'll be able to reach a broader audience. Just being Daptone alone, you want to take a second look at it. I want to see what they come up with because there are a lot of artists that are following along."

"Those cats are from New York; they know what boogaloo smells like, they know what it tastes like. It's not about Daptone being white capitalists, none of that shit, but now there's a major market looking for this," says Joshua, noting that he sent his 2018 ballad "Rose Gold" to all the major soul indies but got rejected. "A lot of these cats [who record with Penrose] don't know Daptone really. They just see a lot of cool analogue gear and someone who wants to do shit for them."

To Indications drummer/singer Aaron Frazer, "Gabe Roth is a cheat code, you know it's gonna sound incredible, and if you keep it simple, you're gonna make something that could fool a collector," he says. "The challenge for those Penrose artists, for our generation, for those kids who are younger, is to keep pushing it forward. Let's see what we can do when we bring everything that we've learned from these nasty 45s, from what Gabe and Daptone built, and see what happens when we don't do exactly what has been done."

Sugarman hopes to help Penrose artists like Thee Sacred Souls have careers similar to the Budos or Menahan Street Band, using label showcases to "inspire more people to make this music." While the subsidiary had big plans for 2020, recording happened sporadically throughout the pandemic—Jason Joshua, The Altons, and Thee Sacred Souls all donned masks during socially distant sessions for forthcoming LPs. Thousands of miles away and working from his own basement studio, Victor Axelrod surmises that Roth was likely mixing at his house and, purely out of necessity, using digital tools.

Daptone's entry into the world of sweet soul is about uplift rather than staking a claim, Roth adds. "We don't do that with any competition with Durand Jones, or Big Crown, or Colemine. We do it together." Colemine and Penrose share Thee Sinseers, for example—anything produced by Roth goes on his label, while Quiñones or Cole productions are released on Colemine. Instead, Penrose provided Daptone with another link in the soul diaspora, broadening their web of collaborators. Los Yesterdays released a record on Mango Hill, though under a different name. Ambitious producer Quiñones put out music on a handful of labels, narrowly skirting his contracts, and has written for or played with locals Trish Toldeo and Mirah Avila. Adds Terry Cole, "I would never imagine that sweet soul would be a thing ten or twelve years ago. And who knows where it's gonna head from there—maybe soul will get more broad."

Of course, Penrose wasn't the only thing in bloom at Daptone. A second record from Cochemea (who continued the soul/hip-hop connection by appearing on Run The Jewels' 2020 album) was recorded at the West Coast studio in February 2020, swapping the intimacy of his first album session for the humble ecstasy of recording amidst California sunshine. Tom Brenneck was working on an album from Billy Swivvs of The Sha La Das utilizing the Budos rhythm section; Seattle guitarist Jimmy James flew down to Penrose to record with touring drummer Brian Wolf. The label was also sitting on a shelf of material from family passed—including much-anticipated live recordings from the Super Soul Revue at the Apollo in 2014—while Wayne Gordon prepped new records from The Mystery Lights, Ar-Kaics, and Michael Rault, as well as a Wick comp. Gordon also added NYC ethereal psych group Steady Sun, singer Eric Mcentee, and a

★ ★ ★ ★ ★ ★

reissue of Ohio teen combo Johnny's Uncalled Four to the Wick lineup.

Meanwhile, members of Antibalas were performing as Keleketla!, a multinational group of studio musicians exploring a wide range of African sounds. Duke Amayo was also stumping for Grammy consideration for the group's latest, *Fu Chronicles*. "After we had been playing that form, following [Fela's] Africa 70, and exploring that shape and stretching it and compressing it, and kind of like twisting around figuring all that out—*Fu Chronicles* was an attempt to extend [Antibalas's sound]; to go further and take it to other places," Amayo says from his Williamsburg apartment. While *Fu* tracks like "Fight Am Finish" were written to prepare listeners "for daily battles, offering encouragement to be steadfast in the dreams you have," according to a Facebook post from the band. Antibalas were also creating music to respond to injustice unfolding in real time. In July, the band released "Say Their Names," a tribute to Black people killed by police and timed to eight minutes and forty-six seconds—the same amount of time that a knee was on George Floyd's neck. In November, *Fu* was nominated for a "Best Global Music Album" Grammy but ultimately lost to Nigerian singer Burna Boy.

But as Coronavirus halted touring plans, production, and record pressing (an industry already devastated by a massive fire at lacquer disk producer Apollo Masters Corp) for the entire world in 2020, Daptone, like many indie labels, had to pivot. With its West Coast Penrose showcase canceled and all performances suspended well into the following year, Daptone teased a handful of new collaborations. Under the banner "Tomorrow's Hits Today," the label released music from Orquesta Akokan, Cheme, Menahan Street Band, and LaRose Jackson—a dear friend of Charles Bradley whose debut album Brenneck described as a cathartic joy. Flint, Michigan, singer Napoleon Demps had earlier befriended The Dap-Kings after an impromptu take of "A Change Is Gonna Come" during soundcheck, evoking the spirit of Willie Hutch on his wailing soul/blues single "Norma Jean." Los Angeles Latin soul band the Boogaloo Assassins came with a Mozambique-style instrumental, while Inland Empire

★ ★ ★ ★ ★ ★

doo-wop singer Vicky Tafoya was announced as the newest member of the Penrose crew—her "Forever" a moody ballad laced with girl group harmonies. Timmion's Pratt & Moody got the Daptone distribution treatment as well, their single "Wheels Turning" bringing a complementary sweet soul vibe from across the Atlantic.

In the fall of 2020, the compilation *... Just Dropped In (To See What Condition My Rendition Was In)* showcased Sharon Jones & The Dap-Kings' ability to harness a wide variety of pop for more soulful purposes; the band recorded thirty or forty covers during their run but chose just twelve for the album. The posthumous LP of unreleased and already popular tracks (including the titular Bettye LaVette cover; the first tune SJDK recorded at the House Of Soul studio in 2002) also demonstrated the breadth of the band's influence and appeal. "Rescue Me" and "In The Bush" were left on the cutting-room floor of *The Wolf Of Wall Street* soundtrack; SJDK took on Gladys Knight's "Giving Up" for a producer who intended to sample it for a Dr. Dre album; the first single, "Signed, Sealed, Delivered," was originally recorded for use in a bank commercial before catching the ear of Mark Ronson. With the larger SJDK family collaged onto the front cover, Binky pouring drinks behind a bar and an oversized image of Sharon floating happily above the crew, *Just Dropped In* brought a brief respite from 2020 chaos—a welcome throwback to a time where fifteen people could stand, shoulder to shoulder, at a bar unencumbered by masks or social distance.

No stranger to chaos, The Budos Band were on a much different tip toward the end of 2020. Their expectedly heavy sixth LP, *Long In The Tooth*, was recorded as the world stood on a precipice, not yet shaken by the Coronavirus pandemic but very much in precarious political times. "When we set out to record this album, we didn't know we would be releasing it during such a dark and ominous period of our history," the band wrote on Instagram in September 2020, noting that the spooky but battle-ready "The Wrangler" "emanates the grand perception of apocalypse we are currently experiencing." Ahead of the 2020 presidential election,

★ ★ ★ ★ ★ ★

which Donald Trump promised would be contested amid false cries of voter fraud, the Budos hoped *Long In The Tooth* would "inspire people to reclaim their power. Vote!!!"

It goes without saying that election night 2016 resulted in a massive political shakeup, and also in the stroke that would eventually kill Sharon Jones. Four years later, vice presidential nominee Kamala Harris paid tribute to the late singer, using the Griptite-penned "Matter Of Time" in a campaign ad. Yet just before the 2020 presidential election results came in favoring Harris and former VP Joe Biden, members of the city council of North Augusta, South Carolina, cast their votes in favor of Sharon Jones—renaming the newly opened Riverside Village Amphitheater the Sharon Jones Amphitheater. Don Rhodes, Jones's friend and an *Augusta Chronicle* columnist, initiated the renaming. "In North Augusta, there's no public park or building named after a Black citizen," he told *Rolling Stone*. "And who else should be it named for? There's nobody else from North Augusta who had that kind of worldwide fame." Jones's sister Willa Stringer added that Sharon "would be flabbergasted right now."[2] The naming might not be a total shock: Sharon was posthumously deemed North Augusta's Citizen of the Year in 2016 and, the year prior, Augusta's mayor proclaimed February 7 "Sharon Jones Day."

The label kept busy throughout the pandemic winter, readying a record from a Grammy-nominated trio of Moroccan expats called Innov Gnawa. The trio's Sufi blues rhythm fest—played on a three-stringed African bass alongside *qraqeb*, metal castanets with a staccato sound representing the shackles of the enslaved—provided an opening meditation for Cochemea Gastelum's record release show and a bold new step in Daptone's "world music" output. Thee Sacred Souls and Los Yesterdays also released new singles that cruised along their expected lowrider lane. Meanwhile, Menahan Street Band prepped the release of its first album since 2012's *The Crossing*.

The Exciting Sounds Of Menahan Street Band received little press but was unsurprisingly grand in scope. The collective wrestled cinematic

★ ★ ★ ★ ★ ★

instrumentals fit for a Western film, Budosy headbangers, and avant-psych takes in the style of El Michels Affair (who released two albums, *Adult Themes* and *Yeti Season*, in as many years) into much shorter arrangements. A few tracks were instrumentals Brenneck originally created for Charles Bradley that the singer didn't quite connect with. "I wasn't into forcing it. It was either magic or not magic," Brenneck told *American Songwriter*. MSB or the Budos backed Charles in studio on all of his releases, and still jammed regularly after he passed. But when the right vibe coalesces to actually record an album, Brenneck continued, "We have to approach it in a different way ... it doesn't just have to be supporting a vocalist and we are basically doing whatever the fuck we want."[3]

Nine days before *Exciting Sounds* came out, Daptone family and friends were struck by the death of Naomi Shelton, who passed away at age seventy-eight. Shelton was a thoughtful, positive force, and, according to an Instagram post from the label, "hands down, the coolest person in the room." Up until the pandemic shuttered venues, she had been doing bi-monthly gospel brunch gigs in Brooklyn—her energy undiminished even though myositis had her mostly confined to a wheelchair. In an Instagram post, Saundra Williams reminisced about Naomi's joyous, life-affirming energy. "She had a smile that filled you up, if you ever had one directed at you," Williams wrote. "Her voice, her singing, was full of heart and that very same intention." Shelton's faith—both in God and in her unshakeable drive to perform—as well as her musicality, was an enormous influence.

Naomi Shelton had lived a hard but determined life. She had secrets; she had a mouth on her and would sneak cigarettes. She also possessed the divine drive it takes to keep at it for decades, cutting her first album at age sixty-seven. The singer "called us all for our birthdays every single year, asked about our kids and significant others, always had a story to tell," Daptone continued on Instagram. "We loved her dearly."

CHAPTER SEVENTEEN LONGER AND STRONGER: DAPTONE AT 20

Daptone Records—the punk soul label that never thought it could be, the auspicious but never presumptive torchbearers of funky soul—celebrated its twentieth anniversary in 2021. In less strange times, where a massive gathering to celebrate two decades of soul wouldn't also be considered a "superspreader" event, the anniversary would certainly befit revelry. Instead, Daptone's twentieth mostly consisted of reminiscing and admiration from fans and colleagues—who in the wake of COVID-19, civil rights uprisings, and more than a year without live music deeply appreciated what Daptone brought to the stage and turntable.

"The musicianship is really amazing; everybody who plays on those records is a great musician and that's been true since the Desco days," says DJ Mr. Fine Wine, over coffee near his house in Windsor Terrace, Brooklyn. He adds that he once had a standing offer to record and produce his own records at Daptone, but regrettably never took the label up on it. "I used to think about this: I like this stuff, but is it as good as the true masters of soul music who were recording in the 60s? And my initial answer was probably not. But now my answer would be, it's every bit as good if not better, and in the musicianship, yes."

Attitudes on the milestone varied within the label, falling along expected personality lines. "We're at a place now that we can do whatever we want to do," Sugarman says. "I feel like we're in a very creative period and aside from COVID, we're making moves." Roth, typically lackadaisical about his label's influence, admits that Daptone are kings of the underground—

★★★★★★

though the label never "really broke out" in his eyes. "We're untouchable in that scene; call it immodest if you want. I think that there's a lot of cool labels that do cool shit—you've got Timmion, you've got Colemine, Truth & Soul, Big Crown—but I think we're still kind of the king of that particular mountain. Still, it's not the same as any of these bands that have one pop hit, or one song on the radio, and all of a sudden everybody in the world knows them."

In the eyes of Dan Auerbach, who in early 2020 produced Aaron Frazer's debut solo album using Nick Movshon and Brenneck as session players, "That natural camaraderie, and also a little bit of competitive spirit, is what's so healthy about this scene. I think that's when things get good, historically speaking." Today's soul scene is rich, Terry Cole notes. "That's the only word that always comes to mind when I think about where the whole scene is. It's a super-rich scene and it touches on lots of parts of the industry now. It's super fun to make music that is relevant."

The camaraderie, competition, and forward momentum that comes with seeing (or hearing) a tight and nasty band has enabled the soul revolution to continue far longer than anyone anticipated it would. "Daptone will never not be the most legendary modern thing, Gabe's never gonna stop putting out really great records," Billy Austik posited, his own Hive Mind studios buzzing. "But the little pause in their domination has led to other people being inspired and a lot of other branches sprouting out—whether it be our little studio, or Kelly's studio in California, or Sergio Rios's studio, Colemine, or Adam Scone's Mango Hill in Miami. We're all at the age or point in our lives where we're all ready to start doing our own things." Bands like The Dip from Seattle, Australia's Dojo Cuts, singer Desi Valentine, and Russian quartet The Soul Surfers continue to iterate on revival sounds; others, like Khruangbin, Kamauu, The Ephemerals, Skinshape, and Seratones, defy categorization but create their most haunting tracks by applying heaping helpings of 60s and 70s funk and soul stylings.

New labels such as the Canadian Kimberlite Records; Lugnut Brand

★ ★ ★ ★ ★ ★

out of Pittsburg, California; Black Bird Records; and Rios's new 3 Palms Records exist among decade-old outfits, all of which are helmed by independent musicians who collaborate across the continent and in a variety of subgenre. In fall 2020, Colemine introduced The Resonaires—a New York five-piece whose single "Standing With You" evoked prime Stylistics with dreamy lead vocals from former Dapette Saundra Williams. Adam Scone's Flamingo Time put the final touches on a remaster of his own Scone Cash Players' *The Mind Blower*—a previously CD-only release recorded in Tom Brenneck's Menahan Street apartment. Mango Hill released a slew of 45s from artists including "Little Did You Know," a sweet Latin-influenced song with Freddy DeBoe's tenor sax floating over summery soul-jazz. "I played with a lot of these soul singers and it's definitely uplifted my life in so many ways," DeBoe says. "And I think there's a whole audience that is just now realizing, *Wow, this happened, like, not that long ago*. They missed out on it while it was happening but they're realizing all these people onstage with someone like Charles have their own stories, and they're continuing to tell their story. We're all young and ambitious, and we're all doing everything we can to stay working."

Daptone continues to be the model for Mango Hill, a self-distributed machine run by Scone and Jason Joshua with A&R help from Joe Quiñones. "Finally, we found somewhere where we can fit in and do shit, and the community is 100 percent behind us," says Joshua. "It's like a big Brown, sweaty dude and another Brown dude doing Chicano and Puerto Rican soul. There's no white, big-boss head honcho sitting there counting the cash." Joshua hails from steamy Haileah, Florida—the home of 1970s funk labels like Alston and clean-up woman Betty Wright. "This is not a race thing at all, but it's hard being a Brown dude and we don't have any Brown leaders. Daptone is my favorite label of all time, and the aesthetic of two dudes trying to make a dope ass label with a certain exclusivity of sound is the inspiration that they gave."

Although Tommy Brenneck continues to pay attention to a wide variety of modern music, the in-demand producer and musician rarely goes out to see bands. "I just don't like the process. My ears are blown out—I've been touring since I was nineteen," he says. "If I want to hear what's going on in the scene, I listen to Binky's radio show on Saturday nights and he's playing whatever new trash is coming out. And I'm like, *I wish he would just not play this trash and play old records.*"

The Daptone-led soul revolution also connected with, and perhaps elevated, revivalist scenes like Latin soul and rocksteady, where a dedication to vinyl, showmanship and big band sound are king. On a pop stage, the driving, raw funk the label helped reinvigorate is heard across genre from London to Los Angeles, Melbourne to Memphis. Brenneck, much like Roth, doesn't often consider the macro view of Daptone's impact on the larger music scene. "I don't really think about music in that broad sense. I just think about songs and in a selfish way, my relationship to the songs, not people's relationship to the songs."

Seated at his large dining room table, Roth asks incredulously, "You think there's a lot of people into soul music now? More than ten years ago? I guess I don't see it; I don't think I've ever been a good judge of what people are doing. I just do the same shit either way.

"One of the things that made this whole path easy for me is I never wanted that. If I wanted fame, I think this would be frustrating. I don't think that the music would have been as good and I think I probably would have spent a lot of money, lost a lot of money," Roth says slowly, his sunglass-less eyes slightly heavy from whiskey and the late hour. "But I think because we never really tried to do that, we can stay in our own lane. We took some risks and we spent some money; we did some promotion, but it was always kind of like, more realistic things. In the end it's an underground scene."

Yet as underground as Roth conceives Daptone to be, manager Austen Holman asserts that everyone knows "there's nothing like Daptone. There will never be anything like that; never, ever, ever. It's like the thing that you love and you hate. Sometimes it's the most frustrating thing because they're so set in the way that they want to do things, that doesn't really

★ ★ ★ ★ ★ ★

reflect what you think the climate is actually like," the now independent manager says. "But I have to sit back and be like, if they didn't do what they did when they did it, we wouldn't know what we missed. We wouldn't have this amazing moment to reflect back on. This, to me, is like New York gold music in the mid-2000s. People have moved, people have passed away, it's changed. Daptone's still alive, they're still doing stuff, but they did something that was total magic."

That magic required immense skill and dedication, but it's deceptively simple. It's the pure joy of screaming horns stepping in time, the ease of nodding along to a groovy baseline, the way innovative and syncopated percussion drives a song home, and the undeniable, smile-plastering propulsive energy of a true showman like Sharon Jones or Charles Bradley.

Speaking over the phone from his home in Zurich, Sugarman reflects on the realities of being one of the kings of the soul revolution. "When I'm hanging out with my friends, especially here in Switzerland or playing music, and The Meters come up and it's like, *Oh yeah, I got to be pretty good friends with Zigaboo Modeliste because we did these gigs together.* It's like, *What?* It's been incredible and I'm not keeping track, so when sometimes it comes up in conversation I even feel like a jerk. But the fact is it happened; The Dap-Kings were nasty and everyone knew it. So we got to be on the same bills and play with tons of people," Sugarman continues. "But I'll be honest, nothing was ever as good as when we were hitting together, just as The Dap-Kings and Sharon." Roth concurs, adding, "The peaks are always those really, really good shows. They weren't necessarily the biggest shows, just shows where the music was the best and the people were the most turned on. Everybody was just, like, sweating and having a good time. We had some good runs where there was a lot of it, and other times it felt more elusive."

Audiences will chase that elusive feeling with a hunger that can only be soothed with the sweet soul music Arthur Conley first screamed about in 1967; Daptone feeds that need. Soul is simply here to stay, says Sugarman. "I think people will always check out Sharon and Charles; they're in this

★ ★ ★ ★ ★ ★

legacy of the genre and I think their stories are still closer than those of Aretha Franklin or the guard who were more superstars. People knock on our door and say, *We're older, and wanna work with Daptone*, and maybe it'll work or maybe it won't. But the fact that they have that faith and hope makes them live longer. And if they don't do it with us, they do it with Colemine or another label opening up next door."

To Terry Cole, the resonance of the soul revival is partially a response to an increasingly digital and distanced world in which everything is at our fingertips. "There's a backlash to this. I *do* want to have a book; I *do* want to disengage from my phone, I *do* want to go out with my friends and not be on Instagram the whole time. I think the success of records ties into that," says Cole who, perhaps more than other soul labels, has used social media most prolifically. "We have this craving for authenticity, whether it's in a physical medium, in the story being told, or where the coffee beans came from. I think that sort of feeds into soul music—it's your feeling and expression through music, and what's more authentic than that? I'm glad to live in a time where there's enough people who want that."

Gabe Roth has a distaste for theorizing about what's next for the constantly evolving genre of soul. He doesn't expect Penrose Records or other sweet soul groups to have much crossover appeal, though anyone with a savvy bend in their sacroiliac wouldn't expect Roth to mind. "I think one of the big things in life is that people fuck with themselves as far as the way they define success. You gotta figure out what success is to you and then don't bullshit yourself. If you decide success is money, then go get some fucking money, you know? If you decide success is trying to make a really good record, then make a really good record and shut the fuck up and don't complain to me about who's buying it," he says, continuing that people assume that a great record will be a financial success. "That's an illusion. There's no fucking correlation between monetary success or fame or something quality. That's the whole illusion of the American Dream, that people get what they deserve. And that's what that whole Sharon record was about."

★ ★ ★ ★ ★ ★

Gabe Roth, Neal Sugarman, and the ever-growing family they developed from the basement studios of Desco Records to Daptone and beyond share no such delusion. Popular taste and big bucks will never prevent the label from putting out records that make them feel good. Daptone and the majority of their contemporaries in the soul revolution remain committed punks—dedicated to putting up soul that strikes a nerve, echoes deep in their bones, and will undoubtedly make its way around the world by operating outside the lane of pop ethos.

ACKNOWLEDGMENTS

It takes a village to create (and write about) a soul revolution. My heartfelt appreciation to Nancy Arteaga, who's long been my champion; to Ben Wright for his keen eye throughout this process; to Craig Campbell, Suzi Grishpul, Andre Cruz and Selam Samuel for their words of wisdom; to Oliver Wang for his insight and Bill Purdy for first turning on the light at Funky Sole.

Thanks to photographers Jacob Blickenstaff and Farah Sosa for capturing sound and emotion so brilliantly; to Robbie Busch, Adam Scone, and Billy Austik for sharing their collections.

My gratitude to Tom Seabrook and Jawbone Press for shepherding this project into the world. Respect to the late Randy Kinavey, who pushed me to be a better writer and is hopefully reading this from the great el queso in the sky. Much love to my family for their support, and my parents in particular for encouraging my passion for music.

This book couldn't exist without the musicians, DJs, and fans who keep dancefloors cooking. Big up yourself and thanks for keeping me grooving.

NOTES AND SOURCES

Unless otherwise noted, all quotations are from original interviews with the following people. *Current and former members of the Daptone family*: Gabe Roth, Neal Sugarman, Homer Steinweiss, Binky Griptite, Tommy Brenneck, Billy Austik, Freddy DeBoe, Charles Bradley, Victor Axelrod, Duke Amayo, Adam Scone, Mikey Post, Jason Joshua, Joe Quiñones, Josh Lane, Todd Simon, Austen Holman, Alex Kadvan, Cochemea Gastelum. *Plus*: Dan Auerbach, Kirk Douglas, Cut Chemist, Danny Akalepse, Terry Cole, Aaron Frazer, Kelly Finnigan, Sergio Rios. *Also*: Jacob Blickenstaff, Nancy Arteaga, Ruben Molina, Clifton Weaver, Miles Tackett, Matt Weingarden, Connie Francis, Sami Kantelinen, Jukka Sarapää.

INTRODUCTION

1 *Living On Soul: The Family Daptone*, 2017. Directed by Jeff Broadway.
2 Stephen Holden, "Holding Nothing In On Love," *New York Times*, December 3, 1995.
3 Brad Farberman, "Behind The 'Scene' With Daptone Records Founder Gabe Roth," *Wax Poetics*, April 6, 2010.
4 *Music Makers and Soul Shakers* podcast, episode 59.
5 Karen Shoember, "A Club Where The Heartbeat Is Soul," *New York Times*, June 17, 1992.
6 Andy Greene, "How 'Meet Me In The Bathroom' Chronicles A Bygone Era Of New York Rock," *Rolling Stone*, June 13, 2017.
7 Jessica Lipsky, "The Root Down Soundsystem Brings The Party To The Virgil For December," *LA Weekly*, December 4, 2017.

CHAPTER ONE

1 Stretch Armstrong, "No Sleep: NYC Nightlife Flyers 1988 To 1999," *Medium*, December 6, 2016.
2 Brian Niemietz, "Blaxploitation, Nightclub Style," *NY Post*, September 27, 2009.
3 giantstep.net/our-story/
4 Saki Knafo, "Soul Reviver," *New York Times*, December 5, 2008.
5 Karen Schoemer, "A Club Where The Heartbeat Is Soul," *New York Times*, June 17, 1992.

★ ★ ★ ★ ★ ★

6 culturesofsoul.com/blogs/news/interview-with-dj-chairman-mao/
7 unrulygallery.com/product/bando/
8 Oliver Wang, "The Poets Of Rhythm: A Troop Of German James Browns," *All Things Considered,* NPR, October 18, 2013.
9 Jon Pareles, "Spinning A Magic Spell For Dancing The Night Away," *New York Times*, February 6, 1998.

CHAPTER TWO

1 Saki Knafo, "Soul Reviver," *New York Times*, December 5, 2008.
2 Ezra Gale, "A Beginner's Guide To The Daktaris," *Village Voice*, March 4, 2009.
3 Paul Sexton, "Lee Fields: At 63, This Soul Survivor Is Finally A Singing Star," *Daily Express*, June 1, 2014.
4 Bill Murphy, "No Sleep 'Til Bushwick: Daptone Records," *Relix*, January 19, 2011.
5 Keith Phipps, "Lee Fields: Let's Get A Groove On," *AV Club*, March 29, 2002.
6 Andy Tennille, "The Return Of Real Funk & Soul Music: Sharon Jones & The Dap Kings," *Best Music Writing 2008* (Da Capo, 2008).
7 Ezra Gale, "A Beginner's Guide To The Daktaris," *Village Voice*, March 4, 2009.
8 Saki Knafo, "Soul Reviver," *New York Times*, December 5, 2008.

CHAPTER THREE

1 "Funk 45s," produced by Tom Parsons for *Nightlife*, ITV London, 2002.
2 "Gabe & Phillip After A Show At Jelly Jazz," courtesy of Pete Isaac, shot May 1999.
3 "Big Ups With Leon Michels," *Flea Market Funk*, July 30, 2020.
4 Miss Shing-a-Ling, "Sharon Jones," *Life & Soul Promotions*, December 2, 2001.
5 Devon Powers, "Red Hot Chili Peppers: Blood Sugar Sex Magik," *PopMatters*, December 2, 2003.
6 enacademic.com/dic.nsf/enwiki/1101726/
7 Carly Carioli, "Soul Fire: Cooking Up The Deep Funk With Daptone Records And The Sugarman 3," *Boston Phoenix*, March 13–20, 2003.
8 "The Roots: Things Fall Apart," *Mojo*, May 1999.
9 Michael D. Ayers, "Sharon Jones's Family Affair," *Village Voice*, April 6, 2010.

CHAPTER FOUR

1 Oliver Wang, *Pop When The World Falls Apart: Music In The Shadow Of Doubt* (Duke Press, 2012).
2 Brad Farberman, "Behind The 'Scene' With Daptone Records Founder Gabe Roth," *Wax Poetics*, April 6, 2010.
3 Miss Shing-a-Ling, "Sharon Jones," *Life & Soul Promotions*, December 2, 2001.
4 "Antibalas—Full Performance," KEPX, recorded February 20, 2020.
5 *Living On Soul: The Family Daptone*, 2017. Directed by Jeff Broadway.
6 Jon Pareles, "Pop And Jazz Guide," *New York Times*, September 14, 2001.
7 Saki Knafo, "Soul Reviver," *New York Times*, December 5, 2008.
8 Toki Wright, "Gabriel Roth Talks About Daptone Records Past, Present And Future," *The Current*, March 14, 2018.
9 Miss Shing-a-Ling, "Sharon Jones," *Life & Soul Promotions*, December 2, 2001.

★ ★ ★ ★ ★ ★

10 Miss Shing-a-Ling, "Sharon Jones," *Life & Soul Promotions*, December 2, 2001.
11 Bill Murphy, "No Sleep 'Til Bushwick: Daptone Records," *Relix*, January 19, 2011.

CHAPTER FIVE

1 antiwarsongs.org
2 Gabriel Roth, "Shitty Is Pretty: Anatomy Of A Funk 45," *Big Daddy* issues 4 and 5, courtesy of funkydown.com.
3 "Sharon Jones & The Dap-Kings: A Little Funk And Soul," interview by Dave Davies, *Fresh Air*, NPR, May 7, 2010.
4 Andrew G. Davis, "Dap-Dippin' Independent Tradition: The Rebirth Of Rhythm And Blues," *Please Allow Me To Introduce Myself: Essays On Debut Albums* (Routledge Press, 2016).
5 *Ten Years Of Daptone Records*, 2017. Directed by Rufus Campbell.
6 *Ten Years Of Daptone Records*, 2017. Directed by Rufus Campbell.
7 *Ten Years Of Daptone Records*, 2017. Directed by Rufus Campbell.
8 *Ten Years Of Daptone Records*, 2017. Directed by Rufus Campbell.
9 Vijith Assar, "Gabriel Roth / Bosco Mann," *Tape Op*, May/June 2007.
10 Steve Guttenberg, "Welcome To Brooklyn's Daptone Records, A Recording Studio That Never Went Digital," CNET, October 8, 2016.
11 Jamison Harvey, "Sharon Jones & The Dap-Kings Live At The Apollo Theater 10.06.07," *Flea Market Funk*, October 8, 2007.
12 Jonathan Zwickel, "Antibalas Afrobeat Orchestra: Who Is This America?" *Pitchfork*, May 18, 2004.
13 Jessica Lipsky, "Binky Griptite: One Man Under A Groove," *Dust And Grooves*, March 15, 2008.
14 Miss Shing-a-Ling, "Sharon Jones," *Life & Soul Promotions*, December 2, 2001.
15 Miss Shing-a-Ling, "Sharon Jones," *Life & Soul Promotions*, December 2, 2001.
16 Miss Shing-a-Ling, "Sharon Jones," *Life & Soul Promotions*, December 2, 2001.
17 Eric Luecking, "Sounding Out The City By El Michels Affair Gets A Deluxe Reissue A Decade Later," *Wax Poetics*, November 6, 2014.

CHAPTER SIX

1 Cameron Macdonald, "Sharon Jones And The Dap-Kings: Naturally," *Pitchfork*, January 24, 2005.
2 Andy Tennille, "The Return Of Real Funk & Soul Music: Sharon Jones & The Dap-Kings," *Best Music Writing 2008* (Da Capo, 2008).
3 Donald Brackett, *Long Slow Train: The Soul Music Of Sharon Jones And The Dap-Kings* (Backbeat Books, 2018).
4 "Remembering Sharon Jones, Soul Singer And Consummate Performer," *Fresh Air*, NPR, November 23, 2016.
5 Michael D. Ayers, "Sharon Jones's Family Affair," *Village Voice*, April 6, 2010.
6 Miss Shing-a-Ling, "Sharon Jones," *Life & Soul Promotions*, December 2, 2001.
7 Lauren Schwartzberg, "Sharon Jones On Beating Cancer, And Her New Album Give The People What They Want," *New York Magazine*, February 2, 2014.
8 Saki Knafo, "Soul Reviver," *New York Times*, December 5, 2008.

★ ★ ★ ★ ★ ★

9 Adam Fulton, "Sharon Jones & The Dap-Kings," *Sydney Morning Herald*, March 8, 2008.
10 "Rare Groove: The 2nd Wave Of Funk & Soul," Grammy Museum panel, March 15, 2018.
11 Lauren Schwartzberg, "Sharon Jones On Beating Cancer, And Her New Album Give The People What They Want," *New York Magazine*, February 2, 2014.
12 Melena Ryzik, "From Jameson To Fela Kuti, Preshow Rites Of A Soul Band," *New York Times*, April 23, 2010.
13 "Grill Yr Idols: Sharon Jones Meets Mavis Staples," *Spin*, April 2010.
14 David Browne, "Schooled In Hard Tries," *New Yorker*, March 24, 2010.
15 Gail Mitchell, "The Kings—And Queen—Of Underground Soul," *Billboard*, June 30, 2007.

CHAPTER SEVEN

1 Andrew Unterberger, "The Spin Interview: Mark Ronson Looks Back On His 20-Year Journey 'Uptown,'" *Spin*, January 8, 2015.
2 "The Story Behind Mark Ronson's Hit Song 'Uptown Funk,'" *All Things Considered*, NPR, April 16, 2015.
3 "The Story Behind Mark Ronson's Hit Song 'Uptown Funk,'" *All Things Considered*, NPR, April 16, 2015.
4 "The Story Behind Mark Ronson's Hit Song 'Uptown Funk,'" *All Things Considered*, NPR, April 16, 2015.
5 Hilary Hughes, "Here's The 'Back To Black' Story That Hit The Amy Winehouse Documentary's Cutting Room Floor," *Village Voice*, July 17, 2015.
6 Tom Payne, "The Curse Of Musical Nostalgia," *New York Times*, August 12, 2011.
7 Mark Ronson, "How Sampling Transformed Music," TED Talk, March 2014.
8 Saki Knafo, "Soul Reviver," *New York Times*, December 5, 2008.
9 Andrew G. Davis, "Dap-Dippin' Independent Tradition: The Rebirth Of Rhythm And Blues," *Please Allow Me To Introduce Myself: Essays On Debut Albums* (Routledge Press, 2016).
10 Amy Linden, "The Slow Blackout Of Amy Winehouse," *Village Voice*, January 15, 2008.
11 Ben Ratliff, "Coachella: A Slightly Dizzying Feeling," *New York Times*, April 28, 2007.
12 David Browne, "Schooled In Hard Tries," *New Yorker*, March 24, 2010.
13 Paul MacInnes, "Amy Winehouse Cancels Rest Of Tour Dates In 2007," *Guardian*, November 27, 2007.
14 Saki Knafo, "Soul Reviver," *New York Times*, December 5, 2008.
15 Alexis Petridis, "Why The Best Album Of The 21st Century Is Amy Winehouse's Back To Black," *Guardian*, September 13, 2019.

CHAPTER EIGHT

1 "Sharon Jones Remembers Meeting, Working And Fighting (A Little) With Lou Reed." *Billboard*, November 1, 2013.
2 Lauren Schwartzberg, "Sharon Jones On Beating Cancer, And Her New Album Give The People What They Want," *New York Magazine*, February 2, 2014.

★ ★ ★ ★ ★ ★

3 Jamison Harvey, "Sharon Jones & The Dap-Kings Live At The Apollo Theater 10.06.07," *Flea Market Funk*, October 8, 2007.

4 Mike Greenhaus, "Sharon Jones: The Dap-Kings, Phish And Other Daptone Gold," Jambands.com, November 16, 2009.

5 Brad Farberman, "Behind The 'Scene' With Daptone Records Founder Gabe Roth," *Wax Poetics*, April 6, 2010.

6 Mike Greenhaus, "Sharon Jones: The Dap-Kings, Phish And Other Daptone Gold," Jambands.com, November 16, 2009.

7 Amanda Petrusich, "Postscript: Sharon Jones, 1956–2016," *New Yorker*, November 19, 2016.

8 Saki Knafo, "Soul Reviver," *New York Times*, December 5, 2008.

9 Matthew R. Warren, "Burglary Stuns A Studio, But Can't Stop The Music," *New York Times*, February 22, 2009.

10 "Daptone Records Robbed," *Brooklyn Vegan*, February 17, 2009.

11 Larry Rohter, "Waiting In Brooklyn For The World To Catch Up," *New York Times*, August 6, 2012.

12 *Living On Soul: The Family Daptone*, 2017. Directed by Jeff Broadway.

13 "Naomi Shelton's Gospel," WBUR, June 30, 2009.

14 Stephen Nessen, "East Village Vinyl Destination For Hit Makers And Global Junkies To Close," WNYC.org, August 6, 2012.

15 Tim Perlich, "Thomas Brenneck," *Now Toronto*, October 21, 2008.

16 "KCRW Presents: Menahan Street Band," interview by Jason Bently, KCRW, February 6, 2013.

CHAPTER NINE

1 Jon Caramanica, "A Journeyman Soul Singer Embraces His Audience In Word And In Deed," *New York Times,* July 27, 2011.

2 Jessica Lipsky, "I'll Just Find A Way To Open My Heart And Keep Going Forward: A Conversation With Charles Bradley," *Vice*, April 4, 2016.

3 Jason Newman, "Charles Bradley On Covering Black Sabbath, Confronting Tragedy On New LP," *Rolling Stone*, May 6, 2016.

4 "Charles Bradley And The Menahan Street Band Live On KEXP," KEXP, recorded December 6, 2012.

5 Jessica Lipsky, "I'll Just Find A Way To Open My Heart And Keep Going Forward: A Conversation With Charles Bradley," *Vice*, April 4, 2016.

6 Sarah Perry, "Smokin' Soul: The Story Of Daptone Records," *Atlas Society*, March 7, 2012.

CHAPTER TEN

1 "Antibalas: NPR Music Tiny Desk Concert," NPR, October 16, 2012.

2 Nate Patrin, "Antibalas," *Pitchfork*, August 2, 2012.

3 "The Budos Band Staten Island Cabal Has A Stranglehold On Sinister Rhythms," *Wax Poetics*, issue 44, 2010.

4 Jody Rosen, "I Learned The Hard Way," *Rolling Stone*, April 6, 2010.

★ ★ ★ ★ ★ ★

5 Raj Dayal, "In A Big Year For New Soul, A Small But Influential Label Turns 10," *Atlantic*, December 28, 2011.

6 Bill Friskics-Warren, "What's Going On? Everything Soul Is New Again," *New York Times*, February 4, 2007.

7 Robert Webb, "Story Of The Song: Crazy In Love, Beyoncé (2003)," *Independent*, November 14, 2008.

8 Bill Friskics-Warren, "What's Going On? Everything Soul Is New Again," *New York Times*, February 4, 2007.

9 "Interview // Leon Michels Of El Michels Affair." *Rollo & Grady*, June 29, 2009.

10 Phillip Mlynar, "Reverse Engineering The Wu-Tang Clan," *Village Voice*, May 12, 2017.

11 Alison Fennerstock, "Sharon Jones Led The Soul Revival To The Dancefloor," *Pitchfork*, November 21, 2016.

12 Raj Dayal, "In A Big Year For New Soul, A Small But Influential Label Turns 10," *Atlantic*, December 28, 2011.

13 Joe Rhodes, "Alabama Shakes's Soul-Stirring, Shape-Shifting New Sound," *New York Times Magazine*, March 18, 2015; Bernadette McNulty, "Alabama Shakes' Brittany Howard: The Lioness Of Soul," *Telegraph*, November 16, 2015.

14 Stacey Anderson, "60s Soul Claims Young Hearts… And Feet," *New York Times*, September 11, 2014.

15 "Sharon Jones Played New Year's Eve, Lee Fields Plays Tonight (WIN TIX) ++ A New Charles Bradley Video," *Brooklyn Vegan*, January 7, 2011.

16 Lauren Friedman, "Why Nostalgia Marketing Works So Well With Millennials, And How Your Brand Can Benefit," *Forbes*, August 6, 2016.

17 Shiddhartha Mitter, "Jones's Soul Revue Is Stuck In Overdrive," *Boston Globe*, November 19, 2005.

CHAPTER ELEVEN

1 "SXSW 2010—Sharon Jones LIVE!" Billboard.com, March 25, 2010.

2 Sarah Perry, "Smokin' Soul: The Story Of Daptone Records," *Atlas Society*, March 7, 2012.

3 Eric Renner Brown, "Sharon Jones Remembers Performing With Prince: He 'Taught Us A Valuable Lesson,'" *Entertainment Weekly*, May 2, 2016.

4 Lou Papineau, "When Sharon Jones Met Prince," *The Current*, February 1, 2017.

5 "SXSW 2010—Sharon Jones LIVE!" Billboard.com, March 25, 2010.

6 Michael A. Gonzalez, "Who Killed The Funk?," *Ebony*, July 24, 2013.

7 Eric Sundermann, "Sharon Jones: Child No More," *Vice*, January 8, 2014.

8 "Film Society Talks," Film At Lincoln Center, uploaded August 8, 2016.

9 "Film Society Talks," Film At Lincoln Center, uploaded August 8, 2016.

10 "Film Society Talks," Film At Lincoln Center, uploaded August 8, 2016.

11 Lauren Schwartzberg, "Sharon Jones On Beating Cancer, And Her New Album Give The People What They Want," *New York Magazine*, February 2, 2014.

12 Hilary Hughes, "Here's The 'Back To Black' Story That Hit The Amy Winehouse Documentary's Cutting Room Floor," *Village Voice*, July 17, 2015.

13 Ben Kaye, "Video: Sharon Jones Performs On Fallon, Sits In With The Roots," *Consequence Of Sound*, January 11, 2014.

14 Eric Sundermann, "Sharon Jones: Child No More," *Vice*, January 8, 2014.

15 Eric Sundermann, "Sharon Jones: Child No More," *Vice*, January 8, 2014.

16 Jason Newmann, "Sharon Jones Fights On: 'I Have Cancer; Cancer Don't Have Me,'" *Rolling Stone*, July 29, 2016.

17 Jessica Lipsky, "'Living On Soul: The Family Daptone' Aims To Be A Concert Film Dream Come True," *Vice*, June 15, 2016.

18 Jessica Lipsky, "'Living On Soul: The Family Daptone' Aims To Be A Concert Film Dream Come True," *Vice*, June 15, 2016.

19 *Living On Soul: The Family Daptone*, 2017. Directed by Jeff Broadway.

CHAPTER TWELVE

1 Maxwell George, "Homecoming Queen," *Oxford American*, January 19, 2015.

2 "Web Exclusive: Sharon Jones Backstage Interview At The Queen Latifah Show." *Queen Latifah Show*, uploaded March 27, 2014.

3 Eric Sundermann, "Sharon Jones: Child No More," *Vice*, January 8, 2014.

4 Gus Marshall, "Phenomenal Guitarist Jimmy James Shreds His Way To Earshot Ballot," *South Seattle Emerald*, April 2, 2018.

5 "The True Loves—Full Performance (Live On KEXP)." KEXP, recorded October 20, 2017.

6 Steven J. Horowitz, "Album Review: Andra Day Channels Amy Winehouse On Debut 'Cheers To The Fall,'" *Billboard*, August 28, 2015.

7 Rod Yates, "Barack Obama's Advice For Musician Leon Bridges," *Sydney Morning Herald*, May 1, 2018.

8 Rebecca Bengal, "The Leon Bridges Phenomenon: Why The Singer's Throwback Soul Sound Is So Right Now," *Vogue*, June 3, 2015.

9 Jessica Lipsky, "Singer Leon Bridges Leaves Soul Revival For Modern R&B On New Album," *Newsweek*, May 2, 2018.

10 Jon Blinstein, "Hear President Obama's Eclectic Summer 2016 Playlist," *Rolling Stone*, August 11, 2016; Joyce Chen, "Michelle Obama Creates 'Forever Mine' Valentine's Day Playlist For Barack," *Rolling Stone*, February 14, 2018.

11 Andrew Unterberger, "The Spin Interview: Mark Ronson Looks Back On His 20-Year Journey 'Uptown,'" *Spin*, January 8, 2015.

12 Matt James, "Mark Ronson: Uptown Special," *PopMatters*, January 23, 2016.

13 Ray Rogers, "Mark Ronson Says New Single With Bruno Mars 'Uptown Funk' Is A Milestone For Both Of Them," *Billboard*, November 10, 2014.

★ ★ ★ ★ ★ ★

14 "A Look Closer With Saun & Starr (Daptone Records)," April 17, 2015.

15 Paul Sexton, "Daptone Records Has Put Authentic Soul Into R&B For 15 Years, From 'Back To Black' To 'Uptown Funk,'" *Independent*, October 16, 2015.

16 Hilary Hughes, "The Tragic Turn Of The Frightnrs' First—And Last—Record," NPR, August 23, 2016.

17 Justin Joffe, "The Frightnrs Find Solace From Tragedy In The Lovesick Longing Of Reggae," *Observer*, September 2, 2016.

18 Jim Farber, "With Wounded Spirits, The Frightnrs Rally Around Their Frontman," *New York Times*, July 8, 2016.

19 Jim Farber, "With Wounded Spirits, The Frightnrs Rally Around Their Frontman," *New York Times*, July 8, 2016.

20 Hilary Hughes, "The Tragic Turn Of The Frightnrs' First—And Last—Record," NPR, August 23, 2016.

CHAPTER THIRTEEN

1 Adrian Lee, "Soul Singer Charles Bradley's Mother Passes Away," *Maclean's*, January 21, 2014.

2 Jessica Lipsky, "I'll Just Find A Way To Open My Heart And Keep Going Forward: A Conversation With Charles Bradley," *Vice*, April 4, 2016.

3 Liz Pelly, "New Imprint Brings Daptone Records' Soul To Analog Rock'n'roll," *Guardian*, July 6, 2016.

4 Nick Krewen, "Meet Toronto's Frank Dukes, The Go-To Producer For Superstars Like Rihanna And Drake," *Toronto Star*, July 12, 2019.

5 Jim Barber, "With Wounded Spirits, The Frightnrs Rally Around Their Frontman," *New York Times*, July 8, 2016.

6 "Soul Singer Sharon Jones: 'The Cancer Is Here, But I Want To Perform,'" *Fresh Air*, NPR, July 28, 2016.

7 "Sharon Jones & The Dap-Kings Performing 'These Tears' Live At KEXP," KEXP, recorded April 16, 2016.

8 Jason Newman, "Sharon Jones, Soul And Funk Singer With Dap-Kings, Dead At 60," *Rolling Stone*, November 19, 2016.

CHAPTER FOURTEEN

1 Fred Pessaro, "That Time The Dap-Kings Played The White House And Met Obama," *Clrvynt*, October 6, 2016.

2 Dean Van Nguyen, "Soul Of A Woman: Sharon Jones's Final, Funky Masterwork, A Year After Her Death," *Irish Times*, November 21, 2017.

3 Jessica Lipsky, "Posthumous Soul: Daptone Will Release A Final Sharon Jones Album," *SF Weekly*, November 10, 2017.

4 Jessica Lipsky, "Double Dap-Dipping: What's Next For Daptone Records," *Consequence Of Sound*, November 14, 2017.

5 Jessica Lipsky, "Double Dap-Dipping: What's Next For Daptone Records," *Consequence Of Sound*, November 14, 2017.

6 Jessica Lipsky, "Double Dap-Dipping: What's Next For Daptone Records," *Consequence Of Sound*, November 14, 2017.

★ ★ ★ ★ ★ ★

7 "The True Loves—Full Performance (Live on KEXP)," KEXP, recorded October 20, 2017.
8 Jessica Lipsky, "Double Dap-Dipping: What's Next For Daptone Records," *Consequence Of Sound*, November 14, 2017.

CHAPTER FIFTEEN

1 "Jon Batiste With The Dap-Kings—Summer Tour," Daptone Records press release, March 26, 2018.
2 Margie Goldsmith, "Batiste: So Much More Than Stephen Colbert's Music Director," *Forbes*, September 9, 2019.
3 Keith Caufield, "US Vinyl Album Sales Grew 15% In 2018, Led By The Beatles, Pink Floyd, David Bowie & Panic! At The Disco," *Billboard*, January 12, 2019.
4 Jessica Lipsky, "Double Dap-Dipping: What's Next For Daptone Records," *Consequence Of Sound*, November 14, 2017.
5 Ryan Leas, "Stream Antibalas Where The Gods Are In Peace," *Stereogum*, September 8, 2017.
6 "Sound & Vision: The Budos Band Saxophonist Jared Tankel On Being Bi-Coastal And New Album V," KEXP, April 19, 2019.
7 Jessica Lipsky, "How Daptone Records Is Betting On Mambo For Its Own Latin Crossover," *Billboard*, March 30, 2018.
8 "Bruno Mars Collaborator And Hit-Maker Mark Ronson Says Success Is Due To Being 'Lucky,' 'Good At Listening,'" CBS Los Angeles, January 29, 2018.
9 Gil Kaufman, "Dap-Kings Sax Player: Kesha Was 'Super-Engaged' During 'Woman' Sessions," *Billboard*, July 14, 2017.
10 Jon Bernstein, "'They Put Us In A Little Box': How Racial Tensions Shape Modern Soul Music," *Guardian*, June 13, 2018.
11 David Browne, "Black Pumas: Rise Of A Psychedelic-Soul Force," *Rolling Stone*, January 21, 2020.

CHAPTER SIXTEEN

1 Jessica Lipsky, "Daptone Records Debuts Penrose Records, New Imprint Dedicated To The Sweeter Side Of Soul," *Billboard*, March 3, 2020.
2 David Browne, "South Carolina Amphitheater To Be Renamed In Honor Of Sharon Jones," *Rolling Stone*, November 3, 2020.
3 Tina Benitez-Eves, "Menahan Street Band Make 'Exciting' Return After Nearly 10 Years," *American Songwriter*, March 1, 2021.

INDEX

★ ★ ★ ★ ★ ★

★ ★ ★ ★ ★ ★

★ ★ ★ ★ ★ ★

ALSO AVAILABLE IN PRINT AND EBOOK EDITIONS FROM JAWBONE

Bowie In Berlin: A New Career In A New Town Thomas Jerome Seabrook

To Live Is To Die: The Life And Death Of Metallica's Cliff Burton Joel McIver

A Wizard, A True Star: Todd Rundgren In The Studio Paul Myers

The Resurrection Of Johnny Cash: Hurt, Redemption, And American Recordings Graeme Thomson

Entertain Us: The Rise Of Nirvana Gillian G. Gaar

Adventures Of A Waterboy Mike Scott

Read & Burn: A Book About Wire Wilson Neate

Recombo DNA: The Story Of Devo, or How The 60s Became The 80s Kevin C. Smith

Who Killed Mister Moonlight? Bauhaus, Black Magick, And Benediction David J. Haskins

Lee, Myself & I: Inside The Very Special World Of Lee Hazlewood Wyndham Wallace

Throwing Frisbees At The Sun: A Book About Beck Rob Jovanovic

Confessions Of A Heretic: The Sacred & The Profane, Behemoth & Beyond Adam Nergal Darski with Mark Eglinton

Complicated Game: Inside The Songs Of XTC Andy Partridge and Todd Bernhardt

Fearless: The Making Of Post-Rock Jeanette Leech

The Yacht Rock Book: The Oral History Of The Soft, Smooth Sounds Of The 70s And 80s Greg Prato

Swans: Sacrifice And Transcendence: The Oral History Nick Soulsby

Small Victories: The True Story Of Faith No More Adrian Harte

King's X: The Oral History Greg Prato

Keep Music Evil: The Brian Jonestown Massacre Story Jesse Valencia

Lunch With The Wild Frontiers: A History Of Britpop And Excess In 13½ Chapters Phill Savidge

Wilcopedia: A Comprehensive Guide To The Music Of America's Best Band Daniel Cook Johnson

I Am Morbid: Ten Lessons Learned From Extreme Metal, Outlaw Country, And The Power Of Self-Determination David Vincent with Joel McIver

Lydia Lunch: The War Is Never Over: A Companion To The Film By Beth B. Nick Soulsby

Zeppelin Over Dayton: Guided By Voices Album By Album Jeff Gomez

What Makes The Monkey Dance: The Life And Music Of Chuck Prophet And Green On Red Stevie Simkin

So Much For The 30 Year Plan: Therapy?—The Authorised Biography Simon Young

She Bop: The Definitive History Of Women In Popular Music: Revised And Updated 25th Anniversary Edition Lucy O'Brien

Relax Baby Be Cool: The Artistry And Audacity Of Serge Gainsbourg Jeremy Allen

Seeing Sideways: A Memoir Of Music And Motherhood Kristin Hersh

Two Steps Forward, One Step Back: My Life In The Music Business Miles A. Copeland III